W9-CTI-303

Premarital Sexuality

Premarital Sexuality

Attitudes, Relationships, Behavior

John DeLamater
Patricia MacCorquodale

The University of Wisconsin Press

Published 1979

The University of Wisconsin Press
114 North Murray Street
Madison, Wisconsin 53715

The University of Wisconsin Press, Ltd.
1 Gower Street
London WC1E 6HA, England

First printing

Printed in the United States of America

For LC CIP information see the colophon

ISBN 0-299-07840-X

Acknowledgments

The research from which this book resulted and preparation of the book itself were made possible by financial support from three sources. The University of Wisconsin Graduate School Research Committee provided funds for preparation of the original grant proposal and for writing of the manuscript. The research and data analysis were supported by a three-year grant from the National Institute of Child Health and Human Development, National Institutes of Health (1 RO1 HD 06264). Financial assistance for the preparation and reproduction of the manuscript was generously given by the Center for Demography and Ecology, in the Department of Sociology, University of Wisconsin–Madison.

Many people have made important contributions over the five years since this research was first conceived. Mary Ann Pate coauthored the original grant proposal, helped to write the original schedule, and supervised the pre-test interviewing and data analyses; without her, the research might never have gotten off the ground. Pat MacCorquodale gave her time, energy, and insights to every phase of the major study and wrote the initial drafts of Chapters 3 and 9 and Appendix II; her invaluable assistance is partially acknowledged by coauthorship. Tony Pate and Jane Traupmann served as research assistants. The careful and conscientious interviewing by our staff of 24 was a major contribution; as indicated in Chapter 3 and Appendix II, the data on interviewing quality uniformly indicate that their work was excellent. Susan Boyle ably fulfilled the delicate role of "paid respondent," which allowed us to determine the reliability of our questions and provide valuable feedback to the 22 interviewers. Three persons contributed to the project as jacks-of-all-trades, through bookkeeping, typing, keypunching, and in general, keeping us afloat: Carolyn Blackánn, Linda Eaves, and especially Jeanne Peterson, who was invaluable during her two years with us. Lyn Kimbrough, Connie Kolpin, and Rose Sommers all earned our sincere appreciation for carefully typing various drafts of the manuscript.

As usual, this research depended on the cooperation of the respondents, particularly the nonstudents who often spent considerable time and effort in coming to the campus to be interviewed. Although all were paid for their participation, the quality of our results is due in part to their genuine interest and willingness to answer questions honestly.

Finally, we wish to express our deepest gratitude to our spouses. They provided the interest, encouragement, and support that helped us sustain the day-to-day activities of this project. In addition, they were understanding of the limitations that the research at times placed on our personal lives.

Without the efforts and support of all these persons, this research would not have been successfully conducted.

Contents

150316

List of Tables

List of Figures

Premarital Sexuality

1

Introduction

SEXUAL BEHAVIOR has been of increasing interest to sociologists over the past twenty years. Perhaps the fundamental reason for this interest lies in the fact that all sexual activity is ordered; this ordering is at least partially a social phenomenon. As Gagnon and Simon (1973) have pointed out, society creates "a narrow domain of *de jure* legitimacy by constraining the age, gender, legal and kin relationships between sexual actors, as well as setting limits on the sites of behavior and the connections between organs." From a sociological viewpoint, sexual activity is ordered or patterned by norms, including laws, and these norms are reinforced by social control: rewards for conformity to and punishments for deviation from them.

This point of view generates two basic questions. First, what are the content and social origins of these norms? Second, how do these norms come to guide or control the behavior of individuals? It is the latter which particularly directs our attention toward the sexual activity of adolescents and young adults, i.e., premarital sexuality. All norms are learned through socialization, and an important aspect of adolescence in our society is the socialization of sexual expression.

For the most part, previous research in premarital sexuality has reflected one of two orientations. The first is sociological and emphasizes the societal or macro correlates of premarital sexual behavior. The underlying interest is in the relationship of sexuality to other institutions in society; thus, such research is directed toward the first question noted above, that of the content and social origins of sexual norms. Research in this tradition is especially concerned with the extent to which sexual behavior differs by variables such as gender, social class, religion, and

3

educational background. Kinsey (Kinsey, Pomeroy, and Martin, 1948; Kinsey et al., 1953) consistently found differences in the incidence and frequency of the behaviors he studied as a function of such variables. His research was the first to document differences in sexual behavior by gender, class, education, etc. More recent work within this perspective includes Schofield's (1965) research on youth in Great Britain, Kantner and Zelnik's (1972) study of single adolescent women in the United States, and work by Udry, Bauman, and Morris (1975). This body of research has clearly demonstrated the influence of such variables on premarital sexuality and led us to incorporate similar variables in our own thinking and research.

A second orientation may be described as sociopsychological. Here, the focus is interpersonal, on the immediate social influences which impinge on the individuals under study. Thus, this research is concerned with the second basic question, the acquisition of norms or standards by individuals. Early research using this perspective was carried out by Ehrmann (1959). He developed measures of parental, peer, and courtship influences and studied their impact on young people's sexual attitudes and behavior. He was concerned with the nature of heterosexual interactions and collected a great deal of information on dating patterns, the emotional quality of male-female relationships, and who initiated and who controlled or stopped various sexual behaviors. Recent investigators employing this general perspective include Simon, Berger, and Gagnon (1972) and Sorensen (1972). A related body of research focuses specifically on the relationship between these social influences and sexual attitudes or standards, and de-emphasizes sexual behavior. This approach was initiated by Reiss (1960, 1967), and his work continues to be very influential. Recent studies utilizing this approach include those by Vandiver (1972), Libby (1974), Perlman (1974), and Walsh, Ferrell, and Tolone (1976). Taken as a whole, this body of research indicates that influences in the individual's immediate social environment affect his or her premarital sexual attitudes and behavior.

Perhaps the major substantive weakness of the extant literature is the lack of a theory or model which integrates these two orientations. Adherents of each have tended to ignore those variables considered most important by the other. Therefore, those who work in the macro tradition explicitly or implicitly assume that the individual's behavior is a function of the norms he or she learns, and that the content of norms varies primarily or only by religion, social class, gender, and educational background. Thus, in their research, they focus on subgroup differences rather than individual differences in standards, heterosexual relationships, and peer group memberships as these relate to behavior. Research in the micro tradition is based on the assumption that individual differences are the major determinant of sexual behavior. Thus, they focus empirically on variation within subgroups, e.g., within male and female or social class groups, and de-emphasize the impact of societal variables. Existing work, therefore, has been severely limited in the comprehensiveness with which it has approached premarital sexual behavior.

At the most general level, the purpose of the research reported here is to integrate these two orientations. Several aspects of our work were directed to this end. First, we developed a general conceptual model of the social influences on premarital sexuality. This model includes both macro and micro variables and specifies a set of relationships between them. This model is presented in detail in the second half of Chapter 2. Second, we included in our research measures of both types of variables. The resulting data set is thus much more comprehensive than is typical of research in this area. Third, we systematically utilized statistical techniques to measure the relative association among variables. Such comparisons provide an indication of the relative contributions of macro and micro influences on premarital sexuality. Last, a general assessment of the contemporary validity of each orientation is one of the foci of the concluding chapter.

Beyond this general purpose, there are three more specific ways in which this research was designed to contribute to the study of premarital sexuality.

Past work, whether focused on societal factors or on aspects of one's immediate social environment, has neglected intraindividual variables. The only characteristic studied with any consistency is the person's attitudes; we review this literature in Chapter 2. Our model is a sociopsychological one and as such suggests that other variables within the person may be systematically related to sexuality. Two studies (Stratton and Spitzer, 1967; Perlman, 1974) have suggested a relationship between self-esteem and sexual standards or behavior. In addition, we included measures of self-image, body image, internal-external control, and sex role attitudes. To our knowledge, this is the first study which has included this last variable. Our results allow us to determine whether these variables are associated with sexuality and are unique in this regard.

A second lacuna in past research has been the study of the concrete interaction within which sexual activity occurs. While the pioneering study of premarital activity (Ehrmann, 1959) measured several aspects of this interaction, subsequent research has ignored it. More specifically, there has been little or no effort to include (1) the partner's social characteristics such as age and social class, (2) the person's perceptions of his or her partner's relevant aspects such as sexual standards, or (3) aspects of the interaction itself such as who initiates and controls sexual activity. We have both included these factors in our conceptual model and incorporated measures of each into our research design.

Thus, in a variety of ways, we have attempted to produce a much more comprehensive analysis, both conceptual and empirical, of premarital sexuality. Our model integrates two formerly disparate orientations and includes both intraindividual and interactional characteristics, factors which have been neglected in the past. The result is a much more complex and sophisticated discussion of the influences on young people's sexuality.

The third specific contribution of the research to be reported here is methodological, though it has important substantive implications. A serious limitation in previous research is in the samples which have been studied. Many of the studies are based on data from college students. Usually the sample is not even random or representative of students but consists simply of those who were present in particular classes on the day the questionnaire was distributed. It is likely that students who take, for example, marriage-and-the-family or human sexuality classes, differ in systematic but unknown ways from other students in the same college. Thus, results from such studies must be viewed as limited in the extent to which they can be generalized. The few studies which are not limited to samples of students have been either of adolescents from 13 to 17 (e.g., Vener and Stewart, 1974) or from 13 to 19 (e.g., Sorensen, 1972), or of adults (e.g., Hunt, 1974). No single study has focused on college-age but nonstudent young people. Our sample was designed to overcome both of these limitations. It includes a stratified, random sample of undergraduate students with almost equal representation of men and women and of the four classes. It also includes a random sample of single men and women, aged 18 to 23, who were not students. We can therefore compare for the first time comparable groups on the same measures. This allows us to determine whether students and nonstudents are subject to different processes of influence, i.e., whether the relationships between variables are different, or whether these groups differ only in the magnitude of various characteristics or relationships. In addition to its comparative value, the inclusion of nonstudents provides information about this hitherto "hidden" population. The substantive value of this sample lies in the fact that any conclusions we reach rest on a much sounder empirical base, and thus we can have greater confidence in their validity and generality.

PLAN OF THE BOOK

Past research has provided us with a general perspective. The individual's sexual behavior has been viewed as a result of two types of social influences. The first is the impact of society as a whole and its major institutions such as religion; this reflects the normative aspects of control over sexuality. The second is the influence of persons and groups with which the individual interacts, or the interpersonal aspects of control over sexuality. At the same time, this past research, which is reviewed in the first half of Chapter 2, has generally been limited in scope. Typically, each study has dealt with only a few relevant aspects. Much of the available literature ignores the individual's partner or the nature of the relationship. A more comprehensive model of sexual socialization or development is needed in order to (1) integrate these diverse pieces and (2) enhance our understanding of the sexual activities of adolescents and young adults. Such a model is presented in the second half of Chapter 2.

Our desire to produce a solid, comprehensive, empirical base raised a number of methodological considerations. The methods employed in studying sexuality have been a source of continuing controversy. Some of the important issues were amenable to study; accordingly, we incorporated a series of "experiments" in our research. The results of these are the focus of Appendix II. A general description of our research methods is the concern of Chapter 3. The measures of basic variables employed in our study are described in Appendix I.

The basic findings are the focus of Chapters 4 through 7. Each chapter considers in detail the data involving a group of related variables and their interrelationships with our measures of sexuality. Chapter 8 reports the results of an overall (regression) analysis which included all of the relevant variables of our model. This analysis constitutes both a summary of our findings and a test of the relative importance of the relationships identified in our model of premarital sexuality. Chapter 9 considers the interrelationships between sexuality and contraceptive use as evidenced in our data. Chapter 10 provides an overview of the research and some conclusions.

Throughout, we have attempted to relate both our model and our results to past work in this area. At the same time, we felt it was important to be selective, to limit ourselves to the most appropriate previous work. The literature which is cited in this book and to which our findings are related was selected according to three criteria.

First, we generally do not cite nonempirical work. Since our concern is to develop a valid model, it is important to rely primarily on empirical research. In addition, reliance on such research helps to eliminate bias due to the analyst's values, a serious problem in materials regarding sexuality.

Second, we emphasize survey and questionnaire studies and do not cite case study and small sample research. Such research has typically been based on an individualistic or psychological perspective, which is an orientation different from our own. While our findings have relevance for those who employ such a perspective, we do not systematically indicate such points of integration.

Third, we place greater emphasis on those surveys which involve representative samples and report multivariate analyses of their data. We can have greater confidence in the validity of such studies; their results, therefore, must be given a prominent place in an empirically based model of premarital sexuality.

The use of these criteria has resulted in the omission of some otherwise relevant articles and books. We are aware of them and of the consequent limitation in our coverage of the literature. However, we have preferred to concentrate our efforts toward building upon and integrating our findings with the most conceptually relevant material and the most empirically sound works in the area.

2

Social Aspects
of Premarital Sexuality

IF SOCIETY controls the expression of sexuality via norms, then the acquisition of these norms by individuals is an important control mechanism. Sociologically oriented writers typically refer to the process involved as "socialization." Individualistically oriented analysts often use the term "development." While this process is not the explicit focus of our research, a conception of it underlies our model and the interpretation of some of our results. Accordingly, we will briefly present this conception of what we term "sociosexual development." Then we will review past research, concentrating on issues to which our own study is relevant. Finally, the last part of this chapter focus on our conceptual model of the major social influences on premarital sexuality.

SOCIOSEXUAL DEVELOPMENT

A basic aspect of societal control over sexuality is the process of socialization. This process consists of the individual learning the norms, information, and behaviors relevant to sexual activity. From the viewpoint of the individual, he or she undergoes a process of sociosexual development.

We believe that this process consists of three stages, which usually occur sequentially. The first stage occurs during childhood. The learning at this time is of two kinds. One kind involves values and norms regarding appropriate and inappropriate sexual expression. These values and norms include specifications of both the behaviors and the types of persons which are acceptable. The other, more general, type of learning is of gender role, the social characteristics and behaviors appropriate for a male

9

or female. The primary socializing agents during this period are parents or parent substitutes. They are the major normative source for the child, and they have considerable control over the types of other influences to which the child is exposed.

The second stage occurs principally during early adolescence. The content of socialization at this time consists of what we refer to as information, about sexual anatomy, physiology, and potential settings for sexual expression. The major socializing agents at this stage are peers, friends of the same age and same gender. The importance of such peer influence is a theme to which we will repeatedly return.

The third stage generally occupies late adolescence and young adulthood. It occurs as the individual engages in sexual activity with a partner, and it consists of learning the interpersonal and behavioral aspects of sexuality. At this stage, the dyad, rather than the peer group or the family, is the principal socializing unit.

Although these stages are discussed as if they are distinct, they undoubtedly overlap to some extent. Parents continue to exert influence, at least as long as the young person lives at home. Initially the influence of peers occurs in addition to rather than instead of parental control. Only with time does their relative weight reverse, and peers become the dominant force. Similarly, partners become more influential as the relationship develops and as the person becomes more accepting of sexual activity.

This three-stage model is summarized in figure 2.1. It is the underlying basis for our approach to premarital sexual activity. As noted above, past research contributed more specific concepts, measures, and results to our own study. We turn now to a selective review of that work.

	Stage	Primary Social Influence	Developmental Focus
I	Normative	Parents	Gender Role, Sexual Values, Norms
II	Informational	Peers	Information
III	Behavioral	Partners	Sexual Expression

FIGURE 2.1. Stages in Sociosexual Development

ISSUES IN THE STUDY OF PREMARITAL SEXUALITY

The Development of Sexuality

Our model identifies the development of sexual expression or behavior as one stage of sociosexual socialization. It begins when the individual begins to "date," that is, to engage in interactions with members of the opposite sex which are viewed by the participants as having romantic and/or sexual potential. Early in this developmental process, the individual engages only in the least intimate behaviors, such as holding hands and kissing. Only with time, as both the individual and his or her relationships develop, do more intimate behaviors, such as breast fondling, commence. The first sexual intercourse occurs late in this developmental process, often several years after the process begins.

Previous work has varied greatly in how this process is considered, if at all. Several authors have focused on norms rather than on behavior. Their implicit or explicit view is that behavior is primarily determined by norms. These authors, e.g., Reiss (1960, 1967), Schofield (1965), and Sorensen (1972), de-emphasize behavior and focus on changes in the content of norms as the young person grows. Others seem to have implicitly assumed that there is a process of behavioral development over time, but have not explicitly discussed it. (See, for example, Ehrmann, 1959, and the discussion below.) Finally, a few authors have focused primarily on behavior (Hardy, 1964; Rains, 1971; Kantner and Zelnik, 1973). These authors ignore norms or standards and focus on variations in behavior as a result of social background or previous sexual experience. Hardy has explicitly proposed a learning model of the development of sexual expression. Thus, a major area of disagreement is the primacy of norms versus behavior in premarital sexuality. Accordingly, we have measured both the individual's standards and behavior and have assessed the relationship between them. In addition, we have employed the behavioral measures necessary to obtain information about the process of behavioral development per se.

Evidence suggestive of the developmental nature of sexual behavior is found in Ehrmann's (1959) data. His research involved questionnaires collected from a non-probability sample of 841 college students, 576 males and 265 females. These data were supplemented with material from interviews with 50 of the men and 50 of the women. He did not assume that there is a developmental sequence, but the measures he introduced are necessary prerequisites to the study of such a process. In particular, he divided sexual behavior into a specific and relatively exhaustive set of "stages," or precisely defined, distinct activities. He presents the rationale for this approach as follows:

> Heterosexual behavior falls into highly compartmentalized *stages* of increasing degrees of intensity, as judged by the young people of our own society, both with respect to physical intimacy and to moral judgment. These stages range from no physical contact, at the one extreme, on through holding hands, kissing, general body embrace, and the fondling of various portions of the body, to sexual intercourse at the other. (1959, p. 2)

Accordingly, his measures identified eight behaviors, and the students were asked a series of questions about their involvement in each. Ehrmann introduced a second innovation which has also been adopted by subsequent researchers. He asked each person whether he or she had *ever* engaged in each of the behaviors; he referred to the most advanced (intimate) stage reported as the person's *lifetime behavior*. In addition, he inquired about the most intimate activity in which the person had engaged on each date in the past month; the most advanced stage reported is referred to as *current behavior*.

Direct evidence of the developmental nature of premarital sexual behavior requires the assessment not only of lifetime behavior measured in stages, but also of the age at which the individual first engages in each type of behavior. Some subsequent investigations have included measures of both. The results obtained by Schofield (1965) are typical. His study involved interviews with 1,873 single British youths aged 15 to 19. He reported the accumulative incidence of each of the eight behaviors included in his measure of sexual activity by age of first experience (Schofield, 1965, tables 3.3, 3.4; figures 3/2, 3/3; pp. 32–37). He found that at a given age, the percentage reporting that they had ever engaged in a given behavior decreased consistently from the least to the most intimate behaviors. At age 18, for example, 92 percent of his male interviewees reported that they had engaged in kissing, with 80 percent reporting "breast stimulation over clothes," 69 percent "breast stimulation under clothes," 56 percent "active genital stimulation," and 34 percent reporting sexual intercourse. He recognized the developmental implications of these and other results and suggested five stages of sexual development through which the individual passes sequentially. They are as follows: "limited or no contact with the opposite sex," "limited experience" (the person has engaged only in kissing or breast fondling), "sexual intimacies . . . short of intercourse," intercourse with only one partner, and coitus with more than one partner.

Complete evidence of such a developmental process requires two pieces of data. Using a scale of behavior which includes stages (activities ordered from least to most intimate), one must first show that all those who report a given behavior also report having engaged in all of the less intimate behaviors in the scale. Schofield stated that this was true of his data. Second, one must show that if an individual has not engaged in a given behavior, he or she has also *not* engaged in more intimate behaviors. While Schofield asserted that this was true of his respondents, an earlier methodological decision made it impossible for him to determine whether it was empirically valid. Schofield was understandably concerned about the problem of embarrassing his respondents and thus reducing their willingness to answer questions. He was particularly concerned that asking about behaviors in which they had not engaged would produce embarrassment. Accordingly, he ordered his questions about sexual behavior from least to most intimate, and when a respondent reported having not engaged in a given activity, he or she was not asked about participation in more intimate ones. Schofield recognized that this procedure may produce the sequential properties of his scale by making it impossible to determine whether individuals had engaged in more intimate behaviors without having participated in less intimate ones. This is one of many examples in which concern about the sensitivity of respondents to questions about sexuality produced limitations in the data obtained. We shall consider this topic in detail in Chapter 3 and in Appendix II.

A variety of other findings are consistent with a developmental interpretation. Ehrmann (1959) reported a positive relationship between age at first date and participation in more intimate sexual activities for males. Schofield (1965) found a positive relationship between age at first date and experience in sexual intercourse. Sorensen (1972) presented his results in a way which suggests a developmental process, although he did not explicitly discuss one. His research involved interviews with a national sample of 393 adolescents (aged 13–19)[1]. He divided respondents into four "sexual behavior groups," and devoted a chapter to the characteristics of each group. The groups were ordered in terms of extent of sexual experience and included "sexually inexperienced," "beginners" (those who had engaged in sexual activities but not intercourse), "serial monogamists" (essentially nonvirgins whose activities were primarily with one partner), and "sexual adventurers." These groups are very similar to four of the five stages of development discussed by Schofield. Sorensen's results indicate that adventurers begin to have intercourse earlier and report larger numbers of sexual partners and greater frequency of intercourse than monogamists.

Thus, there are a variety of findings consistent with a developmental hypothesis regarding the occurrence of sexual behavior. However, there are no published studies which have clearly demonstrated a developmental process in premarital sexual activity. The data and the analytic techniques employed in the present research allow us to assess the extent to which such a process occurs. In particular, we can determine the extent to which involvement in various behaviors occurs sequentially and ascertain the relationship between past experience and present behavior.

There has been relatively little effort directed toward conceptualizing this process. Perhaps the most parsimonious statement is found in Hardy (1964). He suggests an approach-avoidance motivational paradigm, in

1. Sorensen's sample may not be representative of American adolescents. DeLamater (1974b) indicates that interviews were completed with less than 50 percent of the young people who resided in the sampled dwelling units.

which an individual is motivated to engage in a particular sexual activity by positive expectations about its outcome, and simultaneously inhibited by moral concerns and various fears. If the individual engages in a given behavior, for example, kissing, the consequences will typically reinforce the positive expectations and to some extent, extinguish the negative ones. The individual begins with the least intimate behavior because it is associated with the fewest inhibitions; only when the person becomes comfortable with that behavior, that is, has experienced positive reinforcement and a decline in inhibitions due to fear, etc., does he or she progress to the next behavior. This conceptualization is consistent with much of the anecdotal material reported by both Ehrmann (1959) and Sorensen (1972), and with the various findings discussed earlier.

Attitudes and Sexual Behavior

The concept of attitudes has played an important role in previous work. Generally, those investigators who have used it have done so in one of two ways. One group has assumed that one's attitudes determine his or her sexual behavior. The other group has attempted to relate much more general attitudes to sexual activity. These two bodies of literature are quite distinct, and we shall review them in turn.

Attitudes as a Determinant of Sexual Behavior

To the extent that investigators have attempted to explain premarital sexual behavior, to identify the reason why some individuals engage in various behaviors and others do not, those working within the micro orientation have usually relied on the individual's attitudes or beliefs. As we shall see, different investigators have identified and/or measured the relevant attitudes in various ways, but several have shared the assumption that a person's beliefs about the acceptability of a behavior before marriage are a major influence on his or her behavior.

From our perspective, these beliefs or attitudes are the result of socialization and are the representation within the individual of social norms. Once acquired, these norms are the basis for self-control over one's sexual activity. Since sexual behavior is private in our society, no potential control agents, other than the participating individuals, are present when it occurs. Thus, if control is to occur, it must be via influence in the individuals through self-control or negotiation between partners. Parents and other agents thus focus their influence on attitudes. But it should be remembered that the source of normative learning is the society and its agents, and thus control via attitudes represents societal control as well.

Ehrmann.   In his work, Ehrmann (1959) has employed the terms "sex codes of conduct" or "code of sexual morality" to refer to these attitudes. He identified three specific codes. The first is the social code, the code of conduct "embodied in the folkways and mores" (p. 171); this is clearly the equivalent of the sociological concept of norm. In a static society with high levels of consensus and strong social controls on premarital behavior, one could presumably infer young people's attitudes directly from the norm; that is, we would expect people's attitudes to merely reflect prevailing societal norms or standards. But Ehrmann has pointed out that in a society experiencing change, there may be ambiguity as to the content of the social code. In this situation we cannot assume that there is a single set of societal norms and that individual attitudes are identical to it. Accordingly, he identified two other codes: personal code, "what the individual considers to be right and proper heterosexual conduct for himself or herself"; and peer code, "what the individual considers to be permissible and acceptable conduct for his or her associates in the peer group" (p. 174). On the basis of his exploratory or pre-test interviews, he distinguished three types of relationships: acquaintance (someone "toward whom one does not feel very familiar" [p. 174]), friend, and lover (one with whom the person is or was in love). Ehrmann stated that these terms were in common use among the student population studied. Questions about personal and peer codes were not included in the questionnaires, but only in the interviews with the subsamples of 50 males and 50 females. With respect to these measures within the interviews, "In every case there was sufficient discussion to determine that the subject clearly understood the characteristics of each of these [three] relationships . . . " (p. 176). Ehrmann assessed peer and personal codes in terms of the same activities included in his behavioral measure: he asked for each individual's opinion of acceptable behavior for friends and for himself or herself in each of the three relationships, and coded the responses in terms of his eight-stage scale.

An entire chapter in Ehrmann's book (Chapter 5) is devoted to the relationships between lifetime behavior, peer code, and personal code. In general, Ehrmann found that the individual's peer code was somewhat more liberal, that is, allowed more intimate behavior within a particular type of relationship, than was his or her personal code. He also reported a number of analyses of the relationship between codes and lifetime behavior. His results show a close correspondence between personal code and lifetime behavior, that is, between what respondents say they believe is acceptable behavior with acquaintances, friends, and lovers and the most intimate behavior in which they report having ever engaged in each type of relationship. Personal code and lifetime behavior were the same in 71 to 98 percent of the cases (see Ehrmann, 1959, table 5.4, p. 185); departures from identity occurred primarily among males, where from 6 to 29 percent reported a code which allowed more intimate behavior than that in which they had ever engaged.

Thus, Ehrmann's results demonstrated correspondence between the person's attitudes concerning the acceptability of particular sexual behaviors ("personal code") and his or her lifetime sexual behavior. He also found that both standards and behavior varied as a function of the nature of the heterosexual relationship. However, these results were based on small samples of only 50 males and 50 females; the relationship needs to be verified on larger, more representative samples. Subsequent research has often included measures of the attitudinal phenomenon that he designates "personal code."

Reiss. The most extensive and widely known work on attitudinal phenomena has been conducted by Ira Reiss. The major statement of his conceptual position is found in *Premarital Sexual Standards in America* (1960). Reiss has employed the term *standards* to refer to an individual's beliefs about the acceptability of various sexual behaviors before marriage. This approach is sociological, in contrast to one which stresses "the psychological and biological determinants" of sexual behavior. Thus, Reiss's "main interest is in the shared cultural standards underlying the patterns of sexual behavior which occur in society" (p. 81). He has argued that the standards held by individuals are derived from the culture and that these standards regulate sexual behavior. He has identified four premarital standards which he argued were (are) predominant in American society. The four types are as follows: abstinence, the double standard, permissiveness (the acceptance of intercourse) with affection, and permissiveness without affection.

The relevant empirical data are reported in his later book, *The Social Context of Premarital Sexual Permissiveness* (1967). The measure of premarital standards was based on a perspective similar to Ehrmann's; it assumed that the acceptability of a given behavior depends upon the nature of the heterosexual relationship. Whereas Ehrmann specified only the relationship and asked what behavior was acceptable, Reiss specified both relationships and behavior. Reiss employed three behaviors: kissing, petting, and coitus ("full sexual relations"). The definition of petting was included in the instructions to the respondent for completing the scale: "Petting means sexually stimulating behavior more intimate than kissing and simple hugging, but not including full sexual relations" (p. 22). Reiss recognized that this definition was broad and included breast and genital fondling (and perhaps oral-genital sexuality), activities which other behavioral measures distinguish. He also specified four relationships:

engaged, in love, strong affection, and no affection; definitions of love and strong affection were also included in the instructions (pp. 21–22). The measure itself included 12 items, each of which specified one of the behaviors and one of the relationship categories. The 12 items were assessed twice, once with males and once with females as the referent. Each item was of the form "I believe that *(behavior)* is acceptable for the male/ female before marriage when *(description of the relationship)*" Response choices ranged from "strongly agree" to "strongly disagree."

The data reported were obtained from seven samples: white and black high school students in Virginia; white and black college students in Virginia; white college students in New York and in Iowa; and a national sample of adults. All of the student data was collected through questionnaires, and all but the Iowa college sample were probability samples. The adult sample involved interviews conducted by the National Opinion Research Center, from a quota sample within selected city blocks $(N = 1,515)$. For purposes of analysis, Reiss employed Guttman scaling techniques to reduce the responses to the 12 items for each sex to a single measure, scored to reflect "permissiveness," the extent to which the three behaviors are acceptable before marriage.

Much of the book is devoted to analysis of the relationship between permissiveness and various social characteristics. Permissiveness was shown to be related to various sociological variables, particularly gender, race, religiosity and religious attendance, and social class. Reiss argued that the differing racial, religious, and class groupings are the source and transmitters of differing sexual standards. More specifically, each family belongs to some set of these groups from which it derives the standards which are transmitted to children. Reiss demonstrated that, in addition to the family's sociological characteristics, the role relationships within it also are related to the individual's permissiveness. As the individual enters the courtship process in adolescence, peers become important influences on standards, and Reiss discussed the relationship between the individual's permissiveness and the permissiveness which he or she perceives among peers. Reiss reported that most young people perceive their parents as less permissive and their peers as more permissive than themselves; the latter was also found by Ehrmann.

Reiss included measures of sexual behavior only in the questionnaire employed with the Iowa student sample (the only sample which was not a probability one). Most of the respondents were juniors and seniors at the time of the data collection. Reiss found a high correspondence between current standards and current behavior. Majorities of from 64 to 78 percent of those holding a given standard reported that behavior as their most intimate current activity. Minorities reported both more or less intimate behavior than that allowed by their standard. Reiss discussed this relationship relatively briefly. His main emphasis was on the standards themselves and their cultural and social sources. Within that context, both of his books argue for the importance of studying premarital sexual standards. A number of subsequent studies have expanded on Reiss's basic model. These researchers assume that the individual's standards do determine his or her behavior and in general, report strong relationships between the two. Of particular concern in more recent work has been the relative influence of various sources on standards, or on the relationship between standards and behavior. Thus, research has assessed the role of campus standards (Clayton, 1972), peers (Mirande, 1968; Vandiver, 1972; Walsh, Ferrell, and Tolone, 1976), and parents (Walsh, 1970; Burgess, 1973) as influences on the individual's standards.

Other evidence for the role of attitudes as determinants of premarital sexual behavior is found in articles by Christensen and Gregg (1970) and Kaats and Davis (1972). The latter identified the individual's standards as one of three determinants and concluded that "the most powerful predictor of the extent of sexual experience among these three factors is the person's own judgement of its acceptability" (p. 565).

General Attitudes and Sexual Behavior

Two major studies have assessed other, more general attitudes and have attempted to relate them to premarital sexual behavior. Schofield (1965) included a wide variety of items in his interviews, such as questions dealing with marriage, sex education, virginity, and general attitudes toward premarital sex (e.g., whether "sexual intercourse before marriage is wrong"). Schofield factor analyzed responses to the items and discussed primarily those factors which differentiated respondents at different stages of sexual experience. He found 15 first-order factors for males and 16 for females. He subsequently analyzed the matrix of correlations between first-order factors and identified five factors which were significantly and positively associated with sexual experience for each sex. For males, the factors listed were support for teenagers, distaste for mass media, respect for adults, support for boys' sexual freedom, and support for moral restrictions. For females, they were antipathy towards the family, opposition to sex instruction, belief in personal moral responsibility, belief in double standards, and opposition to girls' sexual freedom. Finally, analysis of the intercorrelations of these factors resulted in two third-order factors, which were quite similar for both sexes: teenage ethnocentrism ("the extent to which teenagers are for their own group and opposed to all others") and restrictiveness ("with opinions on honesty, control of teenagers, and a strict moral code at one end, to permissiveness in all these topics at the other end") (pp. 205–6). With controlling for age, restrictiveness was negatively correlated with sexual experience for both sexes, particularly for males. The restrictive-permissive factor seemed in part to represent sexual permissiveness as studied by Reiss; a major item loading on this factor for both sexes was "Sexual intercourse before marriage is wrong." The relationship between restrictiveness and sexual behavior in Schofield's data also reflected Reiss's finding that "general liberalism" was associated with greater premarital sexual permissiveness.

Sorensen (1972) included a variety of attitudinal items in his questionnaire. Again, these tended to be general attitudinal statements; he did not include an Ehrmann/Reiss type measure of the individual's sexual standards. A major attitudinal dimension which Sorensen emphasized was called "generational chauvinism"; the belief by adolescents "that their values are different from those of their elders . . . [and] that their values are superior to those of the older generation" (p. 42). He discussed nine items, each of which contrasted "young people" or "people in my generation" with "older people in their forties and fifties." His measure was simply the number of items which the respondent answered in the direction (agree/disagree) which affirmed the superiority of young people's values and orientations. He reported that chauvinism thus measured was positively associated with lifetime sexual experience.

Vandiver (1972) examined the interrelationships of three belief systems and sexual permissiveness, and the relative influence of peers and parents. He examined religious ideology, general ideology of social institutions, and self-identification with student subcultures. In general, he found that the relationship of these dimensions to general liberal-conservative ideology was weak. Also, peers were more similar and had more influence on standards and ideology than parents did. His approach is similar to those above in that it focuses on youth, student groups, on the one hand, and general social institutions on the other.

Sorensen's measure of chauvinism is conceptually very similar to Schofield's ethnocentrism factor. Both seem to be measures of the extent to which a young person identifies with and accepts the attitudes and values of peers, in contrast to parents, "older people," and society in general. Their findings can thus be readily interpreted within our conceptual framework. Reiss's data indicate that parents are generally among the least permissive persons in our society; he argues that young people who remain attached primarily to their families will also be relatively less permissive. As an adolescent moves into the courtship institution, he or she increasingly comes in contact with peers and their more permissive attitudes. Thus, measures of chauvinism or ethnocentrism probably reflect the extent of the young person's identification with the values of these peer groups and rejection of their parents' less permissive ones. This, in turn is related to the holding of more permissive personal standards. Walsh, Ferrell, and Tolone (1976), based on longitudinal data, have reported that a shift in reference group from parents to peers is associated with an increase in permissiveness. Had Schofield or Sorensen included a measure of standards, sexual permissiveness would have undoubtedly been positively related to chauvinism and ethnocentrism. From our perspective, these last factors are measures of the importance or credibility of parents and peers as sources of influence over one's sexuality.

In summary, two types of attitudes have been measured in past research and found to be related to sexual experience. Both Sorensen and Schofield reported that attitudes reflecting identification with peers and a feeling of superiority to, or rejection of, other groups within society were positively associated with lifetime sexual experience. Reiss and Ehrmann focused more specifically on young people's attitudes about their own premarital sexual behavior, and Ehrmann reported considerable data which demonstrated a close correspondence between the individual's standards or "code" and his or her lifetime sexual behavior. The value of these findings is reduced in all cases by limitations in the various studies. In particular, Ehrmann's data were based on samples of only 50 males and 50 females, and were collected between 1947 and 1950. Reiss reported only briefly on the relationship between standards and behavior, and datum was based on a nonprobability sample of college students. In both of these studies, the analytic technique employed was cross-tabular, and it is impossible to determine the relative influence of attitudes about the acceptability of behavior compared to other variables which are also related to sexual experience. More recent studies have tended to employ "convenience" samples, students present in particular classes on the day questionnaires are administered. As yet, no definitive and detailed analysis of the interrelationship of premarital standards and behavior has been published. One of the aims of the present research was to fill this lacuna. We assessed both the standards and behavior of large, random samples of single, young adults. We utilized techniques of data analysis which allowed us to determine the relative influence of several variables on behavior. Our finding with regard to the relationship between attitudes and behavior is one of the foci of Chapter 5.

The Premarital Dyad or Couple

We have seen that attitudes about the acceptability of various sexual behaviors seem to depend on the nature of the heterosexual relationship.

Both Reiss and Ehrmann specified particular types of relationships in their measures and found that young people indeed accept a given behavior, e.g., intercourse, in one type of relationship but not in another. The clear implication is that a major determinant of one's current sexual activity is the nature of the relationship with the person(s) one is dating.

Our own model assumes that sexual expression reflects the socialization which occurs in the dating relationship. Our respondents were 18-to-23-year-old single persons. We expected the vast majority of them to be dating, i.e., to be in Stage III of the model. Thus, their partner should have been the most important influence on their sexuality and have had relatively greater control over their present behavior than parents or peers.

As one reviews the research, it is striking that in general, current sexual behavior has not been analyzed from this point of view. Ehrmann reported *lifetime* behavior within the three types of relationships specified in his measure of personal code. In analyzing current behavior, however, he discussed the influence of going steady (a type of relationship not included in his measure of codes), relative social class of male and female, and number of dates and number of persons dated recently. Apparently, he did not ask the questionnaire respondents to classify their current relationships in terms of their emotional intimacy. As noted earlier, Reiss only briefly discussed the relationship between premarital standards and behavior and did not consider the quality of the relationship independently of these measures. Schofield and Sorensen assessed the quality of the relationship only for one's first partner in genital stimulation and apposition (Schofield) and intercourse (both).

More recent studies based on Reiss's permissiveness model (Mirande, 1968; Vandiver, 1972; Walsh, 1970; Walsh, Ferrell, and Tolone, 1976) generally have not assessed the intimacy of respondent's heterosexual relationships. They have also ignored various other potentially relevant characteristics of partners, such as age, social class, and religious background. Two studies which have assessed the relationship have focused on whether one is going steady or engaged rather than on emotional intimacy (Carns, 1973; Bell and Chaskes, 1970). In addition Carns reports data only for first coitus.

It seems essential to include measures of current relationships in research on current sexual behavior and to employ them systematically in analyses. Ehrmann, Schofield, and Sorensen have all relied heavily on number of dates, number of persons dated, and number of dates with each partner in analyzing current behavior. Certainly, one must date in order to engage in heterosexual activities, but the logic of measures of codes and standards argues that the quality of these relationships rather than sheer frequencies is a major determinant of current premarital activity. Kaats and Davis

(1972) have argued that, given a standard which allows certain behaviors, one must have the "opportunity" to engage in them, i.e., to be involved in a heterosexual relation of the appropriate type. Without such opportunity, the behaviors presumably will not occur.

Thus, past research has tended to overlook the emotional quality of the couple's relationship. It is difficult if not impossible to obtain any objective measure of this parameter; particularly in a survey context, one can only inquire about the respondent's perception of the extent of intimacy. But it is argued here that that perception is in fact a phenomenon of concern. If the individual believes that intercourse is appropriate with a person he or she loves, then whether or not coitus occurs should be in part determined by how feelings for the partner and the partner's feelings are defined. Some studies have assessed the level of commitment or exclusivity of the relationship by asking whether the couple are friends, going steady, or engaged. We believe that such commitment is less important than emotional involvement in determining the couple's sexual activity.

Accordingly, we have focused on the couple or dyad in analyzing current sexual behavior. We have included a variety of questions about the partner and the relationship in our research. In the analysis of current behavior, we have emphasized the partner more and characteristics of the individual, such as dating patterns, general attitudes, and personality, less than did past research. In this sense, our perspective is sociopsychological or micro, emphasizing social relationships and influences in the immediate social environment. This approach is in contrast to a more macro and behavioral focus, like Kinsey's emphasis on outlet, in which only two of the six behaviors of concern are heterosexual (petting and intercourse). It is also in contrast to the psychological approach which characterizes Sorensen's and Schofield's research, where the emphasis is on the individual, and his or her background characteristics, social attitudes, and personality (Schofield).

CONCEPTUAL PERSPECTIVE

The present research focuses on heterosexual activity. Thus, the presentation of the model upon which it is based is limited to such phenomena. We believe that the influences and processes discussed may occur in or be relevant to other areas of sexuality, such as homosexual activity and relationships and swinging or mate swapping. However, heterosexuality is clearly the modal pattern in our society and is of primary interest. In addition, we were limited in what could be included in the interview schedule by constraints of length and accordingly focused on heterosexual relationships and behavior.

The model, which combines the developmental perspective discussed earlier and relevant aspects of past research, identifies six classes of variables. It includes three sources of social influence or socializing agents: parents, peers, and partner within the dyadic relationship. In addition, we conceptualize the individual as having two sets of characteristics which may be important determinants of his or her sexuality. The first is previous sexual experience; the second is a set of sociopsychological characteristics, such as self-image and gender role orientations. The final class of variables is the person's current sexuality, which has two components: his or her attitudes or standards and sexual activity. The model is summarized in figure 2.2.

In one sense, our model exemplifies the truism that "there is nothing new under the sun." Each class of variables and each of the major relationships between classes has been suggested by someone at some time. Generally, our discussion of the model will credit these sources. At the same time, some of the measures, as has been discussed, have never before been included in research on premarital sexuality. Their inclusion is thus novel, and the results involving them unique and important independently of the model itself. Beyond that, this conceptualization represents a synthesis of disparate studies and is much more comprehensive than past work.

In the presentation which follows and in the discussion of the results in Chapters 4 through 7, we consider these classes of variables in developmental sequence, as they occur in an idealized pattern of individual socialization.

The earliest social influences on an individual come from the family. With regard to sexuality, the most important family characteristics are the standards held by the parents and the quality of the person's relationship with mother and father. As discussed above, parental standards in turn are influenced by the family's religious, racial, socioeconomic, and other characteristics. These determine the individual's initial sexual standards and thus are a major influence on his or her early sexual behavior. Although we cannot measure a young adult's earlier standards, we can consider previous sexual experience in relation to familial characteristics (Chapter 4).

The other aspects of the person which the family influences, and which may effect sexuality, are a set of sociopsychological variables. Five were included in this research: self-image, self-esteem, body image, internal-external locus of control, and gender role orientation. Their relationships with sexual ideology and current behavior are the focus of Chapter 5.

A second major source of influence on current sexuality is one's peers, as indicated in our developmental model and suggested by past research. We look at several ways of conceptualizing and measuring peer influence, and consider in detail their interrelationship with the person's standards and behavior (Chapter 6).

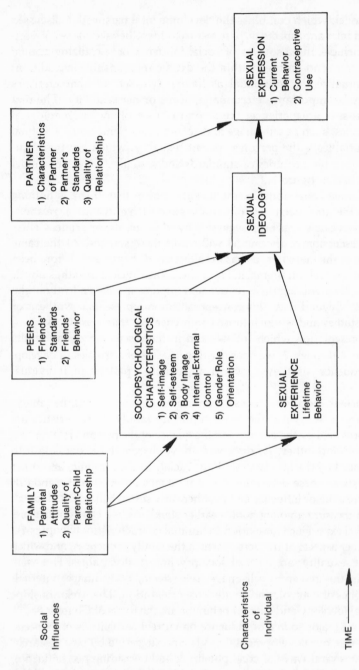

FIGURE 2.2. Conceptual Model and Principal Measures

The last set of variables are those characterizing the young adult's partner and the relationship. As noted above, we believe that this interpersonal context, in conjunction with one's premarital standards, should be the primary or most immediate determinant of his or her current heterosexual activity (Chapter 7).

We turn now to a more detailed discussion of each of these sets or classes.

Family Characteristics

There are a variety of potentially relevant family characteristics. We have argued that parental standards are very important, since they are the earliest to which the child is exposed and thus provide the foundation for subsequent sociosexual development. In addition, Burgess (1973) has reported evidence from small samples of students that the quality of the young person's relationship with parents is important. Those who experience a closer relationship may be more influenced by parental standards. Thus, we included various measures of quality of relationships with parents. Finally, previous research (for example, Reiss, 1967) has found relationships between various social characteristics of the family— class, religion, educational attainment of parents—and premarital standards.

Sexual Experience

We assume that the individual's current sexual behavior is indirectly the result of his or her previous sexual experience. More specifically, we believe that most persons undergo a process of behavioral development; this process begins with participation in the least intimate behaviors and proceeds through involvement in one or more experiences with sexual intercourse. From a biological perspective, almost all postpubescent males and females could engage in coitus and experience sexual excitement and release. The fact that sexual behavior develops more slowly, as a result of experiences over time, suggests that a process of socialization occurs. This process of social learning is the means by which society controls the individual's sexuality. It would require careful and extensive longitudinal research to identify precisely the individual's characteristics which are involved in this process; cross-sectional research, such as the present study, can at best index the process by retrospective assessment.

Information about this process comes from our measures of lifetime heterosexual activity. We are particularly interested in the extent to which involvement in sexual activities occurs sequentially, as evidenced by the individual's age at the time of his or her first experience with behaviors involving increasing physical intimacy. In addition, we have employed scaling and statistical techniques which measure the extent to which individuals uniformly engage in one behavior prior to their involvement in another. As noted earlier, in order to show sequential patterns of development, we need to demonstrate not only that individuals who engage in a given behavior all have experienced the less intimate ones, but also that no one who has not experienced that behavior has participated in more intimate ones.

Sociopsychological Characteristics of the Individual

In addition to attitudes, which are discussed below, this research measured several other characteristics of the person. We believe that characteristics such as self-image, body image, and whether the individual perceives himself or herself as controlling his or her own behavior are important influences on that behavior. These cognitions are products of one's experiences of socialization and thus, may provide additional vehicles for social control. If particular images are associated with particular behaviors, as will be argued below, society can influence behavior by influencing the content of these cognitions. Only one such sociopsychological aspect has been included in past research, self-esteem (Stratton and Spitzer, 1967; Perlman, 1974). The inclusion of the other measures described in this section is a unique aspect of this research.

The underlying perspective is symbolic interactionism (Shibutani, 1961). This orientation to social behavior begins with the assumption that there is no inherent meaning in social phenomena—behavior, relationships, and settings. Meaning is developed through social interaction and maintained over time by members of the group or society adhering to and basing actions upon these meanings.

Self-image and Self-esteem

The individual's identity is the set of beliefs or cognitions held about himself or herself; it is the definition of oneself as a social object and tells the person who he or she is. The self is also a social product; the individual learns this identity only through others' reactions, what they communicate explicitly or implicitly about the kind of person he or she is. It is argued that, once a self begins to develop, the individual begins to select situations and behaviors on the basis of his or her identity; one seeks out behavior compatible with self-image and avoids behavior which is incompatible with it. "Each man also has a stable sense of personal identity. What he is willing or unwilling to do depends upon the kind of human being he thinks he is" (Shibutani, 1961, p. 214).

A number of authors have suggested that whether an individual engages in various deviant or delinquent activities may be influenced by his or her self concept (for example, Schwartz and Stryker, 1970). It was this reasoning that first suggested to us that self-image might be related to premarital sexuality; certainly many adults view premarital intercourse as deviant as they view many activities which are legally defined as delinquency. Thus, we believed that some self-images might be associated with extensive premarital sexual behavior, and that others might be related to abstinence from physical intimacy. We had no specific hypotheses. For every plausible prediction, e.g., that persons who view themselves as highly likable, desirable, and attractive will have had greater dating and courtship experience and, therefore, more extensive sexual activity, the alternative was equally plausible, e.g., that persons with these characteristics would be assured of social popularity on nonsexual grounds and thus might participate less in sexual activities.

Many discussions of self-image or identity also consider the related phenomenon of self-esteem, "the manner in which a person evaluates himself" (Shibutani, 1961, p. 235). Self-esteem is generally conceptualized as ranging from high to low or positive to negative, reflecting the extent to which the individual sees himself or herself as a good, acceptable, desirable human being. Self-esteem is the result of others' reactions to the individual, specifically their communications about whether he or she is a worthwhile person. In recent years, self-esteem has been used as a major explanatory concept by social psychologists (a thorough review of this literature is included in Wells and Marwell, 1976). It seemed that self-esteem might be related to premarital sexuality. Again, no specific hypotheses were articulated in advance. People with low self-esteem might avoid intimate relationships because of fear that partners would respond negatively to them, or would not like them; alternatively, such persons might be more likely to engage in premarital sexuality in an attempt to obtain feedback about their social worth.[2]

Relationships between self-image and self-esteem on the one hand and premarital sexuality, on the other, seemed particularly likely because self-perceptions are social products and are assumed to influence social

2. A recent study suggests that the relationship between self-esteem and sexuality depends on the group standards and on whether behavior or attitudes are measured. Perlman (1974) found a positive relationship between esteem and number of coital partners in a small sample of students at a "liberal" college, but no relationship between these variables in a sample of students at a "moderate" college. He found no association in either sample between self-esteem and premarital standards as measured by Reiss's scale.

behavior. Once established, these aspects of self may be bases of self-control which reinforce social controls. In addition, they are important attributes which the person brings to heterosexual relationships. To the extent that past experience influences present social relationships, it may do so by affecting one's conception of self and evaluation of self as a social object. An alternative perspective has been employed by psychologists, who often conceptualize the characteristics which persons bring to situations in terms of personality and personality traits. These traits, or cognitive and behavioral orientations, are generally viewed as less subject to social influences, and perhaps, therefore, as more stable over time. Substantial relationships between personality traits and premarital sexuality have not been found. One relevant study which included personality measures is Vincent's (1961) *Unmarried Mothers*. His research involved in part a comparison of 100 unwed mothers and a matched sample of 100 single, never pregnant, high school senior females. Both groups completed the *California Psychological Inventory* which includes 18 personality scales. These scales comprise four general "classes": Poise, Ascendancy, and Self-assurance; Socialization, Maturity, and Responsibility; Achievement Potential and Intellectual Efficiency; and Intellectual and Interest Modes. In general, Vincent did not find substantial differences in scale scores or profiles; his results suggest that personality variables are not a major determinant of unwed motherhood.

Borgatta and Bohrnstedt (1970), in their longitudinal study of university undergraduates, included measures of personality characteristics and of participation in premarital intercourse. They found no substantial relationships between various scales designed to measure social orientations and general values, and the incidence of premarital intercourse. These findings, in conjunction with our focus on the interpersonal aspects of premarital sexuality, led us to focus primarily on characteristics which are a function of social interaction.

Body Image

Most discussions of self-image or identity focus on the individual's perceptions of self as a social actor, and the vast majority of empirical measures assess such perceptions exclusively. However, in some situations, the cognitions which one develops through interaction about his or her physical characteristics may influence behavior. For example, whether individuals choose to participate in athletics may be heavily influenced by their perceptions of relevant physical attributes such as strength, speed, and physique. Similarly, sexual attitudes and behavior may be influenced by a person's evaluation of his or her body, evaluations which to a considerable extent are influenced by the reactions of others to physical attributes. To our knowledge, such a relationship has never been researched. We therefore included a body-image scale which measured the extent to which the individual is satisfied with a variety of physical characteristics.

Internal-External Control

During the past decade, there has been considerable interest in the concept of internal-external control (Rotter, 1966) and associated measures. Internal control refers to the perception or belief that reinforcement, or more generally, the consequences, of behavior are due to the person's skills and abilities; external control refers to the belief that reinforcement or outcomes are due to others' actions or to chance factors. Elder (1968) has reviewed a number of studies which have linked adolescent socialization, particularly moral development, to internal-external control. It is possible that internal-external control influences premarital sexuality. The extent to which the individual adheres to his or her sexual code or standards may be mediated by perception of control; we might find that there is generally a closer correspondence between attitudes and behavior for those with a greater sense of personal control. We also anticipated that internal-external control might be related to contraceptive practices. Rains (1971) has argued that women begin to use contraceptives effectively only when they expect to have sexual intercourse; if they perceive intercourse as due to situational or chance factors, it is illogical to plan for it. It seems that contraceptive use might be more frequent when one generally has a sense that outcomes, in this case pregnancy, are under his or her control.

Definitions of Gender Roles

A final sociopsychological characteristic which may relate to premarital sexuality is the individual's perceptions of male and female roles. Ehrmann (1959) found that, in general, males initiated sexual activities, but females were the ones who stopped at particular behaviors. He argued that this was consistent with broader definitions of gender roles in our society. In the past decade, many young people have questioned the "traditional" role definitions, and some have developed a more egalitarian view of male-female relationships, rights, and duties. One might expect a different pattern of control over sexuality to be associated with balanced role definitions, characterized by more initiation by females and more termination by males. We also expected that role definitions might be related to contraceptive practice; thus, there might be more discussion about and, therefore, effective contraceptive use when the individual holds an egalitarian view of heterosexual relationships.

Thus, the research to be reported here included measures of a variety of sociopsychological characteristics: self-image and self-esteem, body image, internal-external control, and definitions of male and female roles. Each of these is conceptualized as a relatively stable aspect of the person, as a product of social learning generally and social interaction in particular, and as a potential influence on the individual's sexuality. None of these has been systematically studied in the context of sexual behavior, and it seemed important to determine whether and how they relate to premarital standards and/or sexual activity. Previous studies which have attempted to relate such variables, particularly self-image and self-esteem, to social behavior have yielded inconsistent findings. However, Ward (1974) has suggested that many of the behaviors typically studied are either habitual or governed by norms and sanctions. In such situations, habit or normative considerations may override the potential influence of characteristics of the person. He has argued that such attributes may have a much stronger influence in situations where the individual can exercise choice, i.e., control. Premarital sexuality, particularly the more intimate behaviors such as intercourse, is an area in which the individual has potentially complete control, and we therefore may be able to demonstrate such influences in this context.

Peer Group Memberships

So far, we have discussed attributes of the person, i.e., previous development in the realm of sexuality and several classes of perceptions. While all of these are social products, at any given time individuals bring these into their relationships with other persons or groups. It is within the framework of these characteristics that more immediate social influences operate.

We reviewed above the literature on the influence of the group. Analytically, the starting point is Ehrmann's (1959) observation that in a static, highly cohesive society, societal norms and individual standards would be identical, since individuals would be supported both by social consensus and by sanctions for violations of the norms. Ehrmann suggested that it is only when society is changing, with the result that the social code becomes ambiguous or seems to be invalid, that personal standards can diverge from the social code. Reiss (1960) identified four types of premarital standards which he believed were developing within American society. In his subsequent research (1967), he argued that primary groups are the major source of the individual's standards and that as the person becomes involved in the courtship institutions in society, he or she is increasingly influenced by the peer group. Reiss interpreted a variety of his data as consistent with the proposition that:

> The degree of acceptable premarital sexual permissiveness in a courtship group varies directly with the degree of autonomy of the courtship group and with the degree of acceptable premarital sexual permissiveness in the social and cultural setting outside the group. (p. 167)

Reiss views permissiveness in an individual's standards as primarily being the result of peer group influences while the group's permissiveness is a joint function of its autonomy from other institutions, especially the family, and of levels of permissiveness in its social milieu.

This argument is closely related to the symbolic interactionist assumption that meaning is socially determined. One corollary of that premise is that different social groups have different definitions of, i.e., norms about, the same behavior. For example, some groups (including certain religions) define sexual intercourse before marriage as unacceptable or wrong; for a variety of reasons, they argue that this behavior is acceptable only in the context of a marital relationship. Other groups define coitus as an appropriate part of a loving relationship, where the two people are "in love" with each other, whether they are married or not. Such groups may also provide definitions of being in love and give the individual cues and attributes to look for, both within the self and in the other person, that indicate whether they are in love. Finally, some groups might define intercourse as acceptable whenever both parties desire it regardless of the emotional intimacy or legal or religious status of the relationship. Thus, the existence of varying sexual standards is viewed as a consequence of different groups developing and maintaining different definitions of the appropriateness of certain sexual behaviors. Although there may be considerable variation in the social definition of when intercourse is acceptable, these groups might agree on the appropriateness or inappropriateness of other sexual phenomena. All would probably agree that sexual activity involving force, i.e., rape, is wrong. A majority might agree that intercourse is acceptable only in heterosexual couples and have a very negative view of homosexuality. And while they vary in requiring the couple to be married to each other, they might agree that adultery is wrong. So while groups may differ in the meaning they give to premarital heterosexual intercourse, there may be consensus or agreement about other aspects of sexuality. Thus, groups are the source of definitions of social behaviors, and of our beliefs about the nature and meaning of various behaviors and the conditions under which they are appropriate.

In theory, there is no limit to the meanings which might be associated with particular behaviors; there is a tremendous range of potential definitions. In reality, however, symbolic interactionists argue that only a very limited set of definitions are developed and sustained. Societal values are one important basis of limitation; values, or general beliefs about desirable goals or states, limit the range of potential definitions. Thus, our general values of individual freedom (when applied equally without regard to gender) lead us to view sexual activities involving force as undesirable, and as criminal behavior under certain circumstances. Similarly, the high value we place on the family leads us to define incest as unacceptable and often to define sexual activity between persons who are not married to each other as inappropriate. Of greater importance in the present context is the symbolic interactionist assumption that if meanings are to be valid for individuals, they must be shared, there must be *consensus* or agreement among those with whom a person interacts. Truly idiosyncratic beliefs or definitions are a logical impossibility, since all meaning is viewed as socially derived. Individuals have only a limited set of definitions available to them by virtue of their membership in various groups.

This analysis is fundamental to our perspective. We expect the individual's permissiveness to be related to the permissiveness of his or her peer groups. Since our research involved students at a large university, most of our respondents were relatively independent of their parents, lived away from home, and were subject to little direct influence of the university as an institution on their heterosexual activities. Peer groups in this setting have a great deal of autonomy, and therefore we can expect them to be relatively permissive. We planned to measure three aspects of peers' permissiveness and one aspect of permissiveness in the social setting of these groups, and expected them to be related to premarital standards.

As noted earlier, several studies have been based on Reiss's model and have focused on the social sources of permissive standards. Five of these have included some measure of peers' standards or behavior, and the individual's standards or behavior (Clayton, 1972; Mirande, 1968; Vandiver, 1972; Walsh, 1970; and Walsh, Ferrell, and Tolone, 1976). In general, all report correspondence between the peer and individual measures. Again, however, the value of these findings is often limited by (1) variability in the measures employed, and (2) limitations in the samples studied. The only study based on a random sample is Vandiver's. The others are all based on nonrandom samples of students living in dormitories or present in selected classes. A systematic analysis of this relationship based on representative samples of both students and nonstudents is one of the contributions of this research. This analysis is presented in the second half of Chapter 6.

The influence of groups on an individual's attitudes and behavior has repeatedly been demonstrated in laboratory research. When we move into "real world" settings, however, we cannot necessarily assume that similarity or identity between group norms, beliefs, or behavior and the individual's attitudes or actions reflects group influence. This interpretation is confounded by the fact that individuals often choose their friends and may initially select persons and groups who are similar to themselves. One of the most relevant studies demonstrating the occurrence of such a selection process over time leading to high degrees of similarity between friends is Newcomb's (1961) research. Thus, individual-group similarities may reflect "socialization," the influence of the group on a person who initially held different standards, or selection on the basis of similarity by the individual. Reiss's model and subsequent research assumes that increased permissiveness reflects socialization. This assumption is only provisionally made here, and we shall return to this issue in our concluding remarks.

Sexual Ideology

The individual's beliefs about the acceptability of various sexual behaviors before marriage is termed his or her *sexual ideology*. Conceptually, this is the equivalent of Ehrmann's "personal code" and Reiss's "premarital standards." In our research, we used a somewhat different set of questions to assess such beliefs, and it seemed desirable to stress that difference in naming the variables rather than to mask it by using, for example, sexual standards. We believe we are measuring the same underlying phenomenon, though we cannot demonstrate the equivalence empirically.

We assume that at any given time one's premarital ideology is the result of three classes of influences: previous sexual experience, the individual's characteristics such as self and body image, and the influence of his or her peer groups. Note that we do not include family influences as a direct influence. Conceptually, we assume that as the individual develops sexually, as socialization processes influence one's sense of self and of control over the outcomes of his or her behavior, and as peer groups assume increasing importance as agents of socialization, the influence of parents and other aspects of family background becomes increasingly muted or indirect. Family characteristics may be a major influence on entry into the courtship process, the amount of sexual experience and the speed with which it is gained, and the kinds of groups with which the person affiliates. These in turn influence sexual ideology. Thus, we would anticipate direct family influence primarily through early adolescence, and then a steady decline in its importance relative to more recent and immediate influences. Once the person leaves home and establishes an independent residence, we expect only indirect influences of family and background factors on premarital sexuality.

Sexual ideology is considered in two contexts. First, we consider ideology as an outcome, or dependent variable, and report a variety of data concerning its determinants. As indicated above, we are particularly interested in the relationships between sexual experience, sociopsychological characteristics, and peer group influences, on the one hand, and ideology, on the other. This focus on the correlates or determinants of sexual ideology is similar to Reiss's work on the determinants of premarital permissiveness. We did not have an adult sample and thus could not replicate many of his analyses, but we can assess some of the relationships he found in the data from his Iowa college sample (1967, Chapter 7).

Beyond this focus, we are also particularly interested in the relationship between sexual ideology and current sexual behavior. We believe that ideology is one of the major determinants of behavior, a belief shared by others (for example, Kaats and Davis, 1972). Ehrmann (1959) and Reiss (1967) have both reported data concerning the relationship between attitudes regarding the acceptability of behavior and behavior itself; in both cases, however, the data were obtained from limited samples and were not analyzed in a way that allows one to assess the strength and indepependence of this relationship. It is anticipated that a major contribution of the present research will be the systematic and extensive analysis of this interrelation using data from large samples of single young people.

Heterosexual Relationships

We discussed earlier the fact that attitudes about the acceptability of specific behaviors depend upon the nature of the relationship. In the context of standards or an ideology which allows certain behavior, the nature of the person's present relationship is presumably an important determinant of which sexual activities actually occur. We anticipated that the emotional quality or intimacy of a relationship intervenes or mediates between attitudes and behavior. We therefore measured the respondent's perception of emotional quality and included this measure in analyses of current sexual behavior. In addition, we have assessed other characteristics of heterosexual partners, such as relative age and social class; Erhmann (1959) found consistent relationships between such characteristics and the individual's sexual behavior.

We included one other measure which we believed might be relevant but has not been used previously. We asked each person to report his or her partner's sexual ideology. We cannot determine whether this report is valid, whether it accurately reflects the partner's sexual standards; its validity in this sense depends upon the extent of communication about sexuality, the past sexual activity of the couple, and probably other factors as well. Presumably, it does reflect the individual's perception of his or her partner's attitudes, and that perception may be an important influence on the person's behavior. Our assumption in this regard follows W. I.

Thomas's famous dictum: "If men define situations as real, they are real in their consequences" (1928). This is the fundamental basis for our belief that perceptions—of self, partners, parents, and peers—are important objects of study.

The inclusion of these measures of characteristics of the partner and the relationship and our emphasis upon them in our model and analyses are unique aspects of our research.

Current Sexual Behavior

The last variable in our model is current sexual behavior. As indicated, we expect sexual ideology and the quality of present relationships to be strongly related to present heterosexual activities. In addition, we believe that past heterosexual experience, sociopsychological characteristics, and group memberships may have a direct effect on current behavior, or may indirectly affect it through their influence on sexual standards.

Contraceptive Use

Given the occurrence of sexual intercourse, we were also interested in contraception. We know from recent research (Kantner and Zelnik, 1973) and from earlier data on abortions that many single young people who engage in intercourse do not use contraceptives. There were two reasons why we felt that contraceptive use should be included in our research. First, contraceptive use is similar to other sexual behavior in that there are particular norms and laws regarding contraceptive use to which the individual is socialized. Thus, variables which influence sexual activity may influence the use of birth control. Second, contraceptive use or nonuse occurs in the context of a particular relationship and is thus influenced by characteristics of the sexual partners as well as by characteristics of the relationship. Previous research has looked only at individual characteristics; we believed that our data on partners and relationships might be more useful in explaining contraceptive behavior.

Our purpose is twofold in the analysis (Chapter 9) of contraception. First, we want to focus on attitudes toward contraception; we consider familiarity with various techniques, sources of knowledge and devices, and previous experience with pregnancy or feared pregnancy. This section is primarily descriptive. Second, we are interested in the characteristics of the individual and the relationship which may be related to the use or nonuse of contraception. In particular, we anticipated that sociopsychological characteristics such as internal, as opposed to external, control and egalitarian role definitions might be important correlates. In the

context of the particular relationship, contraceptive use implies the expectation of sexual intercourse and thus may be related to the expected continua-
tion and the sexual and emotional intimacy of the relationship. Many of
these variables have never been analyzed in relation to contraceptive
uses. Generally, our concern was to see if the model of sexuality developed
in Chapters 4 through 8 could be applied to contraceptive use.

3

Research Methods

THE PURPOSE of this chapter is to describe in some detail the methods employed in collecting the data. In recent years social scientists have begun to recognize that the research procedures affect the nature and quality of the information which results. Investigators in the area of sexuality recognized this much earlier, as exemplified by Ehrmann's (1959) careful attention to methodological issues. Subsequent researchers studying premarital behavior, including Schofield (1965) and Sorensen (1972), have been concerned about the same issues but in several cases used different procedures. As one surveys this literature, it becomes evident that there are, in effect, controversies over the most appropriate techniques.

In some cases it was both possible and appropriate to vary systematically some aspects of our methods and measure empirically the effects of these variations on the data obtained. We systematically varied three aspects of the interview schedule: the order of questions about one's current sexual behavior, current partner, and quality of the relationship; use of an interviewer or a self-administered questionnaire to assess behavior; and the placement of the behavioral measures within the interview, to see if responses given at the end differed from those in the middle. We also varied the gender of the interviewer to determine whether respondents were affected by this factor. We developed measures of the interviewer's sexual experience, the rapport established, and the interviewer's technical competence; analyses were performed to determine whether these were related to variations in respondent reports. Each of these variations and measures is relevant to controversies regarding the appropriate methods to be employed in studying human sexual behavior. These controversies are discussed later in this chapter and in Appendix II. The results of these methodological "experiments" and other data relating to the quality of the interviewers are the focus of that appendix. These findings are important in two contexts. First, many of these controversies have never been addressed empirically, and thus the results are of interest in and of themselves. Of equal importance, our confidence in all of the results reported in this volume can be no greater than the quality of the data on which they are based. As we shall see, all indications are that the data are of high quality.

This chapter focuses on methodological issues and procedural matters. While the discussion centers on the topic of this study, premarital sexuality, we believe that it is more broadly relevant to research on "threatening" topics (Sudman and Bradburn, 1974), attitudes and behavior for which there are social definitions of disapproval, including immorality or illegality. This material is therefore relevant for those interested in research on a variety of topics, such as illicit drug use, exposure to "pornography," various forms of deviant or criminal behavior and racial attitudes, as well as to sexuality.

A fundamental goal of the research was to obtain information from four subgroups of single young people: male and female college students and male and female nonstudents. This goal was the basis of many of the more specific decisions we made. It guided our sampling. It was a major influence on decisions about the wording of items: we tried to avoid jargon throughout the interview and to phrase questions so that they would be readily comprehensible to all, not simply to college students. This goal was a major factor in the decision to use interviews. We believed that an interviewer could develop rapport and put the respondent at ease in what, especially for nonstudents, might be a novel situation. Also, by utilizing interviewers, we could use filter questions to eliminate sets of items which were not relevant to particular respondents. Finally, interviewers could answer questions and in other ways individualize the process of data collection.

MEASURES OF PRINCIPAL VARIABLES

The process of developing measures, or of operationalizing the variables of interest, was guided by two considerations. First, we wanted to use existing measures wherever possible, in order to make our findings comparable to those of past studies. As is generally true, progress in developing a unified model or theory of premarital sexuality has been impeded by the fact that different investigators have often used different measures. This makes it difficult to determine whether the findings in one study are consistent or in disagreement with the results of other research. The second concern was to maximize the validity of the data obtained, that is, to use measures which seem most likely to elicit honest and complete responses. Whenever the two seemed incompatible, decisions were weighted more heavily by considerations of the validity of the measure.

Each of our principal measures is discussed in some detail in Appendix I. There, the interested reader will find (1) an assessment of the relevant measures used in earlier studies, (2) the rationale for operationalizing each variable as we did, and (3) a description of the actual questions we employed. Here, we limit ourselves to a brief description of each of these measures.

Sexual Behavior

We asked about the respondent's participation in each of eight sexual activities, from "necking" to oral-genital contact and intercourse. In the questions regarding genital fondling and oral-genital contact, we distinguished between male and female active behaviors. Our questions employed precise, descriptive phrases, rather than vernacular or scientific terminology. (The behaviors included and the phrases employed are listed in table 4.1.)

Lifetime behavior was assessed by the question "How old were you when you first engaged in . . . ?" Current behavior was measured by an inquiry as to whether the respondent had participated in that behavior with the person he or she was currently dating. If he or she was seeing more than one person, behavior was assessed with the partner whom the interviewee had most recently dated. A separate series asked about behavior with other current partners.

Sociopsychological Characteristics

In general, we were able to employ measures of sociopsychological characteristics which had been developed and used by others, with appropriate modifications. Our selection was aided substantially by the reviews of a large number of indices in Robinson and Shaver (1969). The measures selected (the source of each is indicated in Appendix I) were included in a pre-test schedule, which was employed in interviews with a stratified sample of 238 university students. The methodology of the pre-test is described in DeLamater (1974a). For each measure, we factor analyzed the responses to their component items; on the basis of these analyses, we eliminated items which were not related to other items in the scale, and in some cases, revised or constructed new items. The interview included measures of self-image, body image, internal-external control, and definitions of male and female roles. The final measure used for each is reproduced in Appendix I.

Sexual Ideology

We measured the individual's premarital standards as follows. We presented to the interviewee a card listing five categories which represent relationships: not before marriage, if engaged, if in love, if feel affection, and if both want it.[1] We then asked which type of relation was necessary to make each of three behaviors acceptable; the behaviors were breast fondling, genital fondling, and sexual intercourse. The questions were asked twice, first in terms of acceptability for men and second in terms of acceptability for women.

Group Influence

Appendix I includes a discussion of the various definitions and measures of group or peer influence which have been employed. We decided to operationally define peers as "your five best friends of the same sex." Our first measure of influence is termed *friends' ideology*. We used the format described above for assessing the individual's standards, asking when in a relationship the respondent's "five close friends" felt that each of the three behaviors was acceptable. Again we inquired about their ideology for males and for females separately. A respondent probably knew his or her friends' general sexual standards but might have believed that they held different ones for him or her. Accordingly, we also asked the ideology questions in terms of when his or her friends believed each of the behaviors to be "acceptable for you." This measure is referred to as *friends' expectations*.

Both of these measures are of perceptions of peers' attitudes. We believed respondents might be influenced as well by perceptions of the behavior of other young people. Therefore, we asked how many of one's five friends had engaged in each of the heterosexual behaviors included in our behavioral scale. This is referred to as *friends' behavior*. Following

---

1. To characterize the least intimate relationship, Reiss's scale employs the phrase "even if s/he does not feel particularly affectionate toward his/her partner." This seemed undesirable becaue it might be interpreted by respondents as describing promiscuous behavior or an exploitative relationship. Thus, the Simon and Gagnon alternative, "if both want it," seemed preferable. The use of the latter has been criticized on the grounds that it is not mutually exclusive of the remaining categories. However, there are several indications that our respondents understood it to be exclusive. First, the respondent was handed a card which listed the five categories and was asked at what point in the development of a relationship each behavior was appropriate. The clear implication was that the five categories represented a continuum of emotional intimacy. Second, there were no instances of respondents giving more than one answer. Third, the data in table 5.1 indicate that the responses form a Guttman scale, which reflects their unidimensionality.

Simon and Gagnon (1968), we assessed the respondent's perception of the frequency of four sexual activities among young people in the larger community. The questions asked "what percentage of males (females) engage in" breast fondling, genital fondling, oral-genital contact, and intercourse. We call this a measure of *context*.

Characteristics of Relationships

Our measure of emotional intimacy was based on five categories, stated thus: engaged, in love, feel affection, someone you dated once or twice, and paid sexual partner. The respondent was asked to select the one which best described the relationship. This measure was used to assess the quality of the relationship with the person's first coital partner, and with the partner(s) he or she was currently dating.

Family and Personal Characteristics

We included measures of a variety of background characteristics and standard demographic variables. We also assessed the person's perception of his or her mother's and father's sexual ideologies, their reactions to the respondent living with someone, and to the person's involvement in a pregnancy. We also asked a series of questions about the quality of relationships within the family. These will be described in the discussion of the results.

THE INTERVIEW AS A RESEARCH TOOL

Researchers studying premarital sexuality have frequently noted that technical aspects of the data collection may affect the elicited responses. Having selected measures for the variables of interest, we were aware that various techniques of data collection could be used, and that there is disagreement over which techniques are best. We also realized that some of the data collection techniques could be systematically varied and the effects of these methodological variations could be empirically assessed. A specific technique was selected for variation if it was an important potential source of differences in responses and if the empirical evidence would contribute to one of the methodological controversies in this area.

Interviews versus Questionnaires

In the assessment of sexual behavior, a major controversy involves the relative merit of the self-administered questionnaire and the structured interview. Since sexuality is socially defined as a private matter, and various types of sexuality (including premarital and extramarital activity) may be viewed as undesirable or deviant, problems of embarrassment and reluctance to report sexual behavior may be encountered. The self-administered questionnaire has been recommended because it removes the interviewer from participation in the data collection. Therefore, any biases due to characteristics of the interviewer are presumably eliminated. The self-administered questionnaire was used by Ehrmann (1959) and Sorensen (1972); Sorensen asserted that this method increased the validity of responses by reducing the embarrassment presumed to be elicited by direct questioning. Schofield (1965), on the other hand, used interviews in collecting his data. Schofield argued that questionnaires were undesirable since they resulted in both overreporting and underreporting. In addition, self-administered questionnaires are subject to variation in interpretation of key words and phrases. We found these arguments convincing, particularly since our sample would include nonstudents, and thus made use of interviews to collect the data.

Variations Within the Interview

Within the interview framework, there are several sources of potential variation in response. The first concern is that of the order or "sequence" (Gorden, 1969) of the questions. After a respondent has answered some questions, his or her answers to subsequent related ones may be affected. We felt that this concern was particularly applicable to studies of sexuality. The strong positive association between reported intimacy of the relationship and sexual behavior (Ehrmann, 1959; Reiss, 1967) could be due in part to a sequence effect. If, for example, the respondent first reports the extent of physical intimacy in the relationship, he or she may subsequently report the amount of emotional intimacy that he or she feels *should* be associated with the relationship rather than the actual emotional intimacy. Expanding on the pre-test examination of the order of current partner measures (DeLamater, 1974a), we focused on three aspects of the current relationship: current sexual behavior, partner's sexual ideology, and characteristics of the relationship. Six forms of the interview were prepared, representing the six possible orders in which these sets of questions could be asked. By asking an equal number of respondents these questions in each order, we could (1) assess the effect of order on responses and (2) remove any systematic bias in one direction from the data set as a whole.

Two potential sources of bias in the interview are the age and gender of the interviewer. The gender of the interviewer has usually been neglected in past studies; typically the interviewers are all female, although Kinsey and his associates (Kinsey, Pomeroy, and Martin, 1948; Kinsey et al., 1953) used all men. While this procedure in effect standardizes any effect of gender, it does not permit assessment of the possibility that interviewers of a particular gender may be more or less likely to elicit valid responses. Schofield (1965) used both same-sex and cross-sex interviews in his pretest and although not reporting the data, he concluded that "the best results were obtained when men interviewed boys and women interviewed girls" (p. 20). Benney and his associates in an earlier study (Benney, Reisman, and Star, 1956) identified similarity of both age and gender as important characteristics.

We concluded that interviewers of the same age were essential to create the more open, less judgmental atmosphere found among peers. Although we attempted to vary the interviewer gender in the pre-test, the number of respondents interviewed was small and thus the conclusions drawn were only tentative (DeLamater, 1974a). While respondents probably assume that the interviewer has orientations appropriate to the interviewer's gender, it is not clear whether more valid reports are obtained during same-sex interviews. In this situation, if the respondent assumes that the interviewer has a double standard, males may be more truthful while females may be less truthful. Sexually experienced females may fear censure from a female interviewer. In cross-sex interviews as well, there may be underreporting or overreporting depending on the impression the respondent is trying to make on the interviewer. In the interview process, age variation was reduced by using interviewers who were age peers of the respondents. Gender of the interviewer was systematically varied so that 20 percent of the males and females were interviewed by men and the remainder were interviewed by women.

In assessing sexual behavior itself, we decided to collect data relevant to the controversy over whether more valid reports of "sensitive" information are obtained in self-administered questionnaires or in interviews. The collection of information on sexual behavior by questionnaire could result in more valid answers if the respondent was less embarrassed and less reluctant to answer. Alternatively, the respondent could more easily skip items, and it may be easier for some people to lie when not in face-to-face interaction. In order to check for these possible effects, a questionnaire was administered within the interview to half of each sample to measure their lifetime sexual behavior. A self-administered questionnaire had been employed for all respondents in the survey conducted by the Commission on Obscenity and Pornography (LoSciuto et al., 1971), on the assumption that this would result in more valid data. For the other half of each sample, the behavior was assessed by direct questioning by the interviewer. The wording of questions in the two situations was identical.

The final concern is with the reliability of reported sexual behavior. It has been argued that reliability is partly a function of the placement of the question within the interview. Richardson, Dohrenwend, and Klein (1965) assert that the more threatening questions should be placed at the end of the interview. We agreed that the development of some confidence between the respondent and the interviewer was needed, and so the interview proceeded from the less threatening material—demographic items about the respondent, sociopsychological scales, questions about contraceptives, familial characteristics—to the questions on sexual ideology and behavior. In order to test the impact of the location in the interview, two assessments were made of the sexual behavior of each respondent. One assessment was made approximately halfway through the interview and the second at the very end. Lifetime behavior was reassessed for half the respondents and current behavior for the other half. This variation enabled us to measure the reliability of the self-reports of sexual behavior as well as to assess the impact of the location of the questions.

In summary, the methodological variations within the interview allowed for assessment of the effect of question order, gender of interviewer, self-report or interviewer assessment, and reliability of reported sex behavior. The results of these methodological tests are summarized later in this chapter and discussed in detail in Appendix II.

THE SAMPLE

Selection

Data were obtained from two samples of young people. The first was composed of University of Wisconsin-Madison undergraduates and is referred to as the "student" sample or by the letters SM (student male) and SF (student female). The respondents were obtained from a 6 percent random sample of university undergraduates drawn by computer from a complete student file. The sample contained 1,141 possible respondents. Since it was an unweighted representative sample of all undergraduates, the sample consisted of unequal numbers of students in each of the eight class-gender categories. We desired a stratified sample of 1,000 respondents, 125 in each class-gender category, and therefore did not contact members in a given category, e.g., freshman females, after the quota in that group had been filled.

The second group consisted of persons between ages 18 and 23 who resided in Madison but were not students at the university. This sample is referred to as the "nonstudent" sample or NM (nonstudent male) and NF (nonstudent female). These respondents were obtained by calling a systematic probability sample of residences listed in the Madison, Wisconsin, telephone directory. Census figures indicate that 96 percent of the residences in the area had a telephone at the time the research was conducted, so there should be little bias associated with this sampling technique. A screening call was made to each residence to determine whether any of its members were between ages 18 and 23 and were not students at the university. If one such person was in the residence, he or she was automatically included in the sample; if there was more than one, the respondent was selected randomly by a coin toss.

Scheduling

The potential respondents were telephoned by a same-sex person (not an interviewer) who briefly described the research as an interview study about "young peoples' social activities" being conducted by an on-campus research center. If the respondent was reluctant to participate, the caller stressed the need for a random sample and, thus, the importance of each individual's participation. When the respondent agreed to be interviewed, the caller scheduled the interview for a specific time and place. The respondent received a letter in the mail essentially repeating the information given over the phone; a map was included for all nonstudents to help them locate the building and room. If the interview was scheduled more than four days in advance or had to be rescheduled, a postcard reminder was sent to the respondent.

Several precautions were taken to ensure the respondent's anonymity. At the time of scheduling, the respondent was given an identification number by the caller, and steps were taken to be sure that he or she was known to the interviewer *only* by this number. The interview did not include ascertaining the respondent's name, address, or phone number, and this was pointed out to the respondent as an effort to preserve his or her anonymity. Finally, both the interviewer and the respondent were told that the interview was not to be conducted if they were acquainted.

During the scheduling process, the interview was assigned to the particular methodological variations. The order in which the respondents were scheduled determined which of the six forms was used to interview this respondent. Within a class-gender (for the student sample) or an age-gender (for the nonstudents) category, the first and seventh persons scheduled received form A, the second and eighth received form B, and so on. With this process, approximately equal numbers of persons within a given category were interviewed with each form.

The identification number was based on sample, sex, form, and order of scheduling. The last two digits indicated order within the sample and category. Twenty percent of these numbers had been randomly selected for the interviewer gender variation. These were marked accordingly so that the caller could assign the interview to an interviewer of the appropriate gender. For this variation, one-fifth of the female respondents were to be interviewed by males (cross-sex) and one-fifth of the male respondents by males (same-sex).

The last two digits also determined whether the respondent was asked about his or her lifetime sexual behavior by the interviewer (even numbers) or received the self-administered questionnaire (odd numbers). When lifetime behavior was assessed by the interviewer, it was reassessed at the end of the interview. When lifetime behavior was reported on the questionnaire, the second assessment at the end of the interview was of current sexual behavior.

Completion Rates

Table 3.1 presents the completion rates for the student sample, by gender and year in school. These figures exclude persons who could not be contacted. Interviews were completed with 985 respondents. This

TABLE 3.1. Interview completion rates for students by gender and year

	Male		Female		Total	
Students contacted	N	% of contacts	N	% of contacts	N	% of contacts
Interviewed						
Freshmen	130	94.2	116	92.1	246	93.2
Sophomores	120	89.6	129	89.6	249	89.6
Juniors	128	92.7	120	93.1	248	92.9
Seniors	131	81.9	111	76.0	242	79.1
Totals and averages	509	89.3	476	87.3	985	88.4
Not interviewed						
Freshmen	4	2.9	6	4.8	10	3.8
Sophomores	5	3.7	6	4.2	11	4.0
Juniors	3	2.2	2	1.5	5	1.9
Seniors	8	5.0	12	8.2	20	6.5
Totals and averages	20	3.5	26	4.8	46	4.1
Refused						
Freshmen	4	2.9	4	3.1	8	3.0
Sophomores	9	6.7	9	6.2	18	6.4
Juniors	7	5.1	7	5.4	14	5.2
Seniors	21	13.1	23	15.8	44	14.4
Totals and averages	41	7.2	43	7.9	84	7.5
Total contacted	570		545		1115	

represents a completion rate of approximately 82 percent of the total sample. The remainder consists of 10 percent who refused to be interviewed, either initially or after at least two call-backs, and 8 percent who could not be contacted by phone and did not respond to two letters mailed to their last known address.

For the nonstudent sample, 1,134 persons were identified in the screening calls. Seventy-nine of them moved before we could schedule an interview. Table 3.2 presents the completion rates for the nonstudents by gender, age, and number of persons in the residence. Interviews were completed with 663, 62.8 percent of those whom we contacted to schedule an interview. An additional 78 (7.4 percent) could not be scheduled, while the remaining 314 (29.8 percent) refused either initially or after call-backs. Table 3.2 also indicates the characteristics of those nonstudents who were not interviewed; generally they do not differ substantially in age or number of residence mates from those who were interviewed.

TABLE 3.2. Characteristics of nonstudent sample

| | INTERVIEWED | | | | | | NOT INTERVIEWED | | | | | |
| | Number besides respondent in residence | | | | | | Number besides respondent in residence | | | | | |
Age of respondent	0	1	2	3	Row total	% by age	0	1	2	3	Row total	% by age
						MALE						
18	40	10	1	0	51	54.26	36	4	1	2	43	45.74
19	28	5	2	0	35	49.30	24	9	3	0	36	50.70
20	28	7	3	1	39	58.21	24	4	0	0	28	41.79
21	17	16	2	1	36	57.14	17	8	2	0	27	42.86
22	24	18	2	1	45	58.44	18	14	0	0	32	41.56
23 +	27	27	1	1	56	57.73	25	13	3	0	41	42.27
Column total	164	83	11	4	262		144	52	9	2	207	
Percent by residence	53.25	61.48	55.00	66.67			46.75	38.52	45.00	35.33		
						FEMALE						
18	48	8	3	4	63	63.64	31	4	1	0	36	36.36
19	38	13	4	3	58	62.37	22	4	8	1	35	37.63
20	30	19	3	3	55	51.40	32	15	4	1	52	48.60
21	30	25	7	0	62	54.39	29	19	3	1	52	45.61
22	25	36	7	2	70	58.33	40	7	3	0	50	41.67
23 +	36	54	2	1	93	70.45	24	8	4	3	39	29.55
Column total	207	155	26	13	401		178	57	23	6	264	
Percent by residence	53.77	73.11	53.06	68.42			46.23	26.89	46.94	31.58		

The sample was not restricted to single people; married people within these ages were interviewed and asked about their premarital sexual experience. Among the students, 44 men and 28 women were married; married respondents in the nonstudent sample comprised 34 males and 105 females. The married respondents are excluded from all data presented beyond this point because of the small numbers. Whatever impressions could be gathered from the small number of married respondents seemed to indicate that they were not significantly different from persons of the same age who were single.

The data from an additional 43 single student respondents are not included in our analyses because we have reason to question the validity of the responses recorded by their interviewers. Finally, 18 interviews were conducted with persons who seemed to be unable to understand the questions or provide valid responses. Thus, all of the tables and analyses reported below are based on 432 student males, 220 nonstudent males, 431 student females, and 293 nonstudent females.

THE INTERVIEWING PROCESS

In training and selecting interviewers, our efforts were directed toward maximizing the quality of the data. We aimed to select interviewers who would feel comfortable with the interview schedule and put the respondent at ease while not conveying their own attitudes through their appearance or action.

Interviewer Selection and Training

The interviewers were undergraduates, graduate students, and recent graduates of the university; their age distribution was comparable to that of the respondents in order to eliminate any effect of age difference. The interviewers were recruited by posted notices, word of mouth, and faculty recommendations. Of the more than 40 who applied, 27 were selected for training on the basis of past interviewing experience, relevant course or occupational background, and informal appraisal.

The training period lasted for 30 hours. First, there was a general discussion of interviewing techniques and the particular interview schedule. After familiarizing themselves with the interview schedule, the interviewers watched a demonstration interview by staff members. Next, practice interviews were conducted with each other and at least one interview with a member of the research staff. Some of these interviews were conducted in front of a small group who would later discuss the interview. During the final training period, interviews were conducted with pre-test respondents in the facilities used in the study itself. Written comments from pre-test respondents were obtained about the interviewer's style and quality.

During the entire training period, staff members monitored the interviewer's performance and discussed problems and techniques with him or her. Individual conferences were held with the interviewers to help them get an idea of their progress and problems as well as discuss any questions they might have had. Throughout the training and interviewing, the exploratory nature of the research was emphasized. Directional hypotheses were never expressed to the interviewers; it was stressed that most of the specific relationships we were interested in might be positive or negative. Thus, there is no reason to believe that interviewer expectations systematically biased the data.

The atmosphere emphasized in the interviewing situation was a businesslike one in which rapport would develop, as opposed to friendly rapping among friends. Interviewers strove to avoid conveying particular impressions about their own attitudes and behaviors. In their appearance they were supposed to dress in a neat, clean, moderate fashion that would not give rise to any particular images. Married interviewers did not wear wedding bands during the interviews. The interviewers did not give their personal opinions during the interview; however, if the situation warranted it, they could discuss the topics of the interview after the interview was completed.

The Interview

At the end of the training period, three persons were given other jobs on the project. The actual interviewing was done by the remaining 24 persons: 5 males and 19 females. The interviewing lasted over a six-month period, from February through July of 1973. Virtually all interviews were conducted in small rooms in the research wing of a university building. Since each interview was scheduled for a specific room, the interviewer was usually waiting in the room when the respondent arrived. After introducing himself or herself by first name only, the interviewer summarized the various steps which had been taken to preserve the respondent's anonymity. The interviewer usually gave a brief introduction about the general nature of the study, the interview format, and the importance of each individual respondent's answers in determining general patterns. It was emphasized that the interview was not a test, that there were no right or wrong answers, and that the data would only be analyzed in an aggregate fashion.

As soon as the interview began, the interviewer followed the schedule;

this included any transitional sentences, probes, and rephrasings which might be necessary. The interviewers volunteered no personal data or attitudes, and if necessary, asked the respondent to postpone such questions until the interview was over. During the periods when the respondent was filling out the written questionnaires, the interviewer checked through the interview to make sure the answers were recorded correctly and the proper questions had been asked. After the respondent filled out the post-interview reaction sheet, the respondent placed it in the envelope which contained the completed interview. The envelope was then sealed and the interviewer and respondent took it to the project office where it was left and the respondent was paid for participating in the study.

Supervision

We attempted to continue the learning experience beyond the training phase with supervision of the interviewing and continued interaction between the interviewers and staff members. At the beginning of the interviewing phase, staff members checked the completed interviews daily to make sure they were properly completed. Throughout the interviewing, staff members read the post-interview reactions, and any spontaneous comments relating to the interviewer were recorded daily. Periodically, staff members met with the interviewers individually and discussed the reactions that respondents had been expressing. The coders checked all completed interviews, and any errors or omissions were relayed to the interviewers. At several points, general meetings were held to discuss problems, to enable the interviewers to express their feelings about the project, and to discuss the differences when the interviewing shifted from the student sample to the nonstudent sample.

We also believed that there might be subtle differences in the quality of the interviewers, such as facial expression, rapport, or interpretation of some questions. In order to check for these differences, which might not be communicated by the respondents, we hired one person to be interviewed by all the interviewers. This "paid respondent" arrived late to avoid meeting other interviewers. She gave the same responses to each interviewer except for some slight variation in intensity on some scales. These interviews were successfully completed with 22 of the 24 interviewers and provided us with a good check on the reliability of asking the question and recording the answers. The paid respondent also provided lengthy, written comments on each interviewer, which were discussed individually after these interviews were completed.

Overall, the interviewing quality was very high. None of the interviews was terminated by a respondent. The interviewers handled the interview sensitively and seemed to convey an interest in each individual. Several interviewers knew the schedule so well that if a page was missing they would ask the questions anyway and record the answers on the back of another page. The interviewers' skill is reflected in the quality of the data.

Coding

The interviews were coded by three coders; one did a majority of the work. Since two of the three coders had been trained as interviewers, they were already familiar with the schedule. The training for all three began by a review of a completed interview form and a discussion of each question with a staff member. The discussion included definitions of all the possible codes for each question, where blanks were appropriate, and which specific questions should have been asked. The coders were told what pieces of information about the interview to include on the code sheet. It was stressed that they should strive for accuracy and record slowly, particularly at first.

The coders practiced by coding a prototype interview. This prototype was exhaustively annotated with coding instructions and could later be consulted by the coders. Each coder then proceeded to coding other interviews; a staff member was present for the coding of several interviews so that questions could be answered immediately. Any coding conventions were recorded and discussed so that they would be used uniformly.

A 10 percent error check on coding was done for the 1,376 interviews. A 10 percent sample of code sheets were randomly selected from each set of approximately 200 interviews that were completed. Using an estimated 800 codes per interview, the error rate for each coder ranged from 0.0006 to 0.0016 percent.

The interviews with the student sample were keypunched by professional keypunchers at the university computer center. Three to 5 percent were verified, with a very low error rate. The nonstudent interviews were keypunched by a staff member and were all verified. The data were cleaned for inappropriate codes or missing data.

In summary, wherever possible, we used previously employed measures in order to make our findings comparable with those of past studies. An additional consideration was to develop measures so as to maximize the validity of the data. The selection, training, and supervision of the interviewers were designed to eliminate potential uncontrolled interviewer effects. In particular, a nonjudgmental atmosphere was desired, in which the respondent would answer honestly without being concerned with the interviewer's attitudes. The supervision of the interviewing and coding, and the attention paid to accuracy in coding and keypunching, contributed to the quality of the data.

We have discussed a variety of factors which could potentially affect the results. We systematically varied three aspects of our interview schedule: question order, placement of assessment of sexual activity, and self or interviewer assessment. In addition, we varied interviewer gender, obtained information about the interviewers' sexual experiences, and used the "paid" respondent to develop measures of our interviewers' technical and interpersonal competence. Information about the nature of each of those methodological aspects and the results of analyses of their effects are included in Appendix II. In general, there was no substantial variation in reported sexual behavior and attitudes, nor in reactions to the interview, associated with any of these factors. Appendix II also discusses response rates within the interview, the extent to which respondents reported answering honestly, and some comparisons of candid and noncandid respondents. This material indicates that virtually every person answered every question and most answered truthfully. All of this evidence suggests that the data are of high quality.

CHARACTERISTICS OF THE SAMPLE

The data obtained could also be biased because of the quality of the sample. The techniques for obtaining the samples and specific respondents and the completion rates discussed above do not indicate any reason to question its quality. Since the student sample was drawn randomly and the completion rate was high, the sample should be relatively representative of the population from which it was drawn. The nonstudents are somewhat more problematic since our completion rate was about 62 percent. One way to assess its representativeness is to compare its characteristics with comparable data from the 1970 United States Census. This information, for both students and nonstudents, is presented in table 3.3. There are some differences between our sample and the Madison area population as reported in the 1970 census. There was essentially no variation in race; between 96.7 and 99 percent of our samples were white, and the comparable census figure is 97 to 98 percent. On the age variable, our respondents were selected on the basis of age for the nonstudents and year in school for the students. The goal was to interview approximately equal numbers in each gender-class or gender-age group. Therefore, our respondents tended to be more evenly distributed in age than the population as a whole. Among the students, there were very few who were 23 or older. The census figures for the Madison area encompass the ages 18–24 and therefore include more older persons (23 and 24 years old); the age distribu-

TABLE 3.3. Comparison of sample characteristics and census data for the Madison area

	SM	NM	Census males	SF	NF	Census females
Age						
Percent 19 or under	40.97	38.63	24.57	46.64	40.96	24.05
Percent 20 to 24	59.03	61.36	75.43	53.36	59.04	75.95
Mean income (ages 18–24 yrs)	$2662	$3531	$2934	$2316	$3555	$2390
Mean education in years						
(ages 18–24 yrs)	14.49	13.16	13.15	14.54	13.75	13.3
N	432	220	24,095	431	293	25,377
Occupation (in percent)						
Professional/Technical		10.72	20.76		22.15	17.70
Businesspersons/Managers		4.87	4.05		1.17	0.64
Sales		10.23	6.38		13.22	6.27
Clerical		3.41	9.42		28.41	48.14
Craftspersons		15.61	13.85		2.32	0.81
Operatives		19.51	11.38		4.28	3.18
Transportation		a	4.67		a	0.17
Laborers		7.32	7.60		1.56	0.47
Farm operators		1.46	2.78		0.00	0.34
Farm owners		0.00	1.10		0.00	0.02
Service workers		26.83	17.99		26.83	21.84
N		220	14,908		293	16,926

aNo comparable code.

tion shown in table 3.3 indicates that only one-quarter of this population is 19 or under, while 40 percent of our respondents fall in this category. In looking at the other comparisons it should be kept in mind that the census figures include more older persons.

The gender distribution reported in the census is nearly equal for single people: 49.3 percent were females and 50.7 percent were males. In our nonstudent sample, women are overrepresented (57.1 percent), while men are underrepresented (42.9 percent), because of higher rates of refusal by males. Since the data were analyzed separately for each gender, this imbalance is not problematic. The comparison of the nonstudents with the census data on educational attainment reveals that there are virtually no differences. The student samples had higher levels but were stratified on the basis of year in school. If the students and nonstudents were aggregated, the average educational attainment would be somewhat higher for our sample, compared to the census data. The average income figures from the census fall between the averages for students and nonstudents, with students having less money to live on. Nonstudent females, in particular, were employed in better paying jobs. Persons with lower educational status and lower incomes may have been harder to reach, particularly when sampled by telephone, and may have been less willing to participate. The occupational differences are presented in the final section of table 3.3. The nonstudent males are particularly underrepresented in professional/technical and clerical occupations and have more representation in the categories of sales, craftsmen, operatives, and service workers. It seems that the nonstudent males had less prestigious but not necessarily less well paying jobs. The female nonstudents were found more often in the professional/technical, sales, operative, and service worker categories and less in clerical work, compared to the females in the census figures. These differences probably reflect the higher educational levels and incomes of the nonstudents in this sample, compared to the area average. The nonstudent averages for education and income may be somewhat higher because all those persons included in these figures were single, while the census figures contain the married as well. The differences, however, do not seem large enough to significantly affect the quality of the data.

Table 3.4 presents the distributions of interviewees on five demographic variables: religion, family income, perceived social class of the family in the community, monthly income, and age. The student sample tended to have more Jewish people than the nonstudent sample, and in general, the women were more likely than men to express a religious affiliation. The estimates of family income in table 3.4 reflect the middle income origins of the respondents. It should be noted that more of the nonstudents than students were unwilling to make this estimate. There are somewhat more students' families in the higher income categories. The nonstudent females, in particular, tended to come from the lower end of the distribution, with 43 percent estimating their family income at less than $15,000, compared to 30 percent of the nonstudent males and 30 and 35 percent of the student females and males respectively. The third section of table 3.4 shows that the social class of the family perceived by the respondents was similar across the samples, although the nonstudents were more likely to pick middle class and lower middle class, while relatively more of the students picked upper middle class or upper class. The predominance of middle class characteristics is not unexpected, since most of the respondents came from Wisconsin (86 %, SM; 77 %, NM; 91 %, SF; 82 %, NF) and nearly all were white. Thus, the sample characteristics are to be expected for a middle-sized midwestern city.

The obvious question is to what extent sample characteristics limit the generalizability of the results. The sample is restricted to ages between 18 and 23 years. The racial composition is essentially all white. Most of the respondents have no religious preference, although those with religious affiliation are predominantly Catholic and Protestant. The respondents have middle class origins but are themselves low in income level at this point in their careers. The characteristics of the sample do not differ significantly from comparable data available from the 1970 census. Insofar as this midwestern city is similar to other cities throughout the country, one would expect similar results from further research. The results of this study seem to be generalizable at least to other white, high school–educated young people.

In addition, this sample is a more representative data base than are those typically found in research in premarital sexuality. Past studies have used nonprobability samples, such as Ehrmann's (1959) use of volunteers in classes, or have had low completion rates, as in the work by Sorensen (1972), or have included only respondents of one sex, as was done by Kantner and Zelnik (1972). We believe our sample is a significant

TABLE 3.4. Demographic characteristics of respondents by subsample (in percent)

	SM (N = 432)	NM (N = 220)	SF (N = 431)	NF (N = 293)
Religion				
Roman Catholic	22.00	24.55	26.00	22.86
Jewish	5.06	1.36	9.50	3.75
Protestant—traditional	25.01	22.72	22.26	27.63
Protestant—fundamental	7.91	5.91	6.30	11.94
None	38.50	41.36	32.70	31.39
Other	1.52	4.10	3.24	2.43
Family income				
Less than $4,999	2.79	1.82	1.87	1.02
5,000–7,499	3.95	2.27	3.27	6.83
7,500–9,999	7.44	4.55	3.97	9.56
10,000–14,999	19.76	21.36	19.63	25.60
15,000–19,999	20.70	21.36	17.29	18.77
20,000–24,999	13.72	16.82	17.76	12.29
25,000–39,999	19.07	18.18	17.99	10.92
40,000 or over	11.63	8.18	14.95	7.50
Missing[a]	0.93	5.45	3.27	7.50
Perceived social class				
Upper class	4.89	3.18	4.91	2.39
Upper middle class	39.53	33.64	48.83	33.11
Middle class	43.26	50.91	35.75	51.88
Lower middle class	6.74	8.18	7.71	8.87
Working or lower class	5.59	3.64	2.57	3.41
Missing[a]	0.00	0.45	0.23	0.34
Respondent's income/month				
$ 199 or less	46.53	35.45	58.74	39.59
200–399	46.99	28.64	35.66	32.08
400–599	5.10	22.73	5.13	19.79
600–799	0.69	6.82	0.00	7.51
800–999	0.00	2.73	0.00	0.34
1,000–1,199	0.00	1.82	0.00	0.34
1,200–1,499	0.23	0.45	0.00	0.00
Missing[a]	0.46	1.36	0.47	0.34
Age				
18 or under	19.44	23.63	18.65	20.82
19	21.53	15.00	28.21	20.14
20	21.76	15.91	24.48	12.97
21	21.06	11.36	17.02	16.38
22	8.33	16.82	8.16	14.33
23 or over	7.87	17.27	3.49	15.36

[a]Respondent did not answer the item.

improvement over these earlier ones; our completion rates were 82 percent for students and 62 percent for nonstudents, yielding large, randomly chosen, matched subsamples. For these reasons, one focus in our discussion will be on comparisons with findings of previous research.

ANALYSES

In analyzing the data, we had two goals. First, we wanted to exploit the unique sample we were able to obtain and to carefully explore the possibility of differences between men and women and between students and nonstudents. We were interested in differences either in the nature of their sexual standards and behavior or in the way in which sexuality related to their other social and personal characteristics. To this end, every analysis was conducted separately for four subgroups of single persons: male students, female students, male nonstudents, and female nonstudents. The second goal was to assess simultaneously the effects of a variety of variables. Multivariate techniques were thus frequently employed, in contrast to the bivariate, cross-tabular techniques which have been relied upon in some past research.

4

The Development
of Sexuality

WE TURN now to the results. In this chapter, we are concerned with the lifetime sexual activity of our respondents. In Chapters 5, 6, and 7, the focus is upon their current sexual behavior; Chapter 8 describes a regression analysis designed to assess the relative strength of the relationships reported in these three chapters, and thus summarizes our findings with regard to the correlates of current activity. Chapter 9 deals with contraceptive use.

In general, we begin each chapter with the descriptive results on the relevant measures. The purpose of this is twofold: (1) to indicate the character of our measures, and (2) to allow for comparisons of our results with those of prior studies, which have often emphasized such descriptive findings. The middle section of each chapter considers the interrelationships of the relevant variables, the zero-order correlations. Again, this allows us to discuss our results in relation to those of previous research, as well as to provide tentative findings regarding the validity of our conceptual model. Finally, we end each chapter by discussing a regression analysis, which (1) indicates the relative influence of interrelated variables, and thus provides an assessment of the support for our model, and (2) serves as a summary of the main findings of that chapter.

The concern in this chapter is the individual's sexual experience, or lifetime behavior. We believe that this is a major focus of the socialization process which the person undergoes. While we cannot measure it in detail, we can "reconstruct" it by determining whether and at what ages each person has participated in each behavior. The description of these data is the focus of the first part of this chapter. In general, we believe that the further one has progressed in this process, the more extensive his or her current activity will be. As an aspect of the sociosexual development which begins in early adolescence, we expected lifetime experience to be more heavily influenced by family than peers and especially current partners. Accordingly, the second half of this chapter presents data on the interrelationships of lifetime behavior and family characteristics.

We believe that sexual behavior undergoes a developmental process over time. For most people, heterosexual intercourse does not occur on the first date, nor necessarily with one's first dating partner. Instead, as Hardy (1964) has argued, there seems to be a long process beginning with the least intimate physical contact and only very gradually progressing to more intimate behaviors.

In Chapter 2, we reviewed the evidence from past research which is consistent with such a model. We pointed out that a sound assessment of the developmental nature of behavior requires both information about whether the person has ever engaged in each behavior and about the sequence in which each behavior first occurs. Our measure of lifetime behavior provides both, with the temporal measure consisting of the age at which the person first experienced each behavior.

LIFETIME SEXUAL BEHAVIOR

Incidence of Behaviors

Table 4.1 presents two sets of information about the lifetime behavior of our respondents. The data are presented separately for each of the four educational status-gender subsamples. The first column for each group presents the percentage of that subsample who reported ever engaging in the behavior. Nine out of 10 respondents have engaged in the three least intimate behaviors—necking, french kissing, and breast fondling. People in our college age samples are not less likely to participate in breast fondling than in kissing, though it is more specifically sexual than the other two behaviors. There is a decrease in incidence between breast and genital fondling, with 5 to 9 percent fewer young people reporting the latter. From 60 to 80 percent of our respondents have participated in heterosexual intercourse at least once; with the exception of female students, they are about as likely to have engaged in genital apposition as a distinct behavior. The least frequent behaviors are the oral-genital activities.

Three characteristics of these results are worthy of brief discussion. First, there are neither systematic nor substantial differences between the students and nonstudents. Differences larger than 5 percent are found only for intercourse and oral-genital activities, where nonstudents are somewhat more likely to report participation. This finding is quite important in view

TABLE 4.1. Lifetime sexual behavior by gender and educational status

| | MALE | | | | FEMALE | | | |
| | Student | | Nonstudent | | Student | | Nonstudent | |
Behavior	%	Age[a]	%	Age[a]	%	Age[a]	%	Age[a]
Necking	97	14.2	98	13.9	99	14.8	99	14.9
French kissing	93	15.3	95	15.1	95	15.8	95	16.0
Breast fondling	92	15.8	92	15.5	93	16.6	93	16.6
Male fondling of female genitals	86	16.6	87	16.3	82	17.2	86	17.5
Female fondling of male genitals	82	16.8	84	16.7	78	17.4	81	17.8
Genital apposition	77	17.1	81	16.8	72	17.6	78	17.9
Intercourse	75	17.5	79	17.2	60	17.9	72	18.3
Male oral contact with female genitals	60	18.2	68	17.7	59	18.1	67	18.6
Female oral contact with male genitals	61	18.1	70	17.8	54	18.1	63	18.8

[a]Includes only those who have engaged in the behavior.

of the fact that virtually all previous research on premarital behavior has involved either college students or nonstudents but not both. Our results indicate that nonstudent young people of equivalent ages in the same community do not differ in their lifetime sexual behavior.

We included distinctions between male and female active in our behavioral measure. Both Ehrmann (1959) and Simon and Gagnon (1968) found that male active behaviors were more frequent than female active ones. This presumably reflected the fact that males generally took the initiative in heterosexual interactions. (See Ehrmann's discussion of "positive control," pp. 54–60.) In our data, such differences are generally slight and not meaningful. These results indicate that, at least over long time periods, behaviors in which the female is active are as likely as male active activities.

Finally, in a comparison of males and females, there are virtually no differences in the incidence of each of the behaviors. Unlike most earlier studies, which generally reported lower frequencies of more intimate activities among females, we find that women are as likely as men to have ever engaged in these behaviors. The only exception occurs with coitus, which women, particularly in the student sample, are less likely to have experienced. Thus, the gender differences in lifetime behavior which were consistently found in studies conducted in the 1950s and early 1960s have narrowed considerably. This is also an important finding; it suggests that those models which have emphasized gender as an explanatory variable are no longer valid.

In order to truly demonstrate the sequential nature of involvement in behavior, we needed a measure of the unidimensionality of premarital activity. To our knowledge, Podell and Perkins (1957) were the first to employ Guttman scaling techniques with sexual behavior. Basically, a Guttman scale orders attributes, in this case behaviors, in a unidimensional sequence, where a given behavior occurs only when all behaviors lower on the scale, i.e., less intimate activities, have also occurred. Thus, one can apply Guttman scaling techniques and determine the extent to which such a sequence exists in the data. Podell and Perkins found that the lifetime premarital behavior of a sample of males did conform to a Guttman scale. Accordingly, we applied these techniques to the behavioral reports of our respondents. This scale was constructed using the Cornell ranking technique, which assigns weights according to whether or not the person reported engaging in each of the nine behaviors (Edwards, 1957). Since the oral-genital behaviors were the least frequently reported by our sample, the best order for such a scale was that in which the behaviors are listed in table 4.1.

Table 4.2 presents the characteristics of the resulting scales. In addition to the common measures of reproducibility and the percentage of pure cases, we used the factor analytic techniques suggested by Heise and Bohrnstedt (1970) to calculate the coefficients of validity, reliability, and invalidity. All these measures indicate that our scales are quite good, that is, reliable and valid. The very high coefficients of reproducibility and validity indicate that lifetime behavior, as measured here, does form a unidimensional sequence, that almost all individuals engage in each of the behaviors before he or she participates in those higher on the scale, i.e., that less intimate behavior precedes more intimate ones. This is strong evidence for a developmental process in premarital sexual behavior; it supports the assumption discussed in Chapter 2 that such a process is an important aspect of sociosexual socialization.

TABLE 4.2. Characteristics of Guttman scale of lifetime sexual behavior

	SM	NM	SF	NF
Characteristics				
Coefficient of reproducibility	0.981	0.987	0.981	0.985
Minimal marginal reproducibility	0.804	0.836	0.771	0.815
Percentage of pure cases	85.6	86.3	90.5	89.4
Coefficient of				
Validity	0.973	0.954	0.968	0.956
Reliability	0.952	0.961	0.950	0.937
Invalidity	0.006	0.049	0.014	0.024

Age of First Experience

Table 4.1 also presents, in the second column for each group, the average age (to within a tenth of a year) of first participation in each of the nine behaviors. These averages were calculated only for those respondents who had ever engaged in the behavior. Twenty-five to 40 percent had not yet engaged in the more intimate activities; when they do, most of them will be in their twenties. Thus, when everyone in our samples has engaged in a behavior, for example, intercourse, the average age will be greater than those reported here; also, of course, some will not engage in these premaritally.

In general, the results show that a period of four years elapses from first experience with necking to first participation in intercourse. Compared to the age of first necking, the age of first french kissing was typically one year greater; thus, progress from the first to the second of the behaviors occurred slowly, relative to progress later in the developmental process. A second lengthy transition is found between breast and genital fondling, where the latter first occurs 6 to 11 months after the initial experience with the former. The figures on average age suggest that apposition (contact between genitals without penetration) is a distinct behavior; it first occurs several months after the person begins to engage in genital fondling and several months before the initial experience with sexual intercourse.

We noted above that there are no differences in frequency between male and female active genital fondling and oral-genital activity. There is a consistent difference in average age, with both males and females reporting somewhat earlier ages of male active manual-genital activity. We find little or no difference in ages for the two oral-genital contacts, however.

We can also look at the ages themselves. Our respondents were 18 to 23 years old in 1973, and thus were adolescents in the late 1960s. On the average, they began necking at 14, french kissing at 15, engaging in genital fondling at 16 or 17, and participating in intercourse at 17 or 18. Here, there are consistent and fairly substantial gender differences. Overall, women first engage in each of the behaviors at a somewhat older age than men. Among the student sample, women on the average are about six months older at each step; among the nonstudents, the difference is larger, with women generally one year older than men when they first participate in each activity. With the exception of oral-genital contact among students, all of the differences in age of first experience between males and females are statistically significant ($p < 0.01$, i.e., the probability that the difference is due to chance is less than 0.01). Thus, with the exception of coitus, the lifetime incidence of behavior among persons of ages 18 to 23 does not vary with gender; however, the age of first experience varies significantly.

The actual distributions of age at first participation for each behavior are presented in tables 4.3 through 4.6. For each behavior, we included only those who have ever participated in it. For comparison purposes, the data are cumulative percentages.

These tables provide more detailed support for the finding noted above, that young people participate in the more intimate behaviors at older ages. For example, looking at any age (row), we see that the percentages decline steadily from the least intimate behavior (necking) to the most intimate. Similarly, the age at which anyone in our samples first reported a behavior increases, from 9 (or younger) for necking to 11 (for males) and 14 or 15 (for females) for oral-genital contact.

Looking at the ages themselves, we again find evidence of the gender differences which appeared in the average age of first experience. At any given age, fewer women (tables 4.5 and 4.6) than men (tables 4.4 and 4.3) have engaged in each of the behaviors. For example, by 16, about 70 percent of the experienced males had engaged in breast fondling, compared to 45 to 50 percent of the females. By this same age, 23 and 32 percent of the men but only 14 percent of the women had experienced intercourse.

Two additional findings are evident in these tables. First, there were few persons whose first heterosexual activity occurred before age 12. Earlier activity is primarily kissing and petting, though a very few males

TABLE 4.3. Age at first participation in sexual behaviors: student males (cumulative percentages)

Age[a]	Necking	French kissing	Petting	Male fondling of female genitals	Female fondling of male genitals	Apposition	Intercourse	Male active oral-genital contact	Female active oral-genital contact
9	2.40	0.25	0.50	0.54	0.56		0.62		
10	4.79	0.25	0.50	0.54	0.56		0.62		
11	8.38	1.74	1.25	1.08	1.41	.60	1.24		0.38
12	20.13	5.23	3.52	1.89	1.97	1.50	1.55	0.77	0.76
13	35.23	17.42	8.30	4.31	4.23	3.59	2.78	1.15	1.52
14	52.73	33.61	20.64	8.89	8.19	4.78	3.71	1.92	2.28
15	74.07	54.75	41.04	23.21	18.92	13.16	8.34	3.45	4.57
16	88.93	75.39	67.48	47.26	39.54	33.82	23.77	12.26	12.96
17	95.40	87.82	84.86	69.68	65.25	60.47	49.38	32.18	33.19
18	98.99	96.02	94.43	89.14	85.30	82.93	76.23	63.98	60.67
19	99.47	98.01	97.95	96.43	95.19	93.70	88.27	81.99	80.90
20	99.71	98.75	98.96	98.05	98.30	97.29	95.99	94.25	93.88
21	100.00	100.00	99.47	99.13	100.00	99.68	99.07	98.46	98.07
22			99.73	99.40		99.68	99.69	99.60	99.60
23 or over			100.00	100.00		100.00	100.00	100.00	100.00
N	418	402	397	370	354	334	324	261	262

[a]19.49 % of sample 18 or under, 41.07 % under 19, 62.88 % under 20, 83.99 % under 21, and 92.11 % under 22.

report genital contact and intercourse at earlier ages. This undoubtedly reflects the fact that by the age of 12 the biological processes involved in puberty are occurring for many young people. Awareness of these changes, particularly the onset of menstruation (menarche) for women, probably initiates thought about the sexual aspects of oneself and of sexuality. In addition, the social definitions applied to young people begin to change. Parents, peers, and the individual begin to define him or her as someone who can "date," participate in one-to-one heterosexual interactions. Individuals undoubtedly vary in the point or age at which they accept this self-definition, but social groups begin to provide it as a potential one at approximately this age. Certainly, when the person enters high school, he or she is exposed to the "institution" of dating, opportunities to learn new social definitions and heterosexual skills through exposure to older students who are participating in it. Thus, both biological and social changes contribute to the determination of when one enters the stage (III) of behavioral development, as discussed in Chapter 2.

The other finding involves the sharp increase in percentages who have experienced each behavior from ages 17 to 18; these increases reflect the fact that substantial numbers of young people first engage in these activities at 18. This is especially true for genital fondling, apposition, intercourse,

TABLE 4.4. Age at first participation in sexual behaviors:
nonstudent males (cumulative percentages)

Age[a]	Necking	French kissing	Petting	Male fondling of female genitals	Female fondling of male genitals	Apposition	Intercourse	Male active oral-genital contact	Female active oral-genital contact
9	4.62		0.49						
10	7.86	1.43	1.47	0.52					
11	12.49	4.29	1.96	0.52	0.54	1.12	0.57	0.67	
12	24.53	8.58	4.41	2.08	1.08	2.80	1.72	0.67	
13	39.81	19.53	16.67	7.29	5.38	5.05	2.87	2.00	2.58
14	58.79	37.15	27.94	18.23	11.83	11.23	6.89	3.33	3.87
15	75.46	59.53	48.04	30.73	20.97	22.47	17.24	8.66	9.03
16	85.64	77.15	73.04	58.86	44.09	44.94	32.76	23.33	21.93
17	93.97	87.62	86.28	74.49	66.13	66.29	56.32	47.33	46.45
18	97.67	94.76	94.12	86.99	84.95	84.27	81.61	70.66	64.51
19	99.52	97.14	96.57	95.94	91.94	91.57	88.50	80.66	77.41
20	100.00	100.00	100.00	97.92	97.85	97.75	94.25	90.66	93.54
21				99.48	99.46	98.87	98.27	97.66	97.41
22				100.00	100.00	100.00	100.00	99.32	99.35
23 or over								100.00	100.00
N	216	210	203	192	186	178	174	150	155

[a]23.63 % of sample 18 or under, 38.63 % under 19, 54.54 % under 20, 65.9 % under 21, and 82.72 % under 22.

TABLE 4.5. Age at first participation in sexual behaviors:
student females (cumulative percentages)

Age[a]	Necking	French kissing	Petting	Male fondling of female genitals	Female fondling of male genitals	Apposition	Intercourse	Male active oral-genital contact	Female active oral-genital contact
9	0.47								
10	0.94								
11	3.51	0.24							
12	11.27	1.46	0.25						
13	26.09	11.44	5.25	1.42	0.60	0.32	0.38		
14	44.67	24.33	11.50	4.83	2.97	3.20	1.54	1.17	0.86
15	65.61	45.98	24.25	15.34	10.66	10.57	5.43	1.95	1.72
16	82.55	68.85	50.25	32.38	26.34	23.71	14.37	11.32	12.44
17	90.78	81.25	71.25	57.95	51.19	46.46	35.38	30.07	29.18
18	98.07	93.41	88.00	80.68	77.22	74.66	66.90	62.88	63.08
19	99.71	97.55	97.50	93.46	92.90	91.33	87.13	85.54	83.25
20	100.00	98.28	98.25	97.72	96.75	97.10	96.07	94.91	96.55
21		99.50	99.50	99.42	98.82	99.66	99.18	98.81	97.83
22		99.74	99.75	99.70	99.71	100.00	99.56	100.00	100.00
23 or over		100.00	100.00	100.00	100.00		100.00		
N	425	411	400	352	338	312	257	256	233

[a]18.65 % of sample 18 or under, 46.86 % under 19, 71.34 % under 20, 88.36 % under 21, and 96.52 % under 22.

TABLE 4.6. Age at first participation in sexual behaviors:
nonstudent females (cumulative percentages)

Age[a]	Necking	French kissing	Petting	Male fondling of female genitals	Female fondling of male genitals	Apposition	Intercourse	Male active oral-genital contact	Female active oral-genital contact
9	1.37								
10	3.09	0.36							
11	3.77	0.36							
12	9.27	1.44	0.73	0.39	0.43	0.44			
13	24.39	6.83	4.02	1.18	0.86	0.44			
14	42.95	21.58	12.44	5.17	3.39	2.20	0.47		
15	58.07	37.41	25.62	11.54	8.45	7.05	2.84	1.02	1.08
16	81.44	62.59	45.40	28.67	22.37	20.27	14.69	9.18	8.15
17	92.80	79.50	70.67	51.78	41.36	42.30	33.65	24.99	20.65
18	97.93	92.45	87.15	75.68	68.36	70.49	60.19	51.01	45.11
19	98.96	96.04	93.74	87.63	83.13	84.15	76.78	71.93	67.39
20	99.30	98.56	97.77	95.20	91.57	93.84	87.21	85.19	84.24
21	99.64	99.28	98.87	98.39	97.89	98.24	95.75	95.90	95.65
22	100.00	100.00	100.00	99.18	99.15	98.68	98.12	97.94	98.37
23 or over				100.00	100.00	100.00	100.00	100.00	100.00
N	291	278	273	251	237	227	211	196	184

[a]20.81 % of sample 18 or under, 40.94 % under 19, 53.9 % under 20, 70.28 % under 21, and 84.61 % under 22.

and oral-genital contact, where the increases range from 20 to 33 percent. Eighteen has been identified as an important age in previous research. Reiss (1967) reported that most females' standards change at 18 to 19. Simon, Berger, and Gagnon (1972) have indicated that leaving home, which often occurs at 18, is associated with an increase in the influence of courtship processes and a decline in parental influence on sexuality.

Certainly the changes at this age are partly attributable to the fact that many young people establish separate residences after they finish high school. In our study, the majority of students had left home in order to attend the university; only 9 percent of the men and 10 percent of the women lived with parents or relatives at the time of the interview. Among nonstudents, 43 percent of the males and 36 percent of the females reported such a living situation. Living with parents or relatives is significantly correlated with lifetime behavior; those living at home had less experience with intimate sexual activity. The correlations are substantial for nonstudent men (-0.31) and women (-0.34). Our model argues that the importance of the living situation lies in its consequences for social influences and control. Leaving home reduces the potential control of parents over behavior and increases the potential influence of both peers and partners. To the extent that one moves to a new locale, this may end parental effectiveness as socializing agents.

Another factor which may contribute to these changes is changed social definitions. The completion of high school education and becoming 18 are, for many, indicators of achieving adult social status, particularly for those who do not attend college. Defining oneself as an adult may lead to the expectation that one is now ready for or capable of mature heterosexual relationships, for example, "falling in love" instead of "puppy love" or "adolescent infatuation." This process would be hastened by the fact that one has friends who are engaged or marry shortly after completing high school.

Relationship with First Intercourse Partner

Several studies (e.g., Schofield, 1965; Sorensen, 1972) have reported data concerning the individual's relationship with the first person with whom he or she had intercourse. Although these investigators do not discuss the rationale for collecting and presenting such information, it seems important primarily as an indicator of social or group norms or standards. One's first voluntary coitus is an event of considerable psychological significance. The person is undoubtedly aware of various considerations, including imagined reactions of partner and self, how significant others such as parents and close friends would react, and beliefs about potential consequences, as on one's reputation and on the relationship.

All of these reflect social and group standards, and the influence of social control over the individual's sexual activity. Beliefs about how people would react and what effects the act may have will be quite different if those around the person consider the act wrong, than if they accept it. Those who adhere to a norm of premarital chastity will believe that intercourse will harm the person and reduce the partner's respect for him or her, and may be concerned about the possibility of venereal disease or pregnancy. All of these attitudes will be communicated to the individual. Conversely, those who accept the act are likely to believe that it will contribute to the individual's growth, enhance the relationship, and so on. Also, first intercourse is presumably less likely to be influenced by factors such as previous behavior with that partner.

Thus, first experience is to a considerable degree a matter of choice and is more likely to reflect the standards held by the individual, derived from participation in groups. In Chapter 2, we indicated that previous researchers have assumed that standards depend on the type of relationship. Information about the type of relationship with one's first partner reflects in part the standard, as held by the individual *at that time*. We are, of course, aware that many respondents are characterizing a relationship which ended several years ago, and that this introduces the possibility of errors due to memory. We hope that these are minimized by the presumed importance of the experience.

Table 4.7 presents the responses we obtained to the question "How would you describe the nature of your relationship with the first person with whom you had intercourse?" Each person was given a card which listed the categories exactly as they appear in the left side of the table. The percentages in the table are based on the number who have engaged in coitus, and thus total 100 percent. As indicated in the last rows, these constitute 60 to 80 percent of the total number of persons in each subsample.

On the whole, these results indicate that the relationship within which intercourse first occurs is characterized by affection or love. The partner is described as someone the respondent was "emotionally attached to" or "in love with" by majorities of 56 to 72 percent of those who had ever engaged in intercourse. This reflects the standard which Reiss (1960, 1967) termed "permissiveness with affection." In contrast to past research, we find that less than 2 percent of the respondents report "paid sexual partners" (past research included "prostitutes" as an alternative only for males), and less than 4 percent of the women report a fiancé as first partner. Gender differences have not completely disappeared, however. Women are more likely to engage in intercourse for the first time with someone they love (63 and 58 percent), compared to men (36 and 32 percent), while males report that it occurs in casual relationships ("dated only once or twice" or "dated often") much more frequently than do females (28 and 36 percent versus 7 and 11 percent, respectively). These patterns are strong, but less pronounced than in Ehrmann's (1959) data, where males reported that they primarily or exclusively had intercourse with acquaintances and not with lovers, while the reverse was reported by females. The distributions of responses are quite similar to those reported by Sorensen (1972) based on responses of an adolescent sample. Although none of his categories included the term "love," he found that females reported more emotionally intimate relationships with their first partner than did males (see Sorensen, 1972, table on p. 198).

Thus, more recent data indicate that over the past 25 years, the type of relationship with first partner is converging for men and women. Women are becoming, by this measure, more permissive, engaging in intercourse with men they feel affection for rather than waiting for a relationship which they characterize as being in love or until they become engaged. Bell and Chaskes (1970) also found such a change, between 1958 and 1968, based on questionnaire data from small, nonrandom but matched samples of female college students. Men, by contrast, are becoming less permissive, in that they are more likely to report being emotionally attached to or in love with their first partner. Though the trend is clear, the differences have not disappeared. We shall consider this further in the discussion of current sexual ideology.

TABLE 4.7. Relationship with first intercourse partner,
by gender and educational status of respondent

Description of relationship	SM		NM		SF		NF	
	N	%[a]	N	%[a]	N	%[a]	N	%[a]
A paid sexual partner	5	1.54	3	1.72	0	0.00	1	0.47
Someone you date(d) only once or twice	52	16.05	45	25.86	10	3.89	13	6.16
Someone you date(d) often but are/were not emotionally attached to	44	13.58	18	10.35	10	3.89	10	4.74
Someone you are/were emotionally attached to, but not in love with	102	31.48	53	30.45	63	24.51	56	26.54
Someone you are/were in love with but are/were not engaged to	98	30.25	46	26.44	122	47.47	77	36.49
Someone you are/were in love with and expect(ed) to marry	22	6.79	9	5.17	43	16.73	47	22.27
Someone you are/were engaged to	1	0.31	0	0.00	9	3.50	7	3.32
Total ever engaging in intercourse	324		174		257		211	
Percent of total sample		75.00		79.09		59.63		72.01

[a]Percent based on number ever engaging in intercourse.

Lifetime Intercourse

We obtained information about two other aspects of coital activity, estimates of the number of times and the number of partners with whom the person had ever had sexual intercourse. These questions were asked only of respondents who reported ever having participated in this behavior. The data on number of experiences are obviously approximations, since many respondents could only give us estimates. Their responses concerning number of partners are probably more reliable.

Number of Intercourse Experiences

In all four subsamples, the number of experiences reported ranged from one to more than one thousand. Less than 2 percent gave frequencies at either extreme; most of our respondents estimated that they had engaged in intercourse between 5 and 200 times. More informative than the range are the means; the average for male students was 113, for male nonstudents, 175, for female students, 151, and for female nonstudents, 161. Thus, the amount of intercourse experience does not differ much between the female samples; male nonstudents, however, are more experienced by this measure than male college students.

Number of Intercourse Partners

The results obtained for number of partners are presented in table 4.8. During the interview, the number given by the respondent was simply recorded; the categories in the table were constructed after the fact to simplify the presentation. It is apparent that most of our respondents had engaged in coitus with a relatively small number of partners. More than two-thirds of those who had engaged in intercourse had done so with one to five partners; the medians are two or three partners in three of the subsamples. The one exception is found among the nonstudent males; almost half of these men had had more than five partners. This difference also appears in the averages for the four groups; student males reported six partners on the average, compared to almost ten among nonstudent men. The averages for women were quite similar (4.6 for students and 5.2 for nonstudents). To some readers, these means may seem large, given that two-thirds to three-fourths of our respondents had five or fewer partners. The means in this case are increased by the relatively very large numbers reported by a few respondents.

Thus, nonstudent males report relatively more sexual experience than do our other groups, in terms of both number of coital experiences and number of partners. It is possible that they overreported, for example, in an attempt to impress the interviewer, who was usually a woman. However, on the self-administered questionnaire which they completed at the end of the interview, they were no less likely to report that they told the truth. This suggests that the difference is a valid one. One possibility is that male nonstudents differ in background from the college student men we interviewed. There is a tendency for the former to come from families characterized by somewhat lower annual incomes and lower levels of formal education of parents.

On the whole, the data on lifetime sexual behavior indicate that the expression of sexuality develops over a period of several years, as assumed by our model and implied by earlier research. As young people gain sociosexual experience, they begin to engage in more intimate behaviors. The majority engage in premarital intercourse at least once, on the average, by the age of about 18. A few do not engage in it again (less than 2 percent); most do, and in our samples of 18 to 23 year old persons, the average coitally experienced man or woman reported more than 100 experiences. We interpret these results as indicating that these young people had progressed quite far in the process of development, rather than, for example, remaining in Stage II until after marriage, as Ehrmann's (1959) results suggested was true in the period 1947–51. At the same time, two-thirds or more of these persons had had one to five partners, and half reported only one, two, or three. These data do not suggest that the young people we studied were promiscuous, in the sense of engaging in intercourse with casual acquaintances or strangers, or in the sense of engaging in it with a large number of partners. The findings that each person had had few partners and that first intercourse occurred in an emotionally intimate

TABLE 4.8. Number of intercourse partners in lifetime, by gender and educational status of respondent

	SM		NM		SF		NF	
	N	%[a]	N	%[a]	N	%[a]	N	%[a]
1	65	20.08	22	12.64	94	36.57	60	28.43
2	52	16.07	20	11.49	38	14.78	33	15.64
3	50	15.45	24	13.79	36	14.00	23	10.90
4	36	11.12	20	11.49	24	9.35	19	9.00
5	22	6.80	12	6.89	11	4.28	20	9.47
6	17	5.25	9	5.17	6	2.33	12	5.68
7–10	41	12.67	26	14.94	22	8.56	23	10.90
11–15	17	5.25	16	9.19	14	5.45	13	6.16
16–25	14	4.33	14	8.04	7	2.72	5	2.37
26–49	6	1.85	4	2.29	3	1.17	1	0.47
50–99	4	1.24	7	4.02	2	0.78	2	0.94
Total ever engaging in intercourse	324		174		257		211	

[a]Percent based on total ever engaging in intercourse.

relationship are consistent with our assumption that partners are important influences on sexuality. We will return to this in Chapter 7.

BACKGROUND CHARACTERISTICS AND LIFETIME BEHAVIOR

As discussed in Chapter 2, the family is seen as a major socializing agent in our conceptual model. It is the first influence on the individual, and we believe it is the source of the values and norms which the individual learns and subsequently employs as a basis for self-control. Certainly the family provides the foundation upon which the person's sociosexual development is built. We included measures of parental attitudes toward sexuality and of the quality of the young person's relationship with his or her parents: we felt that the latter might influence the impact of the former. We also were interested in "background" characteristics, such as family's religion, social class, and parents' education. In our model, these social variables are assumed to influence parental sexual standards. In addition, earlier research reported some differences in premarital expression as a function of such variables.

Our interview schedule included a large number of questions about the respondent's family background. Most of these questions dealt specifically with aspects of his or her family and relationship with mother and father while he or she was in high school. We felt that it was desirable to limit the temporal frame of reference to facilitate accurate answers. We selected the high school years because we anticipated that this would be the period during which his or her sexuality was developing. In this section we consider the interrelationships of some of these characteristics and lifetime behavior. We did not analyze the relationship between characteristics of the person at the time of the interview—e.g., education or income—and lifetime activity, because for most of our respondents these followed their first participation in the various sexual activities. We will consider subsequently his or her present attributes in relation to current sexual activity.

The first step in analyzing the data involved determining the correlation between the background variables and lifetime behavior. Our basic measure of lifetime behavior is the Guttman scale, discussed earlier in this chapter, constructed from responses to the question asking whether the person had ever participated in each of the nine behaviors. As secondary measures, we included the two discussed in the preceding section, the number of intercourse experiences and partners reported by the respondent. We initially included in our analyses all the background data which we obtained during the interview. Tables 4.9 through 4.13 present all the correlation coefficients, r, for those background variables which were related to one

TABLE 4.9. Background variables

REL ATNHS—attendance at religious functions during high school
FAM INCOME—respondent's estimate of family's annual income
FAM CLASS—perceived family social class
MO ED—mother's education
FA ED—father's education
PAR AFF—parents' display of affection toward each other
FA AFF—father's display of affection toward respondent
MO AFF—mother's display of affection toward respondent
FA UNDER—father's understanding of respondent
MO UNDER—mother's understanding of respondent
FA CLOSE—father's closeness to respondent
MO CLOSE—mother's closeness to respondent
SEXED FA—evaluation of sex education from father
SEXED MO—evaluation of sex education from mother
FA VALUE—value of sex in father's own life
MO VALUE—value of sex in mother's own life
FA REACT—father's reaction to cohabitation
MO REACT—mother's reaction to cohabitation
FA IDEO—father's sexual ideology
MO IDEO—mother's sexual ideology
FA SRC—father as source of moral attitudes toward sex
MO SRC—mother as source of moral attitudes toward sex
MFR SRC—male friends as source of moral attitudes toward sex
FFR SRC—female friends as source of moral attitudes toward sex
LOVER SRC—lover as source of moral attitudes toward sex
PART—number of intercourse partners in lifetime
INTER—number of intercourse experiences in lifetime
LIFE—lifetime sexual behavior—Guttman score

---

or more of our measures of lifetime behavior.[1] Our behavioral measures appear in the last three rows in each table of correlations, and we limit our discussion to those background characteristics which are related to them.

Typically, discussions of results focus on those relationships which are statistically significant, i.e., highly unlikely to occur in the data on chance alone. However, with samples as large as ours (220 to 432), quite small correlation coefficients meet this criterion, for example, a correlation of 0.10 is significant at $p < 0.05$ when the number of cases is 400. We are more interested in the meaningfulness of a relationship; a good measure of this is the coefficient of determination, or r^2, which indicates the extent to which the variance in one measure is explained by the other. The square of the correlation is considered a good measure of the strength or meaningfulness of a relationship. Thus, a correlation of 0.10 is not very mean-

---

1. The correlation coefficient, r, is an index of the extent to which two measures or variables are related. Correlations may range from $+1.00$ through 0 to -1.00; a value of zero indicates that there is no linear relationship between measures. A positive correlation indicates that as the value of one increases, the value of the other also increases; for example, there is a large positive correlation between height and weight. A negative correlation indicates that as one variable increases, the other decreases.

ingful, since its square is 0.01; similarly a correlation of 0.20 yields a coefficient of determination of 0.04. Throughout our presentation, we generally do not emphasize correlations which are smaller than 0.20, unless the absence of a relationship is itself of substantive importance.

Socioeconomic Status

The interview included several questions concerning the socioeconomic status of the respondent's family. Tables 4.10–4.13 include the correlations obtained for three of these measures: income, class, and parents' education.

The income question asked the interviewee to estimate his or her family's total annual income before taxes. Answers were coded into one of eight categories, ranging from less than $5,000 to more than $40,000; the most frequent responses were $10,000 to $15,000 and $15,000 to $20,000, with approximately 20 percent of the respondents in each category; smaller percentages reported both lower and higher incomes. The complete distributions of responses were presented in table 3.4. Most of the correlations obtained are not statistically significant; for these young people, there was little or no relationship between family income and any

TABLE 4.10. Correlations of background variables and lifetime sexual behavior: student males

	REL ATNHS	FAM INCOME	FAM CLASS	MO ED	FA ED	PAR AFF	FA AFF	MO AFF	FA UNDER	MO UNDER	FA CLOSE	MO CLOSE	SEXED FA	
REL ATNHS	—													
FAM INCOME	-.152	—												
FAM CLASS	-.013	.577	—											
MO ED	-.128	.412	.314	—										
FA ED	-.140	.469	.416	.506	—									
PAR AFF	.115	.265	.224	.096	.175	—								
FA AFF	.006	.212	.181	.086	.231	.587	—							
MO AFF	.065	.056	.085	.039	-.010	.371	.365	—						
FA UNDER	.041	.224	.217	.081	.185	.421	.471	.152	—					
MO UNDER	.124	-.061	-.027	.029	-.027	.275	.203	.259	.386	—				
FA CLOSE	.102	.243	.249	.110	.183	.435	.531	.156	.805	.309	—			
MO CLOSE	.160	-.018	.007	.010	-.017	.336	.268	.365	.335	.738	.465	—		
SEXED FA	.082	.195	.217	.074	.201	.372	.432	.117	.408	.203	.412	.229	—	
SEXED MO	.039	.041	.053	.040	-.059	.126	.091	.175	.129	.222	.116	.188		.4
FA VALUE	-.034	.152	.057	.173	.111	.340	.265	.133	.303	.213	.256	.186		.3
MO VALUE	-.012	.142	.143	.142	.085	.314	.197	.162	.184	.239	.166	.207		.1
FA REACT	-.296	-.036	-.118	.032	-.008	-.125	-.101	-.018	-.003	.019	-.089	.004		-.0
MO REACT	-.319	.074	-.046	.099	.053	-.050	-.022	-.070	.012	.083	-.028	-.004		.0
FA IDEO	-.252	.180	.026	.014	.115	.077	.139	.015	.255	.137	.167	.118		.2
MO IDEO	-.253	.112	-.028	.098	.083	.083	-.022	.004	.032	.197	-.020	.081		.0
FA SRC	.183	.119	.177	.040	.083	.235	.318	.106	.345	.189	.359	.226		.4
MO SRC	.235	-.078	.019	.035	-.112	.092	.066	.183	.107	.285	.104	.296		.1
MFR SRC	.000	.022	-.007	.023	-.018	-.051	-.030	.049	-.044	-.064	-.043	-.042		-.0
FFR SRC	-.008	.029	-.008	-.020	-.049	-.009	-.097	.032	-.059	-.057	-.089	-.067		-.0
LOVER SRC	.023	.101	.063	.020	.001	-.045	-.103	.005	-.064	-.103	-.114	-.113		-.08
# PART	-.154	.096	-.038	.054	.007	-.026	-.071	.045	-.131	-.057	-.178	-.050		-.0
# INTER	-.243	.088	-.070	.031	-.026	-.047	-.095	.045	-.110	-.063	-.175	-.048		-.08
LIFE	-.140	.097	.017	-.049	.011	-.011	.042	.027	-.067	-.173	-.100	-.115		-.0

of the three behavioral measures: lifetime behavior, number of coital experiences, and number of coital partners.

We also included a "subjective" measure of social class. Each interviewee was given a card which listed six class groups: upper, upper middle, middle, lower middle, working, and lower. He or she was asked "In your community, in which social class would you say your family is?" There was much less variation in answers to this question than in responses to the income item; from 35 to 50 percent said "middle," and an additional 33 to 50 percent reported "upper middle." The complete distributions were presented in table 3.4. In light of this lack of variation, it is not surprising that there are only small correlations between responses to this item and measures of lifetime sexual behavior.

Finally, we asked how much formal education the respondent's mother and father had completed. The answers ranged from less than eighth grade to graduate or professional education. In general, the parents, particularly fathers, of those in our student sample are more highly educated than the parents of our nonstudent respondents. The most frequent educational attainment of students' fathers is a bachelor's degree (29 percent) whereas for nonstudents it is a high school diploma (25 percent). Again,

TABLE 4.10, continued

SEXED MO	FA VALUE	MO VALUE	FA REACT	MO REACT	FA IDEO	MO IDEO	FA SRC	MO SRC	MFR SRC	FFR SRC	LOVER SRC	# PART	# INTER	LIFE
—														
.166	—													
.159	.546	—												
.014	.125	.033	—											
.101	.127	.132	.708	—										
.031	.223	-.001	.496	.403	—									
.125	.205	-.040	.434	.561	.555	—								
.121	.230	.157	-.078	-.107	.024	-.103	—							
.228	.128	.121	-.048	-.042	-.092	-.028	.618	—						
.055	-.041	-.129	.013	-.016	.066	-.008	.072	.015	—					
.075	.054	-.006	.107	.127	.080	.007	.033	.055	.458	—				
.114	.068	.002	.037	.029	.057	.045	.016	.025	.270	.523	—			
.073	.027	.020	.020	.251	.237	.251	-.106	-.138	-.016	.202	.161	—		
.068	-.006	-.057	-.057	.257	.223	.172	-.123	-.146	-.025	.110	.116	.688	—	
.055	.080	.028	.028	.161	.274	.217	-.168	-.181	.028	.288	.400	.335	.318	—

there is little relationship between either father's or mother's education and reported behavior.

Both Kinsey et al. (1948, 1953) and Ehrmann (1959) reported large differences in sexual behavior with social class. In our results, by contrast, there is little relationship between these indices of class and lifetime behavior. One explanation for the difference in results may be that our samples are heavily middle class; certainly relatively few of our respondents came from families with incomes of less than $5,000 (about 2 percent) or where parents had had an eighth grade education or less (about 7 percent). Thus, our sample may be restricted because the geographic area in which we interviewed is composed primarily of middle class persons. Alternatively, however, Reiss (1967) also found no overall relationship between social class and premarital sexual standards. He did find a positive relationship between class and permissiveness among liberals, and a negative relationship between these variables among conservatives. He suggested that the apparent relationship between class and sexual attitudes or behavior in earlier studies may be due to the fact that the samples were biased on the liberalism-conservatism dimension. Our finding of no relationship is consistent with his analysis.

TABLE 4.11. Correlations of background variables and lifetime sexual behavior: nonstudent males

	REL ATNHS	FAM INCOME	FAM CLASS	MO ED	FA ED	PAR AFF	FA AFF	MO AFF	FA UNDER	MO UNDER	FA CLOSE	MO CLOSE	SEXED FA
REL ATNHS	—												
FAM INCOME	-.016	—											
FAM CLASS	.051	.418	—										
MO ED	-.106	.247	.298	—									
FA ED	-.086	.338	.298	.484	—								
PAR AFF	.154	.285	.151	.109	.279	—							
FA AFF	.105	.221	.173	.111	.288	.609	—						
MO AFF	.038	.130	.085	.114	.144	.326	.507	—					
FA UNDER	.072	.187	.144	.099	.177	.424	.565	.192	—				
MO UNDER	-.037	-.034	.011	.054	-.071	.010	.104	.193	.310	—			
FA CLOSE	.093	.191	.097	.027	.105	.390	.507	.137	.760	.173	—		
MO CLOSE	-.022	-.042	-.007	-.013	-.033	.034	.108	.224	.243	.717	.312	—	
SEXED FA	.109	.170	.066	.023	.182	.312	.361	.200	.378	.030	.330	.016	—
SEXED MO	.085	.106	-.049	.088	.039	.060	.076	.215	.097	.272	.038	.246	.4
FA VALUE	.031	.133	.047	.019	.123	.280	.266	.116	.271	.102	.232	.064	.2
MO VALUE	.053	.135	.034	.071	.115	.245	.231	.165	.200	.209	.183	.215	.2
FA REACT	-.310	-.057	.011	.009	-.022	-.065	-.018	.043	.048	.048	.021	.105	.0
MO REACT	-.219	-.117	-.110	-.033	-.131	-.108	-.117	-.056	-.007	.082	-.007	.090	.0
FA IDEO	-.112	.251	.112	.126	.175	.223	.276	.172	.307	-.034	.303	-.024	-.0
MO IDEO	-.223	.073	-.044	.134	.064	-.086	.074	.182	.082	.177	.050	.165	-.0
FA SRC	.202	.129	.044	.020	.088	.226	.318	.111	.355	.212	.349	.121	.3
MO SRC	.200	.015	-.043	.004	.013	.118	.129	.138	.104	.273	.154	.229	.1
MFR SRC	.094	.103	.027	.046	.117	.170	.155	.056	.044	-.059	.038	-.093	.0
FFR SRC	-.058	.021	.034	.004	.024	.076	.134	-.021	.045	-.028			.0
LOVER SRC	.009	.069	-.016	.041	.064	.042	.072	.045	-.020	-.029	-.038	-.040	.0
# PART	-.147	-.025	-.050	-.013	-.005	-.010	-.100	.053	-.149	.042	-.110	.077	-.0
# INTER	-.114	.017	.017	.047	.029	.021	.050	.041	-.043	-.011	-.046	.003	-.0
LIFE	-.049	-.048	-.020	-.027	-.036	-.103	-.066	.052	-.067	-.122	-.055	-.075	-.0

Religion

Organized religion is a major source of the values and norms to which individuals are socialized. To the extent that denominations vary in sexual norms which they espouse, we would expect adherents to different denominations to differ in their standards and behavior. In the present context, we assume that the norms which parents taught their children vary by parental religious affiliation, and that these norms were reinforced to the extent that the adolescent attended services. We will consider these in relation to lifetime experience.

Earlier research has fairly consistently found relationships between religious background and premarital sexual attitudes or behavior. Ehrmann (1959) found that differences in lifetime behavior were related to religious affiliation (Catholic, Jewish, Protestant) and found a negative relationship between frequency of church attendance and sexual experience. Thus, in his results, those who attended church more regularly were less likely to have engaged in genital stimulation and intercourse. Reiss (1967) viewed religion as one source of sexual attitudes, and found that those who attended services more frequently had less permissive premarital standards. Finally, Sorensen (1972) employed a self-rating of religiosity, asking the

TABLE 4.11, continued

SEXED MO	FA VALUE	MO VALUE	FA REACT	MO REACT	FA IDEO	MO IDEO	FA SRC	MO SRC	MFR SRC	FFR SRC	LOVER SRC	# PART	# INTER	LIFE
—														
.138	—													
.137	.619	—												
.107	.026	.012	—											
.069	-.009	.121	.604	—										
-.086	-.016	.051	.298	.201	—									
-.002	-.069	.053	.351	.249	.443	—								
.248	.210	.211	-.043	.023	.088	-.017	—							
.328	.191	.119	-.045	-.004	-.101	-.031	.644	—						
.001	.046	-.036	-.045	-.094	.061	-.052	.102	.087	—					
-.055	.020	.047	.095	.076	.116	.129	.138	.171	.363	—				
.114	.037	-.012	.207	.153	.160	.086	.075	.068	.249	.461	—			
.026	.101	.078	.220	.225	.149	.323	-.058	-.055	-.084	.145	.108	—		
-.001	.124	.120	.293	.294	.225	.220	-.028	-.065	-.079	.169	.129	.478	—	
-.047	.005	.026	.250	.256	.317	.229	-.200	-.217	.051	.325	.463	.299	.327	—

adolescent whether he or she considered himself or herself very, somewhat, not very, or not at all religious; he reported that those who rated themselves more religious were less sexually experienced.

We included measures of both religious affiliation or denominational preference and frequency of attendance at religious functions. We asked these two questions twice, first in terms of the period when the respondent had attended high school, and second in terms of the period immediately preceding the interviews. We also asked each respondent to rate his or her religiosity at the time of the interview. We analyzed information concerning religious background for its relationship to lifetime sexual behavior; we shall consider later the relationship between the "current" measures of religion and current behavior.

We categorized religious affiliations into six groups: Roman Catholic, Jewish, Traditional Protestant, Fundamental Protestant, other, and none. We distinguished the two types of Protestant denominations in view of Reiss's argument that more fundamentalist religions are associated with more conservative sexual standards. We analyzed the relationship between religious affiliation in high school and lifetime behavior. We first looked at the distributions of Guttman scores for lifetime behavior for each of the six denominational groups. Comparing the entire distributions, using

TABLE 4.12. Correlations of background variables and lifetime sexual behavior: student females

	REL ATNHS	FAM INCOME	FAM CLASS	MO ED	FA ED	PAR AFF	FA AFF	MO AFF	FA UNDER	MO UNDER	FA CLOSE	MO CLOSE
REL ATNHS	—											
FAM INCOME	-.212	—										
FAM CLASS	-.149	.536	—									
MO ED	-.157	.292	.318	—								
FA ED	-.084	.359	.424	.492	—							
PAR AFF	.027	.268	.251	.198	.261	—						
FA AFF	-.058	.333	.292	.151	.244	.622	—					
MO AFF	-.105	.213	.207	.196	.200	.405	.526	—				
FA UNDER	.023	.202	.193	.049	.164	.414	.545	.190	—			
MO UNDER	.052	.059	.100	.155	.130	.287	.208	.311	.309	—		
FA CLOSE	.032	.244	.216	.042	.167	.444	.625	.240	.837	.249	—	
MO CLOSE	.061	.091	.095	.060	.160	.290	.259	.398	.274	.783	.369	—
SEXED FA	-.023	.163	.203	.103	.176	.315	.371	.122	.502	.157	.461	.163
SEXED MO	.048	.054	.080	.129	.101	.261	.210	.200	.198	.384	.201	.327
FA VALUE	-.010	.099	.088	.070	.103	.474	.333	.188	.379	.223	.354	.195
MO VALUE	-.045	.162	.128	.127	.186	.364	.196	.220	.200	.259	.191	.252
FA REACT	-.201	-.045	-.042	.131	.013	-.121	-.083	-.008	.028	.022	-.080	-.086
MO REACT	-.207	-.040	.025	.181	.026	-.003	-.039	.041	-.039	.114	-.079	.032
FA IDEO	-.268	.188	.144	.221	.184	.142	.211	.116	.271	.067	.204	.038
MO IDEO	-.261	.134	.107	.268	.152	.048	.062	.142	.018	.205	.007	.152
FA SRC	.105	.113	.058	-.029	.081	.178	.244	.008	.420	.110	.389	.148
MO SRC	.172	-.008	-.003	-.019	.051	.151	-.098	-.119	.168	.390	.167	.382
MFR SRC	.039	.016	.000	.059	-.006	-.003	-.133	-.094	-.077	-.009	-.119	-.078
FFR SRC	.065	.004	.085	.035	.093	-.009	-.073	-.101	.008	.016	-.046	-.045
LOVER SRC	.027	.073	.056	.065	.051	.010	.003	.085	-.029	-.037	-.061	-.058
# PART	-.168	.041	-.005	.038	.021	-.085	-.042	.004	-.169	-.120	-.147	-.007
# INTER	-.133	.054	.030	.101	-.010	-.069	-.052	.018	-.117	-.123	-.118	-.094
LIFE	-.214	.095	.119	.118	.105	.012	.048	.147	-.110	-.061	-.113	-.046

chi-square statistics, we found that the differences were not significant. However, inspection of the distributions revealed differences similar to those reported by Ehrmann (1959). Although only small percentages of his subjects were Jewish (9 percent of the males and 15 percent of the females), he reported that they had higher rates of lifetime genital activity and intercourse than his Catholic and Protestant respondents. In our data, students from Jewish backgrounds were more likely to report having engaged in intercourse (94 percent of the males, 80 percent of the females) than those from Catholic and Traditional Protestant backgrounds (72 percent of the men, 60 percent of the women). The same pattern is found among the nonstudents, although the differences between denominations are smaller. Females raised in Fundamental Protestant religions in both student and nonstudent samples are less likely to report lifetime coitus than those who report Traditional Protestant affiliations (47 percent student and 65 percent of the nonstudent females). The differences among religious groups are statistically significant in the female student subsample. The percentages of our respondents reporting some other or no religious background are so small (1 to 3 percent) that we cannot meaningfully discuss differences in their behavior.

With regard to religious attendance during high school, the correlations

TABLE 4.12, continued

SEXED MO	FA VALUE	MO VALUE	FA REACT	MO REACT	FA IDEO	MO IDEO	FA SRC	MO SRC	MFR SRC	FFR SRC	LOVER SRC	# PART	# INTER	LIFE
—														
.248	—													
.247	.643	—												
.015	.046	.056	—											
−.002	−.004	.097	.616	—										
.047	.097	.139	.471	.372	—									
.177	.004	.201	.389	.533	.649	—								
.192	.210	.103	.021	−.051	.044	−.076	—							
.408	.178	.141	−.061	−.076	−.126	−.043	.557	—						
−.011	.040	−.008	.089	.093	.004	.085	.057	.084	—					
.017	.019	−.032	.021	−.002	.014	.075	.075	.123	.434	—				
−.089	.002	−.021	.069	.090	.050	.045	−.022	−.039	.459	.210	—			
−.128	−.277	−.107	.150	.187	.185	.182	−.177	−.252	−.050	−.100	.029	—		
−.129	−.159	−.115	.175	.261	.099	.091	−.155	−.250	−.003	−.095	.166	.427	—	
−.138	−.079	.044	.199	.241	.223	.230	−.163	−.244	.241	.010	.525	.333	.379	—

in tables 4.10–4.13 show a consistent negative relationship between attendance and lifetime behavior. Those who attended more frequently reported fewer intercourse experiences, a smaller number of coital partners, and generally had a lower lifetime Guttman score. Ten of the 12 correlations are statistically significant ($p < 0.05$); the strongest relationship is found among female students, where the correlation between attendance and lifetime behavior is −0.21.

Thus, there is some evidence of variation in behavior as a function of the individual's denominational affiliation in high school. There is a stronger relationship between attendance at religious services and behavior, with those who went to church more often reporting less intimate lifetime behavior. Both of these relationships were also found by Ehrmann in data collected 25 years earlier. We interpret these results as reflecting differences in the norms to which the person was socialized during adolescence and his or her consequent exercise of self-control on the basis of these norms.

Relationships with Parents

We assume that parents are important agents of socialization. Their influence on the child may be enhanced if the relationship is relatively

TABLE 4.13. Correlations of background variables and lifetime sexual behavior: nonstudent female

	REL ATNHS	FAM INCOME	FAM CLASS	MO ED	FA ED	PAR AFF	FA AFF	MO AFF	FA UNDER	MO UNDER	FA CLOSE	MO CLOSE	SEXED FA
REL ATNHS	—												
FAM INCOME	.049	—											
FAM CLASS	−.030	.356	—										
MO ED	.012	.266	.409	—									
FA ED	−.032	.247	.417	.582	—								
PAR AFF	.084	.104	.177	.190	.270	—							
FA AFF	.121	.147	.233	.209	.316	.522	—						
MO AFF	.129	.135	.210	.262	.241	.363	.507	—					
FA UNDER	.078	.069	.138	.094	.222	.422	.535	.199	—				
MO UNDER	.146	.207	.275	.243	.181	.376	.319	.445	.330	—			
FA CLOSE	.064	.118	.148	.110	.190	.423	.638	.230	.823	.285	—		
MO CLOSE	.151	.194	.195	.226	.127	.366	.349	.492	.298	.791	.352	—	
SEXED FA	.008	.069	.160	.210	.239	.371	.411	.214	.421	.150	.386	.145	—
SEXED MO	.138	.072	.251	.379	.241	.349	.253	.391	.222	.460	.160	.472	.4
FA VALUE	.046	.106	.103	.185	.209	.391	.236	.088	.313	.160	.273	.144	.2
MO VALUE	−.023	−.027	.091	.145	.150	.329	.183	.178	.169	.270	.182	.207	.2
FA REACT	−.240	−.084	.015	.065	.036	−.107	−.125	−.137	−.043	−.121	−.114	−.147	−.0
MO REACT	−.187	−.031	.014	.016	.005	−.169	−.141	−.039	−.230	.084	−.172	−.023	−.1
FA IDEO	−.197	.088	.049	.104	.264	.138	.095	−.018	.253	−.008	.147	−.003	.2
MO IDEO	−.191	.009	.054	.167	.140	−.056	−.035	.086	−.139	.170	−.149	.128	.0
FA SRC	.130	.014	.124	.091	.102	.301	.287	.141	.339	.139	.367	.121	.4
MO SRC	.107	−.003	.117	.146	.061	.255	.162	.262	.161	.334	.168	.338	.2
MFR SRC	−.052	−.045	.011	−.053	−.068	−.051	.013	−.034	.037	−.009	.088	.033	.0
FFR SRC	−.021	.053	.082	.072	.047	.068	.074	.025	.102	.046	.169	.068	.1
LOVER SRC	−.062	.055	.006	−.050	.094	.065	−.075	−.049	−.047	−.002	−.032	.017	−.0
# PART	−.126	.007	−.130	−.094	−.080	−.095	−.137	−.175	−.074	−.215	−.104	−.185	−.0
# INTER	.162	.109	.088	.055	.049	−.043	−.034	−.008	−.172	−.067	−.144	−.073	−.0
LIFE	−.087	.104	−.033	−.089	−.117	−.184	−.123	−.107	−.143	−.139	−.139	−.094	−.1

good. Burgess (1973) studied small samples of American and Norwegian young people. She reported that there was greater correspondence between parents' and child's standards when their relationship was more open, loving, and characterized by understanding and respect. Given the evidence in Reiss (1967) that parents are generally conservative, we believed that particularly close, warm, and understanding relationships with parents might be associated with less intimate lifetime behavior.

We included questions concerning a number of aspects of the individual's relationships with his or her parents. These variables appear in table 4.9 in the order in which the questions were asked. We asked how often parents displayed affection toward the respondent, how well mother and father understood him or her, and how close he or she was to both mother and father.

For males (both student and nonstudent), all the correlations between the affection questions and lifetime behavior are 0.10 or less, and thus not statistically significant. Some of the correlations for females (tables 4.12 and 4.13) are somewhat larger: among nonstudents, answers to the affection questions are significantly and negatively related to the lifetime behavior score, indicating that those from families where displays of affection were more frequent reported less intimate lifetime behavior.

TABLE 4.13, continued

	SEXED MO	FA VALUE	MO VALUE	FA REACT	MO REACT	FA IDEO	MO IDEO	FA SRC	MO SRC	MFR SRC	FFR SRC	LOVER SRC	# PART	# INTER	LIFE
SEXED MO	—														
FA VALUE	.225	—													
MO VALUE	.303	.513	—												
FA REACT	−.084	.024	.000	—											
MO REACT	−.014	−.133	−.010	.490	—										
FA IDEO	.033	.140	.031	.404	.117	—									
MO IDEO	.174	−.057	.067	.285	.506	.432	—								
FA SRC	.219	.269	.139	−.041	−.124	.082	−.073	—							
MO SRC	.438	.120	.138	−.036	−.022	−.047	.054	.620	—						
MFR SRC	−.070	−.012	−.022	.083	.048	.076	.097	.195	.083	—					
FFR SRC	.056	−.013	−.026	−.048	−.103	−.017	−.011	.164	.205	.305	—				
LOVER SRC	−.055	.030	−.046	.052	.050	.030	.109	.024	−.012	.467	.176	—			
# PART	−.155	−.070	−.105	.126	.072	.063	−.053	−.039	−.119	.041	−.034	−.052	—		
# INTER	−.155	−.013	−.079	.122	.201	−.029	.092	−.147	−.209	.017	−.151	.141	.308	—	
LIFE	−.284	−.022	−.090	.159	.152	.278	.331	−.221	−.249	.155	−.088	.388	.278	.331	—

The extent to which our respondents felt that their mothers and fathers understood them also tends to be negatively related to their sexual behavior, that is, those who felt that each parent understood them more reported less sexual activity. For males, father's understanding is negatively correlated with number of partners for both students and nonstudents and with number of coital experiences for the former. Mother's understanding is negatively related to lifetime behavior for both groups. These relationships are somewhat stronger among both female samples.

Finally, the extent to which the young person feels close to his or her parent also tends to be negatively related to lifetime behavior. Among male students, those who felt closer to their fathers reported fewer intercourse experiences and partners, and less intimate behavior. The comparable correlations for nonstudent men are not significant. Among women, closeness to father consistently shows a significant negative relation to the three measures of lifetime behavior.

Thus, the quality of an individual's relationships with his or her parents is related to lifetime sexual behavior. Although the correlations are neither large nor consistent, there is a pattern in which those reporting more frequent displays of affection by their parents, greater understanding by, and closeness to their parents report less extensive and less intimate lifetime behavior. The pattern is stronger among our female respondents and also occurs more frequently in items dealing with the relationship with the young person's father. If parents are the primary source of less permissive standards, our data suggest that those who have better relationships with their parents are more influenced by their parents' beliefs, and less influenced by the permissive standards of the courtship system, i.e., by peers and partners.

Parents' Attitudes Toward Sexuality

Because parents are important as socializing agents, it is important to know to what standards they socialize the young child, the content of the norms they teach him or her.

We included a number of questions which dealt specifically with parents' sexual attitudes and standards. Eight of these seemed to be related to lifetime behavior, and the relevant correlations are included in tables 4.10–4.13. We asked each person to evaluate the adequacy of the sex education received from father and mother, how his or her father and mother felt about the value of sex in their own lives, and how father and mother would feel if the respondent were living with someone to whom he or she was not married. Finally, we asked the respondent about his or her father's and mother's ideology or standards, using the measure discussed earlier.

The questions about sex education by father and mother asked the individual to characterize it in terms of one of the following categories: completely adequate, good but weak in some areas, weak in many areas, or completely inadequate. The data in tables 4.10 and 4.11 indicate that there is no relationship between answers to these two questions and the three behavioral measures among males. All of the correlations are small and not significant. Among females (both students and nonstudents), there are significant negative correlations between adequacy of education by mothers and behavior; the more adequate they felt their education from their mothers to be, the less extensive and intimate was their lifetime behavior.

For the items asking about the value of sex in parents' lives and parents' reactions to cohabitation, six categories were read, and the respondent was asked to choose the most appropriate one. The categories were: very positive, positive, somewhat positive, somewhat negative, negative, and very negative. The results for the items concerning the value of sexuality in father's and mother's lives are inconsistent. In the student male sample, none of the correlations are significant. Among nonstudent men, there are significant positive correlations between value to father and number of intercourse partners and experiences the son reported. Among women students there are significant negative correlations between number of partners and coital experiences, and value of sex to both mother and father. The reversal of the relationship is suggestive of a differential impact of parental attitude by gender; but the potential significance of the finding is reduced by the fact that this differential correlation is not found in the nonstudent groups.

More consistent results are found in the relationships between items inquiring about parents' reactions to cohabitation and the individual's behavior. The more positive (or less negative) the respondent believed his or her parents would be, the more extensive and intimate was the reported lifetime behavior. Many of the individual correlations are significant, and a number of them are larger than 0.20. Presumably, this item measures in part parental attitudes about the importance of sexuality in their son's or daughter's heterosexual relationships, since cohabitation generally involves ongoing physical intimacy. Parental reactions perhaps also reflect sexual liberalism, since those parents who are less concerned about cohabitation also have more permissive premarital standards.

We also asked each respondent to report his or her parents' sexual ideology, using the same question format as employed later in the interview to ascertain the individual's own standards. Again, we asked separate questions about mother's and father's ideologies. We recognize that this is a measure of our respondent's perceptions of parental attitudes; ideally, one would like to ask these questions of parents themselves. But as discussed earlier, we believe that perceptions of significant other's attitudes may be the most important aspect; as long as respondents report their perceptions accurately, we can consider the relationship between these responses and the individual's behavior important in its own right. Walsh (1970), studying a sample of largely freshman females, found no relationship between parents' standard and same-sex child's attitude, but a strong association between child's perception of parental standard and his or her own standard.

The correlations between father's and mother's ideologies on the one hand and the three behavioral measures on the other are generally the largest we have discussed so far. Among males the correlations are all positive and significant, ranging from 0.15 to 0.32. Father's ideology relates more strongly to lifetime behavior, with correlations of 0.27 for students and 0.32 for nonstudents; mother's ideology shows the highest correlation with number of partners (0.25 and 0.32 respectively). The results for females are less consistent. Among students, father's and mother's standards correlate with both number of partners and lifetime behavior; among nonstudents, ideology correlates only with the lifetime behavior though the coefficients are quite large (0.28 and 0.33). Thus, the more permissive these young people perceived their parents to be, the more intimate their lifetime behavior; in addition, among males, perceived permissiveness of parents is also correlated with the number of premarital intercourse experiences and of partners. Again, we assume that these results reflect parental socialization of children to particular standards, and the subsequent use of those standards as a basis for self-control over sexual expression.

Sources of Information

A fundamental aspect of the model presented in Chapter 2 is the assumption that different agents provide different types of socialization. We asserted that parents focus primarily on the teaching of norms and values, and much of the data presented in this chapter supports that assumption. We believe that peers, by contrast, teach information about sexuality, and that partners are primarily involved in the learning of sexual behavior. Relatively direct evidence of the extent to which the three agents are associated with different types of learning is available from a series of questions we asked about sources of various types of information.

We specified four types of information which a person might have: moral ("what is right and wrong with regard to sex"); the anatomy and physiology of reproduction; the mechanics of sexual behavior; and contraceptives. We also provided a list of potential sources, including mother, father, male and female friends, lover, professionals, sex education courses, and media (books, magazines, and films). For each type of knowledge, we asked the respondent to rate the relative importance of each of the potential sources in contributing to his or her attitudes and information in that area. These questions were asked early in the interview, before more specific questions about sexual ideology and behavior.

We discuss the sources of contraceptive information in Chapter 9. In general, parents were not the primary sources of either mechanical or reproductive knowledge. The three most important sources of these were lover, professionals (doctors, clergy, teachers), and sex education courses. Mother or father was rated "very important" as sources of these by only 4 to 17 percent of our respondents.

On the other hand, mothers and fathers were much more frequently rated "very important" as sources of moral attitudes and values. Twenty-seven to 30 percent of the females so rated their mothers, and 19 to 21 percent so rated their fathers. Males were less likely to name mother or father as primary sources; only about 10 percent indicated that either was very important. Lover was again most frequently rated "very important"; 45 percent of the student men and women and 35 percent of the nonstudents gave this response. The other sources, male and female friends, professionals, and sex education courses, were rated "very important" by 4 to 12 percent.

We included these items concerning the importance of each source for one's moral knowledge in our analyses of lifetime behavior. The respondent rated each source as "very important," "quite important," "slightly important," or "not at all important." The responses given concerning five of the sources were related to lifetime behavior, and the correlations are included in tables 4.10–4.13. In general, the more important the respondent rated mother and father as sources, the less extensive was his or her experience and the less intimate his or her lifetime behavior. Among males, the correlations between mother as a source and the behavioral measures are about the same magnitude as those between ratings of father and behavior; these range from −0.03 to −0.22, and not all are statistically significant. In the data from female respondents, the correlations are generally somewhat stronger; virtually all of them are significant. In addition, there is evidence of a differential in the importance of mothers and fathers, with the ratings of mother as a source generally correlating more strongly with behavior (−0.12 to −0.25) than the ratings of father (−0.04 to −0.22). Thus, for females, the moral standards communicated by mothers are more closely related to their behavior than are those conveyed by fathers. Parents seem to be more important sources of moral attitudes for women than for men. More generally, those who rate parents as very important may be less sexually experienced.

When we look at the importance of friends as sources, we again find a different pattern for male and female respondents. In general, the importance of male friends is not correlated with the behavior of our male respondents; none of the correlations are significant for either student or nonstudent men. On the other hand, the importance men attribute to female friends is positively and significantly associated with their lifetime behavior. Among women respondents, the importance of female friends is generally not related to behavior, while the rating of male friends correlated positively and at times significantly with extent and intimacy of lifetime behavior. Thus, in general, the moral standards communicated by friends of the same gender are not associated with behavior, whereas the importance of opposite-sex friends is associated with more intimate and extensive lifetime sexual experience.

The final item concerned the importance of a lover as a source of moral knowledge. As is evident in tables 4.10–4.13, there are substantial positive correlations between lover as a source and lifetime behavior. The more important a lover is in contributing to moral standards, the larger the individual's lifetime behavior score for both males and females. There is a much smaller but still significant correlation between lover as a source and number of coital experiences. In part, these relationships are no doubt due to the fact that only those who have been involved in relationships of high emotional intimacy could rate lovers as an important source; but those who have had lovers would not necessarily have their own moral standards influenced by that fact alone. Intimate behavior with one's lover may merely reinforce previously existing standards. The size of these correlations suggests, however, that lovers also often influence the individual's attitudes.

These results are quite consistent with the general model of differential social influence of parents, peers, and partners. The importance of parental influence on the individual's moral standards is associated with less lifetime sexual behavior; the influence of mothers on daughters seems to be stronger than the other contributions (mother-son, father-daughter, and father-son). To the extent that friends are rated important as a source, the individual's behavior is more extensive, which is consistent with the assumption that peers are the primary source of more permissive premarital standards. Our results suggest an important qualification, that it is principally opposite-sex friends, and particularly lovers, that are associated with increased permissiveness, and not peers regardless of their gender.

We were also interested in whether these relationships vary with the age of the individual. Reiss (1967) suggested a temporal dimension, that as one becomes more involved in the courtship system, he or she comes more subject to peer influence and less to parental influence. This implies that age would be negatively correlated with importance of parents as a source, and positively correlated with ratings of friends' importance. In our results with a limited range of ages, however, these correlations are generally small and not statistically significant.

Other Characteristics

In our analysis we included a variety of other background variables which might have been related to lifetime behavior. These included size of high school attended, size of the community in which the respondent was raised, family composition—number, sex and relative age of siblings, and mother's occupational activity (if any). None of these were correlated with any of the lifetime behavior measures discussed in this chapter.

Relative Influence of Background Characteristics

We have considered a large number of correlations between background characteristics and three measures of lifetime behavior. A correlational analysis looks at the relationship between only two variables at a time. We found significant associations between each of a variety of measures and one or more of the behavioral variables. The next question is the relative importance of each of these measures. For example, we found relationships between measures of the quality of relationship with parents—displays of affection, closeness, and understanding—and behavior, and between parents' attitudes about sexuality and behavior. Can we determine whether one is more or less important than the other? This is particularly important if some of the background measures are correlated with each other. For example, we reported earlier that parental understanding and closeness to parents were both negatively correlated with lifetime behavior. The correlations in tables 4.10–4.13 show that understanding and closeness are highly positively related. Thus, we want to determine whether each is independently related to behavior, or whether only one is, and the correlations between the other and lifetime experience are due solely to the association between the first and second. Multiple regression analysis is a statistical procedure which allows one to determine the independence of the effect of each variable. It takes into account, or controls for, the correlations between each "independent" variable and the dependent variable of interest, in this case, lifetime sexual behavior.

We performed regression analyses with all of the variables included in our analysis of background characteristics. Table 4.14 presents the results obtained. The numbers entered in the body of the table are the standardized regression coefficients. Only those which are statistically significant are included. Thus, variables for which there are no entries are ones which are not independently associated with lifetime sexual behavior. The last two rows in the table present the multiple correlation coefficient and the (corrected) coefficient of determination; these statistics indicate the extent to which the "independent" variables, taken together, can predict lifetime behavior. We are most interested in the coefficient of determination, which is typically interpreted as the proportion of variation in the dependent variable explained by the variables included in the analysis.

Examination of the table indicates that many of the relationships discussed above are not independent. Thus, there are not significant independent associations of family's socioeconomic status, as measured by income, class and parental education, or of closeness to mother and father or the value of sex to mother and father, and lifetime behavior. None of these coefficients are significant when we analyze the simultaneous relationship of lifetime activity and other independent variables. It is also obvious that some of the relationships are not consistent across the

TABLE 4.14. Regression of background variables on lifetime sexual behavior

Background and parental characteristics	Standardized regression coefficients			
	SM	NM	SF	NF
Attendance at religious functions during high school			$-.1809^d$	
Parental attitudes				
Father's display of affection toward respondent	$.1471^c$			
Mother's display of affection toward respondent			$.1094^b$	
Mother's understanding of respondent	$-.1673^d$			
Evaluation of sex education from father				$.1563^a$
Evaluation of sex education from mother				$-.3230^d$
Mother's reaction to cohabitation		$.1461^a$		
Father's sexual ideology	$.2583^d$	$.2351^d$		
Mother's sexual ideology				$.2017^d$
Father as source of moral attitudes toward sex	$-.1897^d$	$-.2729^d$		$-.2107^d$
Mother as source of moral attitudes toward sex			$-.2057^d$	
Male friends as source of moral attitudes toward sex	$-.1511^c$			
Female friends as source of moral attitudes toward sex	$.1712^c$	$.1648^a$		
Lover as source of moral attitudes toward sex	$.3375^d$	$.3475^d$	$.5123^d$	$.3679^d$
Multiple correlation coefficient	.5638	.6173	.6114	.5521
Corrected coefficient of determination	.3066	.3666	.3180	.2927

$^a p < .01$
$^b p < .005$
$^c p < .001$
$^d p < .0001$

four gender-status groups. Thus, religious attendance in high school is significantly associated with behavior only for student women, and not for the other three groups. Similarly, the adequacy of sex education by parents is related to behavior only in the nonstudent female sample.

There are three consistent relationships in these results. First, one or more of the items measuring quality of relationship with parents is a significant correlate of behavior among student respondents. Second, one or more of the items concerning parental sexual attitudes is associated with lifetime sexual experience; more permissive parental standards are significantly related to more intimate behavior in three of the four groups. In addition, rating of mother or father as a source of moral attitudes is associated with lower lifetime behavior scores. Third, the importance of lover as a source is the factor most strongly and consistently associated with behavior.

These results provide a very concise summary of our data concerning the influence of background characteristics on lifetime sexual experience. The results indicate that to the extent that parents are and remain a primary influence on a young person's sexual standards, his or her sexual behavior is relatively less extensive and intimate than that of others of similar age and sex. Conversely, to the extent that parental influence is replaced by peer influence, particularly lovers, his or her heterosexual behavior becomes more intimate and extensive. These conclusions support our model of differential influence, and the more specific assumptions that family characteristics are a major influence on sexual experience (see figure 2.2). These results also replicate, with large, random, rather than "convenience," samples, the findings reported by Walsh (1970), Vandiver (1972), and Walsh et al. (1976). They also found that an increase in peer or "reference group" influence relative to parental influence was associated with more permissive attitudes (Walsh, 1970; Vandiver, 1972) or attitudes and behavior (Walsh et al., 1976). Finally, these findings characterize both college students and 18-to-23-year-old nonstudents.

SUMMARY

This chapter has examined lifetime sexual behavior. The descriptive data on participation in the nine sexual behaviors reveal similar patterns across the subsamples. The only difference between groups is that a larger proportion of the nonstudents had participated in the most intimate behaviors. Analysis of the individual patterns of participation indicated that lifetime sexual behavior was unidimensional and could be represented by a Guttman scale.

This pattern of premarital participation in sexual behaviors and the data on age of first participation in these activities provide evidence of a developmental process in sexuality. The individual's participation in increasingly more intimate behaviors develops over a period of several years. This increasing participation is part of the socialization to heterosexual relationships and is influenced by both biological factors and social definitions of heterosexual behavior. The pattern of involvement is similar across the subgroups. The range of age at first participation suggests that involvement in heterosexual behavior begins at different points in the lives of various individuals. Overall, females are somewhat older than males when they first participate in any particular behavior. Thus in any particular dyad there may be differences in the extent of sexual experience which potentially contribute to conflict.

Data on the respondent's relationship with the first sexual partner reveal that most initial sexual intercourse takes place in relationships characterized by love or affection. While men seemed to be involved in more emotionally intimate relationships than past research had found, there are still gender differences in the emotional quality of the relationship with first coital partner. Females report more emotional involvement with their first partner than males do.

Comparing the number of lifetime intercourse experiences to the number of lifetime coital partners, the data suggest that the respondents are sexually experienced in terms of intercourse but with only a few partners. The data on lifetime sexual behavior and partners show that sexual development is a patterned process subject to the influence of socialization. Respondents experience more sexual behavior over time, but are not promiscuous in terms of number of partners or emotional involvement.

Examination of background characteristics further substantiates the effect of social influences on sexuality. The consistent independent effects on sexual behavior are found primarily among those variables that reflect social influence. The socioeconomic characteristics of family and community were not related to lifetime behavior in these samples. The results indicate that parents and religious institutions influence individuals to restrict their premarital sexual behavior. The more involved or closer to these sources on a variety of measures, the less intimate the sexual experience. Alternatively, peers and partner are sources influencing the individual toward more premarital sexual activity. Thus in terms of our model, there does seem to be a pattern in sexual behavior, and whether a person has shifted from parents to peers or partner as a primary social influence predicts the extent of sexual experience.

5

Sociopsychological Characteristics and Current Sexuality

WE NOW turn our attention to current sexuality. In our interviews, we obtained more information about the respondent and his or her current social situation, relationships, and sexual behavior than about his or her past. Survey research, like other cross-sectional methods based on data collected at one point in time, is most useful for collecting data about present circumstances. Such information is minimally affected by inability to remember and by error due to selective recall (e.g., remembering primarily good or bad aspects of past experiences). Thus, we have relatively more confidence in the validity of our respondents' answers to questions about present and recent events, and in addition we were able to ask more detailed questions about these matters. Thus, we devote the next three chapters to the relationships between various characteristics and the person's current sexual standards and behavior.

In this chapter we focus on the relationship between the various sociopsychological characteristics we measured and sexual ideology (or premarital standards) and current behavior. First, we describe our respondents' ideology; this indicates the content of this product of their sexual socialization. Next we report their current sexual activity. These results are compared both with the findings of earlier research, and with the reported lifetime behavior discussed in Chapter 4. This material is important because the measures of ideology and behavior are our measures of current sexuality. Next, we report the results of scaling techniques which provide a summary measure of both ideology and behavior. These measures are employed in the analyses reported in the next four chapters. We then turn to the sociopsychological measures (self-image, self-esteem, body image, internal-external control, and role definitions) and report the

TABLE 5.1. Personal sexual ideology (in percent; N = SM, 432; NM, 220; SF, 431; NF, 293)

Acceptability of behavior	Petting involving breast fondling				Petting involving fondling partner's genitals				Intercourse			
	SM	NM	SF	NF	SM	NM	SF	NF	SM	NM	SF	NF
FOR MALES												
Not before marriage	0.93	1.36	1.40	2.73	2.08	3.18	6.49	5.12	5.09	5.45	11.13	13.31
If engaged to be married	0.47	0.91	3.24	2.39	1.85	2.73	3.94	5.12	6.48	6.82	6.26	8.53
If in love and not engaged	10.64	10.00	12.76	17.74	20.83	15.00	26.45	28.66	28.01	24.55	44.08	30.71
If feel affection but not love	26.62	28.64	35.96	31.05	23.14	29.55	26.91	26.62	20.83	18.64	14.15	13.65
If both want it	61.34	59.09	46.17	46.07	52.08	49.55	35.73	34.47	39.58	44.55	23.89	33.78
Missing[a]	0.00	0.00	0.47	0.00	0.00	0.00	0.47	0.00	0.00	0.00	0.47	0.00
FOR FEMALES												
Not before marriage	0.93	1.36	1.40	2.73	2.08	3.18	6.72	5.46	5.09	5.45	13.22	14.33
If engaged to be married	0.69	1.36	3.71	2.73	1.85	3.18	4.64	7.16	7.41	7.27	6.72	8.87
If in love and not engaged	11.57	10.00	17.16	19.11	22.45	17.73	28.53	29.69	29.39	27.72	45.24	34.12
If feel affection but not love	27.31	30.00	34.57	30.71	23.61	28.18	26.68	24.91	19.91	17.73	12.06	11.26
If both want it	59.49	57.27	42.69	44.70	49.76	47.73	32.94	32.76	38.19	41.82	22.27	31.39
Missing[a]	0.00	0.00	0.47	0.00	0.23	0.00	0.47	0.00	0.00	0.00	0.47	0.00

[a]Respondent did not answer the item.

results of factor analyses of responses to them. As discussed in Chapter 2, we believe that sexual ideology is the basis upon which the person exercises self-control over his or her sexual activity; accordingly, we discuss the relationship between ideology and current behavior. We then consider the interrelation of the sociopsychological factors and both ideology and current activity. We expect the sociopsychological characteristics to be related to sexuality because they provide another basis for self-control in social interaction.

SEXUAL STANDARDS OR IDEOLOGY

We reviewed in Chapter 2 the past research which has emphasized the role of attitudes. Our model, presented in figure 2.2, shares the assumption of some of that work that the individual's attitudes about the acceptability of various behaviors determine his or her behavior. Thus, our measure of attitudes, or *sexual ideology*, is assumed in part to reflect the sexual socialization he or she received in the family, which was the focus of Chapter 4, and to affect his or her sexual behavior.

As discussed in Chapter 3, the ideology measure involved presenting five types of relationships, of increasing degrees of emotional intimacy, and asking at what point in the development of a relationship each of three behaviors was acceptable. The question stressed that we wanted to know how the respondent *personally* felt; we ascertained his or her personal standards separately for males and females.

Table 5.1 presents our respondents' ideologies for males and females. The data indicate that our respondents did evaluate sexual activities in the context of the quality of the relationship. Thus, breast fondling was accepted by 80 to 85 percent of these young people if both wanted it or if the two people felt affection. On the average, they required somewhat greater emotional intimacy before genital fondling was accepted. Finally, 35 to 60 percent believed that one should be in love for intercourse to be acceptable.

A consistent finding in past research has been that an individual held different standards for males than females. Generally, it has been found that both young people (Ehrmann, 1959; Reiss, 1967) and adults (Reiss, 1967) have more permissive premarital standards for male sexual behavior than for female behavior. This has frequently been referred to as the "double standard." Comparing the equivalent percentages in table 5.1, it is clear that our respondents did not hold different standards for the two sexes. Males tended to accept a particular behavior at the same point in a relationship for both males and females; similarly, females reported the same standards for both men and women. The absence of differential standards is also reflected in the extremely high correlations between respondents' answers to the items concerning the acceptability of a particular behavior for males and for females. These correlations range from 0.937 to 0.973, indicating virtually no difference in responses. Thus, the "double standard" has essentially disappeared in the groups being studied here, a major difference between these results and those of other studies. The importance of this finding will be discussed in Chapter 10.

Our conclusion that the "double standard" has disappeared is one of the more controversial, judging from reactions when we have presented it in other contexts. It must be stressed that we define "double standard" as Ehrmann (1959) and Reiss (1967) did; "a double standard indicates that there is one code of conduct for one sex and a different one for the other" (Ehrmann, 1959, p. 188). Thus, if people do not have different standards for men and women, there is no double standard, *using this definition*. We recognize that other people, using other types of data, have concluded that the double standard still exists. Carns (1973) has emphasized differences in the quality of the relationship with one's first coital partner; in his data, men report more casual relationships, and he cites this as evidence of a double standard. Ferrell, Tolone, and Walsh (1977) cite differences between men and women in frequency of coitus as evidence of a double standard. These differences are important, but it requires an inference to conclude that they are due to different standards. Our analysis of standards themselves is a much more direct approach, and our results are quite clear.

While there is no evidence that the same individual holds different standards for men and women, the results indicate that the standards held by men (for both sexes) differ from those held by women. For example, the last row in the first section of the table indicates that about 60 percent of the males believed breast fondling to be acceptable if both want it, compared to 46 percent of the females. Similarly, approximately 50 percent of the males accepted genital fondling in such a relationship, while only 35 percent of the females did so. The same differential acceptability is evident in the second section of the table. Thus, the males we interviewed had somewhat more permissive standards for both sexes than did the females.

An additional finding of considerable importance is the absence of substantial differences between students and nonstudents. Particularly in the case of those attending large universities, it has on occasion been argued that students are generally both more liberal and more egalitarian in their attitudes. This position implies that students would accept more intimate sexual behavior (e.g., intercourse) within a relationship of a specific emotional quality, and that they would be less likely to hold differing standards for males and females than a comparable group of nonstudents. There is no evidence of either of these differences in our data. Our nonstudent respondents who were of the same age and lived in the same community were neither less permissive or less egalitarian.

The data in table 5.1 indicate clearly that the young people interviewed for this research had, in Reiss's terms, relatively permissive attitudes. Only 5 percent of the males and 11 to 14 percent of the females believed that intercourse was not acceptable until after marriage. This represents a marked decline in comparison to the results of earlier studies. For example, Simon and Gagnon's data, collected in 1967 and based on representative samples of students at 12 colleges and universities, including the University of Wisconsin, indicated that 24 to 31 percent of the males and more than half of the females believed intercourse before marriage was unacceptable. Majorities of from 48 to 63 percent of our respondents held standards which Reiss terms "permissiveness with affection"; that is, they believed that intercourse would be acceptable if the couple was engaged, or felt strong affection or love for each other. Finally, from 22 to 34 percent of the women and 38 to 45 percent of the men felt that intercourse was appropriate if both wanted it. The comparable results from the Simon and Gagnon research are 4 to 7 percent and 17 to 30 percent, respectively.

In their sexual ideology, then, our respondents were relatively liberal or permissive. The majority of both men and women accepted intercourse when there was affection or love in the relationship; one-third or more did not require affection and one-sixth or less believed one should abstain from intercourse until after marriage. Our data indicate that the "double standard," in the strict or traditional sense of accepting premarital coitus for men but not women, has disappeared, at least in this population; our interviewees reported almost identical personal ideologies for males and females. Similarly, sexual ideologies were not especially different among students compared to nonstudents. We did find that men required less emotional intimacy in the relationship than women for intercourse to be acceptable. This may produce conflict in some couples over appropriate behavior, since males may begin to desire intercourse earlier in a relationship, before it reaches the point where they are "in love." Women who believe that intercourse is not acceptable until that stage is reached may find their standards under pressure from their partners. This is not, however because of a "double standard," at least in the traditional sense.

To simplify the analysis of the data, we desired a single measure of the individual's standards for males and for females, instead of three items for each. Reiss (1967) found that Guttman scaling techniques could be employed with the 12-item measure which he used. With this technique, the pattern of the person's answers to each item is analyzed to determine the extent to which he or she approves of sexual behavior before marriage. A score is assigned on the basis of the person's most liberal or permissive response. Thus, if a particular respondent indicates that none of the behaviors are acceptable prior to marriage, he or she would be given the lowest score. If the respondent believes that, while intercourse is not acceptable before marriage, genital fondling is acceptable if the two are in love, he or she would receive an intermediate score. Finally, if the respondent answers that all behaviors, including intercourse, are acceptable if both want it, he or she would be given the maximum scale score. Reiss found that his respondents' standards did form a scale; respondents required the same or more intimate emotional quality for petting compared to necking, and for intercourse compared to the other two behaviors. Reiss referred to the resulting single score as the "permissive scale." Hampe and Ruppell (1974) factor analyzed responses to Reiss's scale and found a single underlying factor; they concluded that the scale is unidimensional.

The format which we employed to measure sexual standards also allows us to use Guttman scaling techniques to arrive at a summary measure. Again, we employed the Cornell ranking technique to construct the scales (Edwards, 1957). Based on the individual's answers to the three items concerning males, a single score was assigned reflecting his or her standards for men; low scores indicated restrictive attitudes and high scores, permissive ones. Similarly, a single score was given on the basis of responses to the three items for females. The characteristics of the resulting Guttman scales are indicated in table 5.2. The coefficients of reproducibility are quite high and substantially larger than the minimal marginal reproducibility. These indicate a good fit of the unidimensional Guttman scale to the data.

TABLE 5.2. Characteristics of Guttman scale for personal sexual ideology

	SM	NM	SF	NF
Coefficient of reproducibility				
Ideology for males	0.925	0.918	0.915	0.904
Ideology for females	0.924	0.903	0.927	0.902
Minimal marginal reproducibility				
Ideology for males	0.510	0.510	0.419	0.381
Ideology for females	0.489	0.489	0.402	0.372
Percentage of pure cases				
Ideology for males	96.06	92.73	96.75	92.83
Ideology for females	95.83	91.36	96.98	93.86

CURRENT SEXUAL BEHAVIOR

The measure of current behavior is described in detail in Appendix I. The behaviors were the same as those considered in Chapter 4 in discussing lifetime behavior. It is important to stress that we measured essentially the respondent's behavior in his or her current heterosexual relationship; in some cases, this relationship had been ongoing for more than one year (in about one-third of the cases). Within the context of this relationship, we asked whether the respondent and his or her partner had engaged in each of the behaviors and on what percentage of the times they had been together had they engaged in each.

The results are presented in table 5.3. Again, the data indicate that the percentage who reported a given behavior declines steadily as the intimacy of the behavior increases. This is consistent with the assumption discussed in Chapter ·2 and the results reported in Chapter 4, regarding the developmental process in sexual expression. Compared to reported lifetime behavior (table 4.1), current participation is less frequent for every behavior within each of the four gender-status groups. This is consistent with the findings of past studies which have assessed both. With the exception of necking, the differences are consistently 10 percent or larger; for the most intimate behaviors, the frequency of current participation is approximately 20 percent lower than lifetime experience.

In general, the frequency of current activity reflects the same patterns found in the data on lifetime behavior. Considering males and females separately, we find no systematic differences between students and nonstudents. A somewhat larger percentage of female nonstudents reported current participation in the most intimate behaviors than women students. Again there is virtually no difference between male and female active in reported frequency of genital fondling and oral-genital contact. Finally,

TABLE 5.3. Current sexual behavior, by gender and educational status

	MALE				FEMALE			
	Student		Nonstudent		Student		Nonstudent	
Behavior	%	% of times together[a]	%	% of times together[a]	%	% of times together[a]	%	% of times together[a]
Necking	93	71	92	76	94	68	95	73
French kissing	83	61	83	64	86	58	86	64
Breast fondling	75	47	77	52	78	47	83	56
Male fondling of female genitals	65	39	67	42	66	41	74	48
Female fondling of male genitals	62	36	64	41	65	39	70	46
Genital apposition	47	23	47	20	52	23	52	22
Intercourse	55	31	58	38	50	36	63	44
Male oral contact with female genitals	41	19	46	22	42	24	51	25
Female oral contact with male genitals	41	18	46	22	42	24	51	25

[a]Includes only those who reported currently engaging in the behavior.

there are no consistent differences between males and females. This is further evidence that the process of sociosexual development is essentially the same for young men and women, that gender is no longer a significant determinant of premarital experience. Carns (1973) does discuss gender differences in whom persons tell about their first coitus, how soon afterwards they tell, and in the rhetoric men and women employ in discussing the experience. While there are differences, these variables do not seem to be important aspects of sexual development.

One anomaly in the current behavior percentages is that for three of the gender-status groups, genital apposition is less frequent than heterosexual intercourse. Genital apposition was defined as a distinct behavior, excluding genital contact which was incidental to intercourse. The difference in reported frequency affects the Guttman scale employed as a summary measure of current behavior. The Guttman scaling technique orders responses, in this case behavior, in terms of frequency of occurrence in the sample, and assigns a score based on the least frequent behavior reported by the respondent. Thus, for both male samples and for female nonstudents, respondents who reported both apposition and intercourse were given a larger score than those who reported only the latter. This violates the logical ordering which views intercourse as more physically intimate than contact between genitals without penetration. In any event, we applied Guttman scaling techniques to current behavior; with the exception of the difference in relative location of apposition, the procedure scored behaviors in the same order as they are listed in table 5.3 and gave the same score to a given behavior in both the current and lifetime scales. The characteristics of the Guttman scales for current behavior are listed in table 5.4. The coefficients of reproducibility are quite high, indicating a good fit of the unidimensional scale to the data. In addition, the much lower minimal marginal reproducibility indicates that the goodness of fit is not merely due to the marginal distributions. Finally, it should be noted that the percentage of pure cases is lower than for the lifetime scale. This means that there are more "errors," in the limited sense of individuals who say they have not engaged in a given behavior, but report participating in one or more of the more intimate ones.

Table 5.3 also indicates the percentage of the times the respondent had been with his or her partner that they had engaged in each of the nine behaviors. Again we find a steady decrease in frequency from the least to the most intimate behaviors. Only two behaviors are reported by all four groups to occur on more than half the occasions partners are together: necking and french kissing. All of the more intimate behaviors occur less frequently; intercourse is reported on approximately one-third of the times they see each other, and oral-genital contact on 20 to 25 percent of these

TABLE 5.4. Characteristics of Guttman scale for current sexual behavior

	SM	NM	SF	NF
Coefficient of reproducibility	0.972	0.968	0.974	0.970
Minimal marginal reproducibility	0.640	0.647	0.659	0.659
Percentage of pure cases	80.3	73.2	78.9	78.2

occasions. Whether a specific behavior occurs on a particular date undoubtedly reflects in part situational factors, such as the presence or absence of other persons. But it also certainly reflects individual choice or decision; all of our respondents were young adults and within limits could probably arrange appropriate settings if they so desired. Thus, we believe that this decreasing incidence reflects the outcome of self-control, and the influence of the partner on sexual behavior.

Again, there are no substantial differences between men and women, nor are there substantial differences in the incidence of male and female active genital contact behaviors. There is a fairly consistent pattern of differences between students and nonstudents. Both male and female nonstudents reported slightly greater frequencies of behavior than did the comparable student groups. However, the differences are relatively small, ranging from 1 to 8 percent.

On the whole, then, the results indicate that a lower percentage of our respondents were currently engaging in a given behavior than had ever engaged in it. The difference is probably due to the nature of current heterosexual relationships. The lifetime behavior measure includes behavior over a time span of several years; such a period maximizes the probability that any single individual has been involved in a relationship which met his or her standards of emotional intimacy for the various sexual behaviors. The current measure, on the other hand is more limited in its temporal coverage, and thus it is more likely that any single individual is not presently involved in the requisite relationship. We return to this interpretation when we discuss the data on current relationship and current behavior in Chapter 7.

THE INFLUENCE OF SOCIOPSYCHOLOGICAL CHARACTERISTICS

We discussed in Chapter 2 the symbolic interactionist approach to social behavior and its stress on the impact of socially derived meanings on activity. As social psychologists, we felt that the meanings associated with self, especially self-image, body image, and gender role orientation, might provide an alternative basis for self-control over sexuality. The possibility of such interrelationships has rarely been considered in the literature. The inclusion of these variables in our model (figure 2.2) and in our report of the findings is one of the contributions of this project.

The sources and development of the measures of sociopsychological variables is discussed in Appendix I. Briefly, responses to the individual items in each scale were factor analyzed. This technique provides an indication of whether there is some common dimension underlying answers to the individual items. In all cases, the principal factor procedure was used, and the factors were rotated only when doing so increased the total amount of variation in responses to the individual items which could be explained. Analyses were performed separately for each of the four gender-status groups. In selecting items for inclusion in our measures, two criteria were employed: (1) the item had to have a loading of at least 0.4 on one factor, and (2) its loadings on other factors had to be substantially lower, usually less than 0.2. After sets of items which formed unidimensional scales were identified, scores were constructed by summing the numerical values associated with the respondent's answers to the items included in each scale. Greater detail regarding each scale can be found in Appendix I.

Tables 5.5 through 5.9 list the variables and present the correlations of the sociopsychological measures with each other and with current ideology and behavior. We shall focus only on the interrelations between these sets; recall that a correlation of 0.10 is statistically significant, though not very substantial.

Self-Image

The self-concept measure yielded three scales. First, all of the items were highly correlated, and factor analyses indicated a large common factor before any rotations. This factor appears to represent the extent to which the respondent viewed himself or herself positively, and accordingly is employed as the measure of self-esteem. Rotating the factor matrix indicated the presence of two more specific factors. The first consisted of self-ratings on characteristics such as comfortable with others, likable, self-confident, and desirable; the scale composed of items loaded on this factor is termed perceived social desirability. The other factor consisted of ratings on the moral, insightful, honest and fair dimensions; this scale is termed perceived morality. On all three scales, larger scores reflect more positive evaluations of self.

The first three columns in tables 5.6–5.9 present the correlations of these three scales with the other variables. We shall consider first the relationships of these measures with the respondents' personal ideologies. Our model posits a direct relationship between self-image (and the other variables as well) and sexual ideology (see figure 2.2). Scores on the perceived morality scale are not related to ideology. Social desirability scores are generally significantly associated with ideology; respondents in three subsamples who perceived themselves as more desirable tended to have more permissive ideologies for both men and women. The exception is in the student female group, where the correlations are smaller than 0.10. Among males there is also a significant positive relationship between self-esteem scores and ideology for both sexes; those who evaluated themselves more positively had more liberal premarital standards.

Our perspective suggested that the sociopsychological characteristics would be indirectly related to behavior. The largest correlations are between self-image scores and current sexual behavior. Here, it is interesting to note that perceived morality is unrelated to current behavior. This does not mean that sexual activities were unrelated to our respondents' moral evaluations of themselves. From our perspective, one's sexual standards are his or her beliefs regarding the morality of behavior. As long as the person adheres to those standards, there is no reason to perceive himself or herself as more or less moral than others. We would expect a relationship between morality and behavior only among those who departed from their standards. There is a significant correlation in all four subsamples between social desirability scores and behavior. Those who evaluated themselves as more desirable also reported more intimate current behavior. This relationship is larger among males (0.27 and 0.30) than among females (0.12 and 0.12).

Finally, self-esteem is positively related to behavior in three of the subsamples, but not in the nonstudent female group.

Since the three self-measures are highly intercorrelated (0.31 to 0.91), we are particularly interested in the results of the regression analysis discussed at the end of this section. It allows us to identify the extent to which the relationships just discussed are independent.

TABLE 5.5. Sociopsychological variables

Self image
    PER MOR—perceived morality factor score
    PER S.D.—perceived social desirability factor score
    SELF ESTEEM—summary measure of self-esteem

Body image
    BUILD—body build factor score
    FACE—face and genitals factor score

Internal-external control
    PC/PLAN—personal control
    SYSTEM—system control
    INTERPER—interpersonal control
ROLE—gender roles scale
PHY ATTR—interviewer rating of physical attractiveness of respondent
PER IDEO M—personal sexual ideology for males—Guttman score
PER IDEO F—personal sexual ideology for females—Guttman score
CURRENT—current sexual behavior—Guttman score

TABLE 5.6. Correlations of sociopsychological characteristics, sexual ideology, and current sexual behavior: student males

	PER MOR	PER S.D.	SELF ESTEEM	BUILD	FACE	PC/PLAN	SYSTEM	INTERPER	ROLE	PHY ATTR	PER IDEO M	PER IDEO F	CURRENT
PER MOR	—												
PER S.D.	.307	—											
SELF ESTEEM	.688	.848	—										
BUILD	.030	.229	.194	—									
FACE	.096	.330	.304	.391	—								
PC/PLAN	-.153	-.218	-.227	-.024	-.090	—							
SYSTEM	-.043	-.149	-.131	-.083	-.103	.283	—						
INTERPER	-.107	-.201	-.196	-.052	-.089	.076	-.058	—					
ROLE	.188	-.006	.120	-.012	.019	.151	.040	-.113	—				
PHY ATTR	-.066	.051	.005	.168	.184	-.015	.025	.022	-.057	—			
PER IDEO M	.088	.182	.202	.136	.070	.096	.078	-.076	.392	-.029	—		
PER IDEO F	.075	.173	.187	.116	.072	.097	.088	-.075	.420	-.039	.976	—	
CURRENT	.031	.274	.199	.127	.223	.004	.017	-.045	.121	.073	.292	.271	—

TABLE 5.7. Correlations of sociopsychological characteristics, sexual ideology, and current sexual behavior: nonstudent males

	PER MOR	PER S.D.	SELF ESTEEM	BUILD	FACE	PC/PLAN	SYSTEM	INTERPER	ROLE	PHY ATTR	PER IDEO M	PER IDEO F	CURRENT
PER MOR	—												
PER S.D.	.324	—											
SELF ESTEEM	.804	.771	—										
BUILD	.211	.157	.215	—									
FACE	.121	.233	.202	.374	—								
PC/PLAN	-.170	-.203	-.258	-.086	-.013	—							
SYSTEM	-.160	-.245	-.254	-.141	-.087	.341	—						
INTERPER	.003	-.047	-.046	.111	-.009	.065	-.035	—					
ROLE	.090	.087	.167	-.069	-.022	.020	-.151	-.127	—				
PHY ATTR	.057	.138	.127	.342	.200	.002	-.016	-.144	-.004	—			
PER IDEO M	.004	.140	.116	-.074	.058	.178	.027	-.100	.220	-.004	—		
PER IDEO F	.004	.166	.130	-.064	.053	.177	-.024	-.103	.276	.001	.972	—	
CURRENT	.010	.297	.228	-.037	.106	-.062	-.057	-.068	.228	.141	.360	.351	—

TABLE 5.8. Correlations of sociopsychological characteristics, sexual ideology, and current sexual behavior: student females

	PER MOR	PER S.D.	SELF ESTEEM	BUILD	FACE	PC/PLAN	SYSTEM	INTERPER	ROLE	PHY ATTR	PER IDEO M	PER IDEO F	CURRENT
PER MOR	—												
PER S.D.	.394	—											
SELF ESTEEM	.751	.860	—										
BUILD	.045	.151	.141	—									
FACE	.110	.265	.250	.212	—								
PC/PLAN	-.137	-.196	-.198	-.078	-.092	—							
SYSTEM	-.109	-.113	-.138	-.058	-.057	.307	—						
INTERPER	-.108	-.232	-.223	-.070	-.151	.144	.096	—					
ROLE	.027	.104	.099	.090	.152	-.025	.021	-.293	—				
PHY ATTR	-.037	.098	.063	.129	.212	-.002	.004	-.047	.028	—			
PER IDEO M	-.013	.083	.062	.006	.101	.093	.148	-.143	.456	.092	—		
PER IDEO F	-.016	.067	.048	.014	.091	.083	.134	-.150	.481	.110	.936	—	
CURRENT	-.061	.118	.176	.153	.180	.009	.058	-.112	.252	.176	.388	.424	—

TABLE 5.9. Correlations of sociopsychological characteristics, sexual ideology, and current sexual behavior: nonstudent females

	PER MOR	PER S.D.	SELF ESTEEM	BUILD	FACE	PC/PLAN	SYSTEM	INTERPER	ROLE	PHY ATTR	PER IDEO M	PER IDEO F	CURRENT
PER MOR	—												
PER S.D.	.418	—											
SELF ESTEEM	.729	.909	—										
BUILD	.194	.223	.252	—									
FACE	.120	.273	.252	.260	—								
PC/PLAN	.194	-.203	-.234	-.003	-.075	—							
SYSTEM	-.100	-.236	-.216	-.098	-.085	.272	—						
INTERPER	-.022	-.082	-.094	-.093	-.071	.001	.078	—					
ROLE	-.105	.202	.210	.061	.104	-.040	-.029	-.320	—				
PHY ATTR	.008	.154	.118	.167	.123	-.011	-.081	.010	.006	—			
PER IDEO M	-.078	.118	.073	-.044	.150	.116	.021	-.125	.419	.151	—		
PER IDEO F	-.057	.100	.066	-.042	.115	.089	.015	-.154	.443	.113	.961	—	
CURRENT	-.013	.121	.087	.038	.117	.027	.029	-.057	.086	.163	.437	.435	—

Body Image

The analysis of responses to the body-image items identified two factors. One included evaluation of waist, build, hips, legs, weight, and stomach and seems to involve satisfaction with one's overall body build. The second factor consisted of items concerning face, complexion, and genitals. Thus, two scales were constructed; on both, larger scores indicate greater satisfaction with these characteristics.

Generally, the relationships between the two body-image scales and sexual attitudes and behaviors are not substantial. Among nonstudent males, only one of the correlations attains statistical significance. Among females, there is a fairly consistent but weak positive association between scores on the "face" factor, and ideology and current behavior. By contrast, among student men, it is the body build score which is consistently related to the sexual variables; the only correlation larger than 0.20 also occurs in this group, with higher evaluations of face, complexion, and genitals associated with more intimate current behavior.

Internal-External Control

Three factors were identified in the responses to the internal-external control items. The first included several questions concerning the individual's ability to control what happens, and is termed personal control. The second involves the ability of people in general to control events, and is termed system control. The third was composed of items dealing with the influence of others on the person, or interpersonal control. On these scales, the higher scores indicate greater sense of personal control (i.e., less sense of being controlled by luck, the "system," or other people).

The next entries in tables 5.6–5.9 (rows 6–8 and columns 6–8) are the correlations of the three internal-external scores and the dependent variables.

In three of the four subsamples there are statistically significant relationships between ideology for males and two of the internal-external control scores. Among nonstudents (both men and women) there is a positive correlation between personal control and ideology, indicating that the greater their sense of control over what happens to them personally, the more permissive their premarital standards. The positive association between system scores and ideology in the SF subsample reflects a similar relationship, since larger scores indicate less sense of being controlled by events in society and the world. In all three, there is a negative correlation between interpersonal control scores and ideology: the less one's sense of being controlled by others, the more permissive one's standards. The relationship of internal-external control measures and ideology for females follows a very similar pattern.

These results are readily interpretable if one assumes that young people generally believe that the larger society, i.e., most people in society, holds conservative premarital sexual standards. Under these conditions, those who feel little control over their own lives, who feel controlled by the larger social system and other people, would adhere to that conservative ideology. Those with more permissive attitudes might generally sense that this reflected choice, i.e., control, over their own attitudes.

In general, the internal-external control subscales are not significantly related to current behavior. The one exception is a negative correlation between behavior and interpersonal control among women students.

Role Definitions

Analysis of the role-definition items identified only one factor, which reflects the extent to which the respondent answered the items in an egalitarian way; 11 of the items loaded on this factor.

The strongest and most consistent relationships are between the role-definition measue and sexual ideology. The correlations between role definitions and sexual standards for males range from 0.22 to 0.46, all of which are highly significant. The associations with sexual standards for females are consistently larger in all four subsamples, ranging from 0.28 to 0.48. Thus, the more egalitarian (or less traditional) the person's views of male-female roles are, the more permissive are his or her premarital sexual standards. This seems to be a good example of the fact that more specific attitudes are generally supported by or embedded in more general ones. Traditional role definitions embodying male dominance in all spheres—economic, political, interpersonal, as well as sexual—are thus associated with quite different sexual standards than are egalitarian or liberated role definitions. Our results indicate an empirical basis for the assertion by some people in recent years that women's liberation, broadly defined, is related to increasing sexual freedom, at least in the sense here of permissive attitudes.

Interestingly, the relationship between role definitions and behavior is not as strong; the correlations range from 0.09 (which is not significant) to 0.25. Thus, in both male subsamples and in the student female one, more egalitarian views of gender roles are associated with more intimate current behavior, but not very strongly.

Physical Attractiveness

All of the measures discussed so far in this chapter are composed of several items; generally, multiple-item scales are more reliable and potentially more valid than single-item scales, such as the measure of physical attractiveness to be discussed here. However, this item is worth separate attention because of the substantial body of data indicating that physical attractiveness plays an important role in attraction or liking (see Berscheid and Walster, 1978). This measure was obtained by having the interviewer rate the respondent's physical attractiveness on a seven-point scale; this rating was made unobtrusively at the end of the interview. Scores ranged from one (very unattractive) to seven (very attractive).

In general, physical attractiveness is not related to ideology for men; the correlation between the two is significant only among the nonstudent females. Interestingly, the relationship between attractiveness and ideology for women is significant in both female subsamples, but not in the male subsamples. Thus, those females whom interviewers rated as more attractive reported more permissive standards for themselves.

Rated attractiveness is associated positively with current behavior in three of the four subsamples; the largest correlations are only 0.16 and 0.18 and again, occur in the female subsamples. Kaats and Davis (1970) have reported similar results based on a sample of student women.

We expected the sociopsychological measures discussed in this section to be related directly to ideology and only indirectly to behavior. The personal and interpersonal control measures from the internal-external control scale and the role-definition measure are all significantly correlated with premarital standards and only weakly or not interrelated with behavior. These findings are consistent with our expectation. Neither the respondent's body image nor his or her physical attractiveness as rated by the interviewer is strongly related to either aspect of sexuality; in our results, at least, these physical characteristics are not associated with sexual experience. This is an important finding, as earlier research has generally not considered physical aspects of the individual. Finally, we found that the self-image measures were more strongly correlated with behavior than with standards, contrary to our expectation. Since these measures are highly intercorrelated, we are particularly interested in the results of the regression analyses with respect to these variables.

Sexual Ideology and Current Sexual Behavior

Our model assumes that sexual ideology is an important determinant of sexual behavior, and thus the interrelationship of them is of particular importance. It is to this topic that we now turn.

Note first the extremely large correlations (0.94 to 0.98) between the respondent's personal ideology for males and personal ideology for females. This, as indicated earlier, reflects the fact that the young people we interviewed had essentially the same standards for men and women, that they did not hold different premarital standards for the two sexes.

The last two correlations in the bottom row of tables 5.6–5.9 indicate the relationship between ideology and current behavior. The high correlations between ideologies for men and for women are also reflected in the fact that the association between each and current behavior is of similar magnitude in each subsample. These associations range from 0.27 to 0.44, reflecting substantial relationships. The ideology-behavior correlation is somewhat stronger for women (0.39 to 0.44) than for men (.27 to .36), suggesting that women are somewhat more likely to regulate physical intimacy in terms of their standards.

Thus, there is a strong association between attitudes or standards and behavior. On the other hand, ideology accounts for only approximately 10 to 20 percent of the total variance (obtained by squaring the correlation) in sexual intimacy with one's current partner. Therefore, while ideology is an important determinant, it is not the only one; Chapters 6 and 7 will explore the relationship between a variety of other variables and ideology and behavior.

Relative Influence of Sociopsychological Characteristics

As in Chapter 4, we have a number of measures which are individually related to the variables of interest; having surveyed these, we turn now to their relative influence, the extent to which the various characteristics are independently and significantly related to ideology and current behavior. Again, the analytic technique employed was regression analysis; the results are presented in table 5.10. In the analysis of ideology, we included only ideology for persons of the respondent's gender, i.e., for himself or herself. Also we did not include the three measures derived from the internal-external control scale; none of the correlations with ideology or behavior were larger than 0.20, which meant it was unlikely that significant associations would be found in the regression analysis.

The results in the first half of 5.10 indicate that several of the bivariate relationships between the sociopsychological attributes and sexual ideology disappear when we control for the correlation between those attributes. In fact, the regression analysis indicates that there are only four significant and independent relationships. Although there were significant correlations between perceived social desirability and standards for men and women, none of the self-image measures are independently related to ideology. This is consistent with the results reported by Perlman (1974), who found no relationship between self-esteem and premarital sexual standards. Of the two body-image scales, the only association is of build and ideology for men in the SM subsample. The role-definition measure is related to ideology in two of the four groups, NM and SF; for both groups more

TABLE 5.10. Stepwise regression of sociopsychological characteristics on sexual ideology and current sexual behavior

	Males		Females	
	SM	NM	SF	NF
PERSONAL SEXUAL IDEOLOGY—GUTTMAN SCORE				
PER MOR				
PER S.D.				
SELF ESTEEM				
BUILD	$.1362^b$			
FACE				
ROLE		$.2203^c$	$.4811^d$	
PHY ATTR				$.1128^a$
CURRENT SEXUAL BEHAVIOR—GUTTMAN SCORE				
PER MOR				
PER S.D.	$.1869^d$	$.2759^d$		
SELF ESTEEM				
BUILD			$.1182^c$	
FACE	$.1267^b$		$.1034^b$	
ROLE				
PHY ATTR				
PER IDEO M	$.1782^d$			$.4369^d$
PER IDEO F		$.2742^d$	$.3143^d$	

$^a p < .05$
$^b p < .01$
$^c p < .005$
$^d p < .001$

egalitarian views are associated with greater permissiveness. We noted earlier that rated attractiveness was related to ideology for women; the regression analysis indicates that this association is significant only for the NF subsamples. In sum, the relationships between sociopsychological characteristics and premarital sexual standards are neither consistent nor substantial. One's attitudes about the acceptability of various behaviors do not seem to be related to the individual's self-image and self-esteem, evaluation of his or her physical attributes, or rating of his or her physical attractiveness.

These characteristics are more strongly related to current sexual behavior. The results in the second half of table 5.10 support our earlier conclusion that there is no relationship between perceived morality and behavior. Among males, there is a strong association between perceived social desirability and sexual activity; those who evaluate their interpersonal skills more highly report more intimate sexual behavior. We cannot determine from our data which is cause and which is effect. It may be that young men who perceive themselves as more desirable are more likely to seek sexual intimacy and/or initiate it in heterosexual relationships; alternatively, participation in more physically intimate relationships may produce or reinforce the perception that one is more desirable. The comparable association among women is not significant. Reiss, Banewart, and Foreman (1975) found small or no differences between virgins and nonvirgins in their ratings of their own confidence, attractiveness, looks, and popularity. Both sets of findings suggest that women's sense of relative desirability is not related to the extent of physical intimacy.

There are three significant relationships between body-image scores and behavior; all occur in the student subsamples. Relative satisfaction with one's build—waist, hips, legs, weight—is associated with more intimate behavior. The fact that all three of these relationships are not significant among nonstudents suggests that physical features are more important in a large college or university setting. One can speculate that in such an environment one is in physical proximity to large numbers of persons of the opposite sex. One has casual contacts with relatively many persons, for example, in classes, dormitories, eating places, and libraries. The most obvious cues one would use in determining whether or not to initiate more personal contact with another individual would be his or her physical appearance. In contrast, people who are not in such an environment probably have contact with fewer age-peers, and these are generally in settings where one can more quickly gain additional information about the other person, such as at work or in an apartment complex. Physical appearance may be less important.

The role-definition measure is not independently associated with behavior. The correlational results indicate that it is more strongly associated with standards than behavior. The regression analyses indicate that it is not significantly related to either one. Our single-item measure of physical attractiveness is also not associated with sexual activity.

Finally, the last two rows in table 5.10 confirm that the strongest relationships are between ideology and behavior, and that, on the whole, there is a somewhat more substantial association between them for women than for men.

Thus, the findings clearly support the assumption in our model that the relationship between premarital standards or ideology and sexual activity is an important one. There is a strong association between attitudes and behavior which remains when the influence of other variables on behavior is statistically controlled. This is an important part of our results. While past studies, such as those by Reiss (1967), Clayton (1972), and Walsh, Ferrell, and Tolone (1976), have found such a relationship, these studies were limited by their use of nonrandom samples of college students and, in some cases, reliance on single-item measures. Our findings, by contrast, are based on scales with excellent statistical properties and have been shown to apply to random samples of males and females, and students and nonstudents. We assume that this interrelationship reflects the use by individuals of their ideology as a basis for self-control over their sexual activity. We included our measures of self-image, body image, etc., because we felt that these might also influence one's sexuality. Our findings suggest that they do not, since their relationships with the measures of sexual expression are neither substantial nor consistent. We also find no substantial differences between men and women and between students and nonstudents in sexual expression or in the interrelationship of standards and behavior. Thus, it was appropriate to exclude gender and educational status from our explanatory model.

SUMMARY

This chapter began by examining personal ideology. Two important conclusions can be drawn from these data. First, the double standard has declined to the extent that most individuals hold the same sexual standard for men and women. Overall, there still is a gender difference; females require more emotional intimacy in *relationships* as a requisite for sexual behavior than males do. Second, a majority of our respondents accept coitus under conditions of love or affection. Thus, there has been an increase in permissiveness compared to earlier findings.

Current sexual behavior reflects the same pattern as do the data on lifetime behavior although individuals report less current than lifetime activity. No consistent differences are found between males and females, although more nonstudents than students report currently engaging in the more intimate behaviors. The correlations between personal ideology and behavior are substantial. These suggest that individuals are not indiscriminate in their sexual behavior, but rather, regulate their physical intimacy in terms of personal attitudes.

A number of sociopsychological characteristics were examined insofar as they relate to sexual ideology or behavior. Although a number of these characteristics are related when considered singly, few are independently related to ideology. Different characteristics are significant in each subsample, so there are neither consistent nor substantial effects of sociopsychological characteristics on sexual ideology. The sociopsychological characteristics are more strongly related to current sexual behavior. Perceived social desirability and body image are related to current sexual behavior inasmuch as individuals with more positive self-images report more sexual experience. Again, significant associations are scattered across the subsamples.

The strongest, most consistent relationship with current sexual behavior is for personal ideology. Thus, personal ideology is the basis of self-control over current sexual behavior, and the effects of sociopsychological characteristics are substantially less important.

6

Social Influences
on Current Sexuality

LIKE CHAPTER 5, this chapter is concerned with the individual's current sexuality. The data presented here are organized into three sections, each representing a potential social influence on the individual. We first consider the family, which we have argued is the first socializing influence on sexual expression. Since our interviewees were young adults and many had left home, we expect the relationships between family variables and current ideology and behavior to be weaker than the corresponding relationships discussed in Chapter 4, which considered lifetime behavior. We then consider various social characteristics of the person, such as religious affiliation and attendance; these may relate to his or her current sexuality to the extent that they reflect the influence of various social institutions such as the church. The third section focuses on the influence of peers. Our model suggests that one's peer group is a major influence on his or her sexual ideology. The data presented allow us to assess the strength of that relationship, as well as the relationship of peer measures to behavior. At the end of each section, we present the results of regression analyses involving the variables considered in that section.

FAMILIAL AND BACKGROUND INFLUENCES

In this section we consider the interrelationship of family and background variables with sexual ideology and current behavior. We discussed in detail the former in Chapter 4 and the latter in Chapter 5.

Tables 6.1 (students) and 6.2 (nonstudents) present the correlations of background variables with the summary (Guttman scale) measures of personal ideology for males and females and current behavior. The intercorrelations of the background items were presented in tables 4.10–4.13 and are not repeated here.

Socioeconomic Status

While past research has emphasized variations in premarital sexuality by social class, we saw in Chapter 4 that our measures of class were only weakly related to lifetime behavior. Thus, we would not expect these measures to be highly correlated with current sexuality. In general, among males there is no relationship between the respondent's estimate of family income and his ideology and behavior. Among females, the positive correlations between income and ideology are significant for both student and nonstudent samples. In addition, there is a significant correlation of 0.12 between income and current behavior among student women. None of these are substantial, however. The correlations of the subjective measure of class are more consistently nonsignificant; the only exceptions occur in the student female group, where there is a positive association between the respondent's perception of her family's class and both her ideology for men and current behavior.

For mother's and father's education, significant correlations are similarly scattered. Among female students, those whose parents were more educated tended to report more permissive sexual standards. With respect to current behavior, the significant associations are found in the nonstudent female subsample and are negative; those whose parents were more educated reported less intimate current behavior.

Thus, within the limits of our measures and samples, social class background is not related to sexual experience, sexual standards, or current sexual behavior.

Parental Relationships

We noted in Chapter 4 that the quality of the relationship with one's parents might be associated with the strength of their influence on the person and thus, with his or her standards. We found that various measures of that relationship were related to sexual experience. Thus, quality should at least indirectly influence current ideology (see figure 2.2). In addition, we can assess the extent to which there is a direct relationship.

The items measuring the extent to which parents displayed affection to each other, and to which mother and father were affectionate toward the respondent, are not significantly related to our measures of current sexuality. However, mother's and father's understanding of the respondent are consistently correlated with sexual ideology. Interestingly, among males, the significant relationships occur only between mother's understanding of him and his standards; among females, the items concerning both mother and father are associated with ideology. All of the correlations are negative; the greater the reported parental understanding is, the less permissive are one's sexual standards. Among student women, parental understanding is also negatively related to current behavior. Reported closeness between the respondent and his or her parents is also consistently and negatively correlated with sexual standards, and in addition, is negatively associated with behavior among female students. Thus, there is fairly consistent evidence that closer and more understanding relationships with parents are associated with less permissive sexual standards.

Thus, parental socialization continues to exert an influence on the individual's standards. This relationship is at least as strong as the one between parental relationships and lifetime experience discussed in Chapter 4.

Parental Attitudes Toward Sexuality

Parental attitudes toward sexuality reflect the specific norms and values to which they socialize their children. To the extent that measures of these

TABLE 6.1. Correlations of background variables,
sexual ideology, and current sexual behavior: students

	MALES			FEMALES		
	PER IDEO M	PER IDEO F	CURRENT	PER IDEO M	PER IDEO F	CURRENT
SES characteristics						
FAM INCOME	.025	.025	.086	.177	.136	.115
FAM CLASS	−.021	−.044	.066	.123	.078	.102
MO ED	.003	.015	.005	.215	.189	.048
FA ED	.045	.047	.059	.123	.093	.071
Parental relationships						
PAR AFF	−.084	−.079	.049	−.002	−.021	−.011
FA AFF	−.051	−.048	.023	.001	.003	.014
MO AFF	.005	.025	.079	.066	.091	.089
FA UNDER	−.084	−.089	.007	−.151	−.173	−.154
MO UNDER	−.137	−.127	−.042	−.153	−.143	−.125
FA CLOSE	−.146	−.148	−.049	−.111	−.129	−.133
MO CLOSE	−.135	−.121	−.039	−.162	−.138	−.115
Parental attitudes toward sexuality						
SEXED FA	−.095	−.084	−.006	−.132	−.177	−.091
SEXED MO	−.017	−.113	−.025	−.181	−.181	−.086
FA VALUE	−.007	.013	.028	−.072	−.082	−.104
MO VALUE	−.059	.058	.023	−.034	−.046	−.055
FA REACT	.329	.327	.117	.240	.231	.132
MO REACT	.308	.302	.113	.252	.253	.184
FA IDEO	.366	.363	.192	.340	.346	.133
MO IDEO	.323	.325	.157	.350	.387	.117
Sources						
FA SRC	−.270	−.271	−.177	−.232	−.278	−.109
MO SRC	−.267	−.266	−.164	−.328	−.337	−.166
MFR SRC	−.098	.089	.013	.120	.115	.158
FFR SRC	.139	.129	.192	.082	.096	.051
LOVER SRC	.130	.111	.343	.188	.210	.431

are associated with current sexual expression, it suggests the enduring influence of Stage I in our model, parental socialization.

The extent to which respondents felt that the sex education received from each parent was adequate is consistently and substantially related to sexual ideology among women; most of these correlations are non-significant among men. In both female subsamples, those who reported more adequate education held less permissive standards; these correlations are of considerable magnitude (-0.24 to -0.35) in the nonstudent subsample. We unfortunately do not know what standards our respondents employed in judging adequacy. However, all are over 18 years old, and most have participated in various heterosexual activities; presumably they are evaluating adequacy in terms of their experience, which suggests that more complete and realistic sex education would be considered more "adequate" by our respondents.

Answers to the questions about the value of sex in their mothers' and fathers' lives are not consistently related to ideology or current behavior. Responses to these were also not related to lifetime behavior.

TABLE 6.2. Correlations of background variables,
sexual ideology, and current sexual behavior: nonstudents

	MALES			FEMALES		
	PER IDEO M	PER IDEO F	CURRENT	PER IDEO M	PER IDEO F	CURRENT
SES characteristics						
FAM INCOME	.008	.036	.108	.101	.104	.044
FAM CLASS	.023	.048	.063	−.062	.048	−.004
MO ED	.033	.034	.108	−.006	.001	−.135
FA ED	.094	.114	.088	.036	.051	−.130
Parental relationships						
PAR AFF	.006	.032	−.046	−.093	−.089	−.097
FA AFF	−.007	.009	.067	−.062	−.040	−.031
MO AFF	−.007	−.014	.096	.001	.005	−.057
FA UNDER	−.029	−.020	−.056	−.231	−.233	−.086
MO UNDER	−.130	−.129	−.116	−.174	−.188	−.059
FA CLOSE	−.053	−.050	.020	−.186	−.175	−.103
MO CLOSE	−.104	−.101	−.061	−.158	−.170	−.041
Parental attitudes toward sexuality						
SEXED FA	−.026	−.033	−.056	−.235	−.238	−.091
SEXED MO	−.187	−.195	−.035	−.335	−.348	−.213
FA VALUE	.014	.026	.020	−.057	−.079	.037
MO VALUE	−.039	−.044	.158	−.176	−.203	.028
FA REACT	.236	.215	.149	.150	.173	.128
MO REACT	.211	.188	.173	.163	.181	.132
FA IDEO	.342	.340	.279	.169	.187	.083
MO IDEO	.284	.295	.149	.260	.261	.143
Sources						
FA SRC	−.165	−.142	−.052	−.151	−.150	−.220
MO SRC	−.255	−.251	−.187	−.300	−.300	−.255
MFR SRC	.198	.209	.118	.155	.136	.060
FFR SRC	.275	.244	.309	.023	.004	−.144
LOVER SRC	.220	.210	.371	.263	.237	.293

The items which deal more specifically with parental sexual attitudes, that is, with reactions to cohabitation and parents' ideology, show strong correlations with current sexuality. In all four subsamples, those who reported that their parents would react positively to cohabitation had more permissive standards; all of these correlations are significant and many are larger than 0.20. In both student and nonstudent subsamples the correlations for males are larger than those for females; the relationships also are somewhat stronger among students than among nonstudents. Parental reactions and ideology are also positively correlated with current behavior; the values are generally between 0.1 and 0.2. Thus, there is a substantial and positive relationship between parental and respondent sexual attitudes, and the correspondence seems to be greater for men.

Sources of Information

We noted above that more adequate education by parents about sexuality was associated with less permissive premarital standards. Another indicator of parental influence on the individual is the importance he or she attributes to them as sources of information. Our data on these items substantiate the earlier finding. Both men and women who rated their mothers and fathers as more important sources had less permissive ideologies; these correlations are generally substantial, ranging from -0.14 to -0.34. In addition, whereas adequacy of sex education was not associated with behavior, those respondents who rated their parents more influential as sources reported less intimate current sexual behavior.

By contrast, greater influence by peers and by a lover is associated with more permissive standards. More specifically, among women (both student and nonstudent), rating of male friends as a source is positively correlated with ideology. Among men, the importance of female friends is positively associated with standards in both subsamples, and among nonstudents, rating of male friends is correlated as well. The pattern of relationships with behavior is less consistent. Among students, importance of opposite-gender friends is positively correlated with behavior. For nonstudents, both female and male friends' influence are associated with more intimate behavior among males; among female nonstudents, those who rate female friends as more important report less intimate current activity.

Finally, the influence of lover as a source is positively related to both ideology and behavior in all four subsamples; the correlations are generally stronger with current activity (0.29 to 0.43) than with attitudes.

These results support our model, which asserts that parents, peers, and partners are the primary sources of influence on premarital sexuality.

Relative Influence

Again, regression analyses were performed in order to determine the independent and relative influence of these various characteristics. These results are presented in table 6.3.

Sexual Ideology

The data indicate a fairly consistent pattern of relationships between background characteristics and sexual ideology. For males, father's understanding (students) or closeness (nonstudents) is associated with less permissive attitudes. Conversely, more permissive parental attitudes toward cohabitation and premarital sexual activity are positively related to personal standards; the regression coefficients for perceived father's ideology are among the largest of those found among males. The importance of father (for student males) and mother (for nonstudent males) as sources is also negatively related to personal premarital standards. There is a positive association between ideology and male friends as important sources in both male subsamples and female friends in the nonstudent sample.

In the data for our female respondents, parental affection is related positively to ideology; among students, the significant coefficient is for father's affection, while among nonstudents it is the coefficients for parental affection toward each other and mother's affection toward the respondent that are significant. Conversely, father's understanding of the respondent is negatively related to her personal standards. The coefficients associated with adequacy of sex education are negative and significant for both female subsamples; in fact, for nonstudent women, the coefficient for this variable (-0.332) is the largest found in this subsample. Perceived parental ideology also has a substantial relationship with personal standards, with the coefficients associated with mother in both subsamples and with father among students all highly significant ($p < 0.001$). The coefficients for importance of mother as a source are also substantial, but negative, in both groups, whereas lover in both groups and female friends among students are positively related to the respondent's permissiveness.

Thus, the data are consistent with the conclusion that parents are an influence on sexual ideology. More permissive parental attitudes toward premarital sexuality are strongly related to more permissive personal ideologies. While Libby (1974) found that perceived mother's standards were important for both sexes, our data indicate that it is the standard of the same-sex parent which is most influential. Also, the more important parents are as information sources and the more adequate the sex education

TABLE 6.3. Stepwise regression of background variables on sexual ideology and current sexual behavior

| | STUDENTS | | | | NONSTUDENTS | | | |
| | Male | | Female | | Male | | Female | |
	PER IDEO M	CURRENT	PER IDEO F	CURRENT	PER IDEO M	CURRENT	PER IDEO F	CURRENT
SES characteristics								
FAM INCOME								
FAM CLASS								
MO ED			.1501[d]					
FA ED								
Parental relationships								
PAR AFF							.1214[a]	
FA AFF		.1067[a]	.1298[b]	.1328[c]				
MO AFF			-.1722[d]	-.1893[d]			.1863[d]	
FA UNDER	-.1440[c]						-.1659[c]	
MO UNDER								
FA CLOSE					-.1228[a]			
MO CLOSE								
Parental attitudes toward sexuality								
SEXED FA			-.1805[d]		-.1429[a]	-.1553[b]	-.3308[d]	-.1410[a]
SEXED MO							.1192[a]	
FA VALUE	.1282[b]				.1510[b]		-.1937[d]	
MO VALUE					.3064[d]	.1890[c]		
FA REACT				.1360[c]				
MO REACT	.2212[d]	.1624[d]	.2180[d]			.2140[d]	.2840[d]	.1424[b]
FA IDEO	.1241[a]		.2309[d]					
MO IDEO								
Sources								
FA SRC	-.2327[d]	-.2203[d]	-.2592[d]	-.1208[c]	-.2054[c]	-.2218[d]	-.2009[d]	-.1658[b]
MO SRC	.1015[a]				.1396[a]			
MFR SRC			.1069[b]		.2096[d]	.1910[c]	.1640[d]	-.1527[b]
FFR SRC			.1385[c]			.2668[d]		.2945[d]
LOVER SRC		.3484[d]		.4079[d]				

[a] p < .05
[b] p < .01
[c] p < .005
[d] p < .001

they provide, the less permissive the respondent's attitudes. At the same time, greater importance of peers and lovers as sources of information is associated with more permissive ideologies.

Current Behavior

The pattern of relationships between background variables and current behavior is somewhat less consistent across the four subsamples. Among students, the extent to which fathers displayed affection for the person is positively associated with behavior. For female students, greater understanding by father is associated with less intimate current activity. Among nonstudents, none of the measures of relationship with parents were significantly associated with behavior. Adequacy of sex education is negatively related to behavior among nonstudents, but the same coefficients are not significant in analyses of the student data.

In all four groups, at least one measure of parental attitudes is significantly related to behavior, though the measure varies. For both male subsamples, father's ideology is positively related to current activity. For female students, it is mother's reaction to cohabitation, while for female nonstudents it is mother's ideology. These results indicate that it is the same-sex parent whose attitudes are more important. Note also that the coefficients involving parental attitudes are generally smaller for current behavior than for ideology. This was also true of the correlations reported in tables 6.1 and 6.2 and suggests that parental attitudes have a greater impact on the person's attitudes than on his or her behavior.

The regression coefficients for the source-of-information questions reflect the pattern discussed above. The importance of parents as a source is negatively related to current behavior; in all but the student male sample, rating of mother as a source is associated with the significant coefficient. On the other hand, the importance attributed to lover as a source is positively associated with current activity in all four subsamples.

These results generally support our model, as did the findings regarding these variables and lifetime behavior discussed in Chapter 4. The quality of the person's relationship with parents, as measured by extent of mutual understanding and closeness, is positively associated with personal standards. Similarly, to the extent that parents are a primary source of information and provide more adequate sex education, the individual's ideology is less permissive. We have argued that parents are the first socializing agents; to the extent that they remain influential, respondents seem to continue to hold less permissive attitudes. Within this context, however, respondent attitudes are positively related to parental ones; parents with more liberal standards seem to socialize their children to more liberal ones. If the person becomes increasingly involved in peer and heterosexual relationships so that they become important sources, he or she is even more likely to hold a permissive personal ideology.

INDIVIDUAL CHARACTERISTICS AND CURRENT SEXUALITY

In this section, we consider several characteristics of our respondents, including age, religiosity, political orientation, and various measures of lifetime behavior. Over time, these factors generally mediate between family influences and the respondent's current or recent heterosexual relationships and sexuality.

Tables 6.4 through 6.8 list the variables and present their intercorrelations and correlations with ideology and current behavior.

Age

There are significant, positive correlations between age and all three of the sexuality measures: personal ideology for males, for females, and current sexual behavior. In three subsamples, the correlation of age with behavior is slightly larger than its association with sexual standards; however, this differential is reversed in the NF subsample.

It is perhaps obvious that it is not biological age per se which produces more permissive attitudes and more intimate behavior. Rather, age here is assumed to be an indicator of social phenomena which are associated with growing older. Some of the relationship is probably due to the relation between age and lifetime behavior (0.14 to 0.29) and the very high correlations between lifetime and current behavior (0.68 to 0.77). Thus, older persons are more sexually experienced (lifetime), and more experienced people have more liberal standards and currently engage in more

TABLE 6.4. Variables pertaining to respondent's characteristics

---

AGE—respondent's age
EXP MARRY—length of time respondent thinks it will be before he or she marries
REL ATN—how often respondent attends religious functions
RELIG—respondent's reported religiosity
POLIT—respondent's political rating on conservative-liberal dimension
CIV DISOB—participation in nonviolent acts of civil disobedience
SEXED CRS—amount of new information in sex education course(s) taken
FEAR VD—perceived probability that person who engages in intercourse will get VD
EVER INTER—whether respondent reported ever engaging in intercourse
AGE FIRST—age of respondent when first engaged in intercourse
PART—number of intercourse partners in lifetime
INTER—number of intercourse experiences in lifetime
LIFE—lifetime sexual behavior—Guttman score
PER IDEO M—personal sexual ideology for males—Guttman score
PER IDEO F—personal sexual ideology for females—Guttman score
CURRENT—current sexual behavior—Guttman score

---

intimate behavior. To some extent, age is also an index of the relative influence of parents and peers; in terms of our model, as persons age during adolescence and young adulthood, they become less influenced by parents and more influenced by other young people.

Time Until Marriage

We asked all persons how long they thought it would be until they married. Some analysts have attributed part of the increase in frequency of premarital sexual behavior among college students to the fact that they typically delay marriage until after they finish school and thus do not have access to intercourse within marriage. Answers to the question were coded into categories ranging from less than six months to more than four and one-half years; "never" was included and was the answer given by 3 to 4 percent of the students, and about 7 percent of the non-students. Between 36 and 46 percent gave answers coded as more than four and one-half years; the remainder (50 to 60 percent) expected to marry within a shorter period of time.

The correlations in tables 6.5–6.8 indicate no association between answers to this question and sexual ideology. There is a significant negative relationship between when the person expects to marry and his or her current sexual behavior in all four subgroups. Thus, the sooner one expects to marry, the more intimate his or her current activity. This clearly indicates that delaying marriage is associated with less rather than more sexual behavior. Kinsey et al. (1953), utilizing age of marriage rather than expectation, found a similar association for females; in our data, the correlations are significant for both men and women. This finding is consistent with the assumption that, as heterosexual relationships become more intimate and move toward marriage, physical intimacy increases. In this context, the correlations discussed here probably reflect the fact that those who expect to marry sooner are involved in more intimate relationships; this interpretation is borne out by the very high .correlations between when one expects to marry and quality of current relationship (−0.40 to −0.54; see Chapter 7).

Religion

Religion is an important influence on sexual standards and behavior. In Chapter 4, we found that involvement in the organized church was associated with less lifetime experience. We are now interested in the inter-relation of religion and current standards and behavior. We asked each person what his or her denominational affiliation was at the time of the

TABLE 6.5. Correlations of respondent characteristics, sexual Ideology, and current sexual behavior: student males

	AGE	EXP MARRY	REL ATN	RELIG	POLIT	CIV DISOB	SEXED CRS	FEAR VD	EVER INTER	AGE FIRST	# PART	# INTER	LIFE	PER IDEO M	PER IDEO F	CURRENT
AGE	—															
EXP MARRY	-.233	—														
REL ATN	-.138	-.005	—													
RELIG	.017	.024	.425	—												
POLIT	.066	.033	-.244	-.210	—											
CIV DISOB	.106	.001	-.215	-.173	.357	—										
SEXED CRS	-.042	-.041	.059	.093	.093	-.083	—									
FEAR VD	.120	-.136	.072	.087	-.152	.015	.022	—								
EVER INTER	.258	-.127	-.281	-.210	.237	.268	.058	.008	—							
AGE FIRST	.297	-.158	-.259	-.192	.209	.241	.055	.021	.978	—						
# PART	.374	-.056	-.211	-.059	.159	.218	.003	-.041	.348	.265	—					
# INTER	.342	-.095	-.212	-.133	.174	.169	-.057	.029	.299	.231	.688	—				
LIFE	.264	-.128	-.228	-.161	.224	.253	-.047	.038	.825	.806	.335	.318	—			
PER IDEO M	.165	-.004	-.406	-.234	.288	.273	-.048	-.047	.404	.383	.263	.250	.385	—		
PER IDEO F	.162	-.003	-.401	-.223	.295	.267	-.060	-.034	.388	.370	.259	.235	.361	.976	—	
CURRENT	.211	-.198	-.151	-.140	.155	.207	-.068	.054	.563	.545	.305	.374	.690	.292	.277	—

TABLE 6.6. Correlations of respondent characteristics, sexual ideology, and current sexual behavior: nonstudent males

	AGE	EXP MARRY	REL ATN	RELIG	POLIT	CIV DISOB	SEXED CRS	FEAR VD	EVER INTER	AGE FIRST	# PART	# INTER	LIFE	PER IDEO M	PER IDEO F	CURRENT
AGE	—															
EXP MARRY	-.154	—														
REL ATN	-.153	-.158	—													
RELIG	.055	-.069	.320	—												
POLIT	.102	.056	-.188	.067	—											
CIV DISOB	.267	.040	-.199	-.006	.374	—										
SEXED CRS	-.141	-.028	-.101	.071	-.039	.043	—									
FEAR VD	.065	-.068	.127	.109	-.101	-.007	.001	—								
EVER INTER	.292	-.179	-.269	-.002	.225	.341	-.026	-.143	—							
AGE FIRST	.363	-.195	-.242	.006	.232	.359	-.030	-.109	.971	—						
# PART	.234	-.011	-.002	.029	.039	.159	-.055	-.140	.282	.166	—					
# INTER	.237	.022	-.161	.138	.104	.211	-.091	-.041	.306	.208	.478	—				
LIFE	.222	-.194	-.206	-.012	.200	.320	.003	-.165	.888	.854	.299	.327	—			
PER IDEO M	.186	.029	-.326	-.041	.240	.317	-.023	-.178	.427	.382	.316	.288	.427	—		
PER IDEO F	.191	.050	-.309	-.037	.263	.336	-.028	-.179	.400	.364	.307	.256	.399	.974	—	
CURRENT	.224	-.156	-.095	-.028	.183	.235	-.082	-.133	.582	.549	.260	.426	.676	.348	.340	—

TABLE 6.7. Correlations of respondent characteristics, sexual ideology, and current sexual behavior: student females

	AGE	EXP MARRY	REL ATN	RELIG	POLIT	CIV DISOB	SEXED CRS	FEAR VD	EVER INTER	AGE FIRST	# PART	# INTER	LIFE	PER IDEO M	PER IDEO F	CURRENT
AGE	—															
EXP MARRY	-.183	—														
REL ATN	-.062	-.050	—													
RELIG	-.006	-.061	.540	—												
POLIT	.115	.148	.347	-.246	—											
CIV DISOB	.236	.090	-.305	-.258	.499	—										
SEXED CRS	-.071	-.020	-.007	.086	-.033	-.053	—									
FEAR VD	-.059	-.126	.005	.018	-.022	-.162	-.039	—								
EVER INTER	.153	-.103	-.458	-.287	.300	.357	-.043	-.032	—							
AGE FIRST	.188	-.117	-.447	-.276	.290	.345	-.037	-.024	.987	—						
# PART	.246	.025	-.288	-.194	.183	.255	-.052	-.161	.371	.315	—					
# INTER	.274	-.103	-.271	-.168	.154	.263	-.028	-.057	.411	.375	.427	—				
LIFE	.137	-.115	-.431	-.287	.315	.366	-.030	-.020	.787	.776	.333	.379	—			
PER IDEO M	.162	.032	-.523	-.389	.362	.326	-.022	-.002	.449	.425	.319	.320	.531	—		
PER IDEO F	.150	.028	-.531	-.391	.391	.360	.018	.009	.475	.449	.338	.342	.567	.939	—	
CURRENT	.170	-.209	-.349	-.193	.234	.261	-.031	.043	.582	.577	.294	.355	.746	.402	.437	—

124

TABLE 6.8. Correlations of respondent characteristics, sexual ideology, and current sexual behavior: nonstudent females

	AGE	EXP MARRY	REL ATN	RELIG	POLIT	CIV DISOB	SEXED CRS	FEAR VD	EVER INTER	AGE FIRST	# PART	# INTER	LIFE	PER IDEO M	PER IDEO F	CURRENT
AGE	—															
EXP MARRY	-.059	—														
REL ATN	-.207	-.252	—													
RELIG	-.091	-.179	.381	—												
POLIT	.258	.327	-.340	-.225	—											
CIV DISOB	.318	.229	-.385	-.169	.508	—										
SEXED CRS	-.262	-.136	.229	.109	-.155	-.117	—									
FEAR VD	.030	-.209	.154	.230	-.158	-.052	.010	—								
EVER INTER	.290	-.126	-.316	-.203	.245	.189	-.062	-.086	—							
AGE FIRST	.360	-.138	-.282	-.165	.223	.175	-.088	-.059	.968	—						
# PART	.117	.037	-.227	-.223	.204	.181	-.041	-.251	.304	.248	—					
# INTER	.292	.053	-.313	-.320	.233	.339	.164	-.078	.347	.293	.308	—				
LIFE	.289	-.171	-.256	-.167	.217	.228	-.079	-.060	.837	.823	.278	.331	—			
PER IDEO M	.328	-.069	-.375	-.359	.415	.391	-.122	-.191	.519	.494	.278	.350	.580	—		
PER IDEO F	.331	.081	-.403	-.388	.435	.399	-.121	-.213	.528	.506	.293	.358	.580	.961	—	
CURRENT	.191	-.257	-.218	-.116	.154	.195	-.019	.020	.675	.656	.253	.369	.774	.437	.435	—

125

interview; the same six categories were used as for affiliation during adolescence. We compared the overall distribution of Guttman scores for current behavior by religious preference; again, the differences were not statistically significant. If we consider only whether the person is currently engaged in intercourse, there are significant differences among student women; those who indicate a fundamentalist denomination are least likely (47 percent) and those with no preference most likely (83 percent) to have engaged in coitus, with Catholics intermediate (60 percent).

We also have two measures of religiosity, frequency of attendance at religious functions in the past two months, and self-rating as very, quite, slightly, or not at all religious. Not surprisingly, the two are highly related; those who attend services more frequently rate themselves as more religious ($r = 0.32$ to 0.54).

Religious attendance is highly correlated with ideology, from -0.30 to -0.53 in all four subsamples. Participation in services is also correlated significantly with current behavior in three groups, though the correlations are consistently smaller. Thus, more frequent church attendance is particularly associated with less permissive attitudes. Attendance undoubtedly reflects commitment to organized religion, and we have already discussed Reiss's position that religion is associated with traditional, i.e., nonpermissive, sexual standards in American society.

The self-rating is negatively related to both ideology and behavior in three of the subsamples. Again, the correlations with standards are consistently larger than those with behavior. For this measure, there is some indication of gender differences with the correlations between religiosity and ideology generally larger for women (-0.36 to -0.39) than for men (-0.04 to -0.23).

Political Orientation

We included several items concerning political orientation and activities. One question asked the respondent to classify himself or herself as right radical, very conservative, moderately conservative, moderately liberal, very liberal, or left radical. In all four subsamples, approximately half rated themselves moderately liberal, 20 percent said very liberal, and another 20 percent said moderately conservative. The remainder in each group characterized themselves as very conservative (1 to 2 percent) or left radical (6 to 11 percent). We also inquired about the individual's participation in nonviolent civil disobedience, partisan political activities, and environmental activities. Involvement in the last two were not related to the variables of interest.

The results in tables 6.5–6.8 indicate a strong relationship between the individual's rating of political orientation and his or her sexual ideology; those who rated themselves more liberal politically were much more likely to have permissive standards. Again, there is evidence of gender differences, with the intercorrelations for women (0.36 to 0.43) larger than those for men (0.24 to 0.29). The correlations of orientation and behavior are also significant in all four subsamples, though consistently smaller. Essentially the same pattern and magnitude of correlations are found with respect to reported participation in acts of civil disobedience. This is at least partially due to the strong relationship between orientation and involvement in such acts (0.36 to 0.51).

Thus, political liberalism, measured both by self-rating and reported activity, is associated with greater premarital sexual permissiveness. This finding is consistent with earlier research, which has frequently discussed such a relationship (see Chapter 2).

Sex Education

We asked several questions dealing with sex education, including whether the individual had taken a course "which dealt at least in part with human sexual behavior," when the course was taken, and the extent to which the information presented was new to the person. We also inquired about familiarity with various contraceptive techniques; these results are discussed in Chapter 9. Finally, we asked how likely the person thought it was that "a person like you who engaged in intercourse will get venereal disease." In asking this question we were interested in whether, in view of the publicity over rising rates of VD among young people, concern about contracting such a disease was related to sexual activity. We thought that such fears might be a factor in self-control, at least over the more physically intimate activities.

Sixty to 65 percent of our respondents reported taking a course which dealt in part with sexuality; the vast majority of these (two-thirds) reported that one-fourth or less of the course was devoted to this topic. Only 8 to 13 percent reported taking an entire course in this area. One third took the course in eleventh or twelfth grade, and most of the others took the course either in ninth or tenth grade or in college. Tables 6.5–6.8 indicate that there is generally no relationship between whether the person had had such a course and either ideology or behavior. Only two correlations are statistically significant, and both are in the nonstudent female subsample; those who had had a sex education course had somewhat less permissive standards.

The implications of the lack of a relationship between having taken a sex education course and sexual attitudes and behavior are not clear. First, collectively our respondents took many different courses, with different material, viewpoints, and instructors. Thus, the absence of an overall relationship may simply reflect the variability in courses and should not be taken as evidence that particular courses have no effect on those who take them. In addition, it is not obvious that one should expect sex education courses to affect standards and behavior. Certainly those who oppose the teaching of such courses argue that standards should be learned in the home, not in the schools. Proponents usually stress the need for such courses in terms of factual knowledge, for example, about physiology, pregnancy, or contraception. One would not expect a factual course to affect moral attitudes or behavior. We might expect such a course to influence contraceptive knowledge, use, and choices, relationships which are examined in Chapter 9. Finally, many of the respondents indicated that the course they took was of low quality and therefore they may not have been affected by it.

There is no correlation between responses to the item concerning the perceived likelihood of contracting VD and sexual standards or behavior among students. In the nonstudent sample, those who perceived a greater likelihood had less permissive standards; in addition, there is a negative correlation with lifetime behavior among the males.

Previous Sexual Experience

We assume that previous sexual experience is a major determinant of current sexuality. As indicated in figure 2.2, we expect lifetime behavior to be directly related to sexual ideology and, through its influence on ideology, to affect the individual's current sexual activity. In our discussion of lifetime behavior (Chapter 4), we considered three measures of sexual experience: number of persons with whom the individual had had coitus, an estimate of the number of times he or she had ever engaged in intercourse, and the Guttman measure of lifetime behavior. Here, we consider the relationship between these variables and current sexuality. In addition, we have included whether or not the person had ever had intercourse and his or her age at first coitus.

The interrelationships of these variables and their correlations with the current sexuality measures appear in the right-hand triangle in tables 6.5–6.8. All five of the sexual experience measures are highly intercorrelated; thus, the results of the regression analysis, presented later, are especially interesting, since they indicate the extent to which the associations discussed here are independent.

The reader will recall that 60 to 80 percent of our respondents had engaged in intercourse at least once. Our measure of experience with intercourse merely distinguishes nonvirgins from virgins. In addition, as we saw in tables 4.3–4.6, the percentage engaging in each behavior increases with increase in age; thus, there are extremely high correlations (0.97 to 0.99) between these two, and their influence is obviously not independent. The correlational results indicate substantial positive relationships between the two measures of initial coital experience and both ideology and current behavior. Thus, the younger the person was when he or she first experienced intercourse, the more permissive were his or her sexual standards (r ranges from 0.36 to 0.51). The association with current behavior is even stronger (0.55 to 0.66).

The correlations of the two frequency measures, numbers of partners and of experiences, with ideology are smaller but still substantial (0.24 to 0.35). The association between frequency and current behavior is of about the same magnitude.

Finally, the lifetime behavior score is strongly related to sexual ideology; those who had participated in the more intimate behaviors had more permissive premarital standards. Generally the correlations are greater for female respondents (0.53 to 0.58) than for males (0.36 to 0.43). Among the strongest relationships in the data are those between lifetime and current behavior; those correlations are also slightly larger for women (0.75 and 0.77) than for men (0.69 and 0.68). Thus, the more intimate one's most advanced behavior in his or her life, the more intimate his or her current behavior; the square of the correlation, the coefficient of determination, indicates that between 46 and 60 percent of the variation in current activity is explained by lifetime behavior.

Ideology

The last data in tables 6.5–6.8 are the correlations between sexual ideology and current behavior. We are most interested in the relationship between ideology for one's own gender and respondent's own behavior. The correlation between ideology for men and current activity is 0.29 for students and 0.35 for nonstudents. The correlations are again larger for women, 0.44 for both students and nonstudents. Thus, there is a substantial relationship between one's atitudes and one's behavior, though it is not nearly as strong as the relationship between past and present sexual activity. This is good evidence for our belief that one's standards serve as a basis for exercising self-control over sexual behavior. In addition, these attitude-behavior relationships are much stronger than those typically reported in the literature.

TABLE 6.9. Stepwise regression of respondent characteristics on sexual ideology and current sexual behavior

| | STUDENTS | | | | NONSTUDENTS | | | |
| | Male | | Female | | Male | | Female | |
	PER IDEO M	CURRENT	PER IDEO F	CURRENT	PER IDEO M	CURRENT	PER IDEO F	CURRENT
AGE								
EXP MARRY		.1183[b]		-.2191[d]		.1958[c]		-.3219[d]
REL ATN	-.4057[d]	-.1621[d]	-.5200[d]	-.1434[c]	-.0406[b]		-.0369[a]	-.1479[b]
RELIG		-.0972[a]					-.0381[a]	
POLIT		.1018[a]	.0434[a]	.1022[a]				
CIV DISOB								
SEXED CRS								
FEAR VD								
EVER INT	.6076[d]	.3931[d]	.7840[d]	.3010[d]	.2523[c]	.4018[d]	.8927[d]	.5194[d]
AGE FIRST					.1714[b]			
# PART	.1293[c]	.1944[d]	.1533[c]	.1018[d]		.2319[d]	.1803[d]	.1211[b]
# INTER		.1782[d]		.3143[d]		.2742[d]		.4034[d]
PER IDEO	—		—		—		—	

[a] $p < .05$
[b] $p < .01$
[c] $p < .005$
[d] $p < .001$

Relative Influence

The results of the regression analyses of these respondent characteristics on sexual ideology and current behavior are presented in table 6.9. We did not include the lifetime behavior measure in these analyses; if we had, it would have reduced the remaining variation to such an extent that it would have been difficult to identify meaningful relationships between other variables and our measures of current sexuality.

Sexual Ideology

The regression coefficients indicate that only two of the sets of variables discussed in this section are independently associated with personal ideology, religion and lifetime experience.

In all four subsamples, recent attendance at religious services is significantly and negatively related to ideology; among nonstudent females, one's rating of her religiosity is also negatively related to premarital standards. Thus, involvement in organized religion is an important influence on one's premarital standards; those who are more involved are less permissive than those who are less involved. It is surprising that the coefficients are so much larger among students (-0.406 and -0.520) than nonstudents (-0.041 and -0.037); this indicates that religion is much more closely related to standards for the former than for the latter. The two samples do not differ substantially in frequency of attendance at services or rated religiosity, so it does not seem that such differences account for the differential impact.

Of the lifetime experience measures, whether or not the respondent had ever had intercourse is most consistently related to ideology. Compared to the other regression coefficients within each subsample, those for having had intercourse are consistently the largest, indicating that this is the strongest association with standards of all the variables in this analysis. Intercourse is one of the three behaviors included in the measures of ideology; only those who accept intercourse before marriage attain high scores on the Guttman scale. Thus, it is not surprising that high permissiveness is associated with the individual's having had intercourse. In three of the subsamples, number of intercourse experiences is also positively associated with premarital standards; in the fourth (nonstudent males), number of partners is positively related, while number of experiences is not. These coefficients are much smaller, though still significant. The results indicate that whether one has intercourse is closely related to standards; given that he or she does, the extensiveness of subsequent experience plays an additional but less substantial role. In our perspective, greater lifetime experience implies more exposure to the influence of partners, that is, progress into Stage III of our developmental model. As indicated in Chapter 2, we expect that this is in turn associated with more permissive ideology.

Current Behavior

The correlational data in tables 6.5–6.8 indicated a positive relationship between age and the measures of current sexuality. The regression coefficients of age on ideology were not significant, indicating that the effects of the former on the latter were an artifact of other relationships, primarily the association between age and sexual experience. There is a significant positive coefficient for age on current behavior in both male subsamples, but not in the female groups; this indicates an independent effect of age on men's behavior.

In three of the four subsamples, there is a negative relationship between length of time before one expects to marry and sexual activity. As noted earlier, there is a strong positive correlation between the former and the quality of the present relationship. The latter is not included in the present analysis but will be considered in Chapter 7. It is probable that this association between length of time before marriage and behavior is not significant when quality of relationship is controlled.

With respect to religion, attendance at services is negatively related to current behavior among women but not men. Among men, one's rating of his religiosity is related to behavior only for male students.

Concerning the political measures, the regression coefficients for self-rating of political orientation on behavior are not significant (nor were those on ideology). The bivariate correlations discussed earlier are thus due to the interrelationships of political orientation and other variables and not to independent associations between political orientation and current sexuality. Interestingly, among students the coefficients of reported participation in civil disobedience on behavior are significant. Such activities were particularly available to students on the University of Wisconsin–Madison campus during the late 1960s and in early 1970. Participation in these activities probably reflects a greater liberalism than is found among students as a whole. The regression results indicate that those who did participate reported more intimate current sexual behavior.

We have discussed the substantial relationship between all five of the measures of lifetime sexual experience and current behavior. The regression results indicate that in three of the subsamples the primary association is between current behavior and whether the person had engaged in intercourse; the coefficients range from 0.393 to 0.519 indicating that a considerable amount of the variation in current behavior is associated with whether or not one is a virgin. Interestingly, in the female student sub-sample, it is age of first intercourse rather than the virgin-nonvirgin distinction which is associated with current activity. The fact that age of first coitus is significant in only one of the four groups calls into question the generality of the findings reported by both Schofield (1965) and Sorensen (1972). They both concluded that relatively early first experience is associated with more intimate subsequent behavior. That may be true among adolescents, who exclusively composed the samples, but the effect seems to be no longer substantial among 18-to-23-year-olds.

Number of intercourse experiences is associated with current behavior in all four subsamples. Those respondents with relatively greater coital experience were engaged in more intimate current behavior. The regression coefficients are larger for men than for women.

Finally, personal ideology for one's own gender, that is, for oneself, is significantly and independently related to current behavior in all four subsamples. Thus, our respondents' attitudes and behavior were fairly consistent. We assume that this reflects the individual's use of his or her standards as a basis for self-control. The coefficients are larger for women than for men; a similar size differential was noted in the correlations between these two variables. This suggests that personal standards are a more important determinant of behavior for women. We will consider other evidence which seems to reflect such differential importance later.

Thus, the results in this section support two of the linkages specified in our model (figure 2.2). They indicate strong relationships between sexual experience and ideology and between ideology and current behavior. As noted in Chapter 2, the second relationship has been assumed in previous work or documented only on small samples. The present study is the first to demonstrate this interrelation, using large, random samples, detailed measures, and multivariate analyses.

PEER GROUPS AND CURRENT SEXUALITY

In Chapter 2, we discussed the importance of peer influences. Our model posits that peers are, developmentally, the second major social influence on the individual's sexuality. Reiss (1967), Vandiver (1972), and Walsh (1970) have indicated that adolescent and young-adult peer groups have more permissive premarital standards than those of parents and institutions such as religion. Thus, the fact that a young person becomes more permissive in his or her sexual ideology during adolescence and young adulthood is due partly to the increasing influence of other young people.

In Chapter 3, we described briefly four different measures of peers' standards, three of which have been used in earlier research; we included all four in the hope that our data would allow us to assess their differential relevance. The first is referred to as *context*, or the extent to which the individual perceives that others of his or her age in the same community are engaging in various behaviors; we asked each respondent what percentage of males and females of the same age he or she thought were engaging in breast fondling, genital fondling, oral-genital contact, and intercourse [cf. Clayton's (1972) discussion of campus standard]. The second measure is *friends' behavior*; we asked each respondent how many of his or her five best friends of the same sex had engaged in each of seven behaviors (those included in our other behavioral scales with the exception of french kissing and apposition). Mirande (1968) also assessed the behavior of respondents' friends. The third is *friends' ideology* which involved the same series of questions about the acceptability of behavior used to assess personal ideology. This is similar to the measures typically used in studies of peer-group or reference-group influence on premarital sexuality, e.g., by Vandiver (1972) and Walsh, Ferrell, and Tolone (1976). The fourth measure is termed *friends' expectations*; whereas the friend's ideology items inquired about their attitudes in general, this measure asked specifically about when in a relationship they felt it was appropriate for the respondent to engage in breast fondling, genital fondling, and intercourse. To our knowledge, such a measure has not been employed in previous research.

The peer group variables examined in the interview are listed in table 6.10.

TABLE 6.10. Peer-group variables

% F PET—estimated percentage of females engaging in light petting
% M PET—estimated percentage of males engaging in light petting
% F FOND—estimated percentage of females engaging in fondling a male's genitals
% M FOND—estimated percentage of males engaging in fondling a female's genitals
% F ORAL—estimated percentage of females engaging in oral-genital contact
% M ORAL—estimated percentage of males engaging in oral-genital contact
% F INTER—estimated percentage of females engaging in intercourse
% M INTER—estimated percentage of males engaging in intercourse
FR NECK—number of five best, same-gender friends engaging in necking
FR FOND B—number of friends engaging in breast fondling
FR M FOND—number of friends engaging in male fondling of female genitals
FR F FOND—number of friends engaging in female fondling of male genitals
FR F ORAL—number of friends engaging in female active oral-genital contact
FR M ORAL—number of friends engaging in male active oral-genital contact
FR INTER—number of friends engaging in intercourse
FR IDEO M—friends' sexual ideology for males—Guttman score
FR IDEO F—friends' sexual ideology for females—Guttman score
FR EXPECT—friends' expectations for respondent's behavior—Guttman score
PER IDEO M—personal sexual ideology for males—Guttman score
PER IDEO F—personal sexual ideology for females—Guttman score
CURRENT—current sexual behavior—Guttman score

Context

The first eight columns (and rows) of tables 6.11 through 6.14 present the correlations obtained with the context measures. One aspect of the intercorrelations of responses to these eight items is worth noting. We inquired separately about the percentage of males and females who engaged in each of the four behaviors. The correlations between the percentages of males and of females whom the respondent believed were engaging in each are all between 0.80 and 0.90 and indicate that our respondents believed that males and females did not differ substantially in their behavior. This is consistent with our earlier discussion of the decline of differences by gender and the disappearance of the "double standard."

There are substantial correlations between the context measures and the respondents' personal ideologies for males and females. They are of about the same magnitude in all four subsamples, that is, they do not seem to differ between men and women or students and nonstudents. It does seem that the association between ideology and estimated frequency of behavior is larger for breast and genital fondling than for oral-genital contact and intercourse. This may reflect the fact that the first two behaviors are both included in our measure of ideology, compared to only one of the last two. In any case, it is clear that young people who reported more permissive personal standards perceived a greater incidence of these sexual activities among their age peers than those who held less permissive standards.

The correlations between context and current behavior are also substantial; they range from 0.18 to 0.41, with the majority between 0.30 and 0.40. These are similar in size to the association between context and ideology. In general, there are no consistent differences between genders or between student and nonstudent groups.

Thus, perceptions of sexual behavior in the community relate about equally to the individual's attitudes and his or her own sexual activities.

Friends' Behavior

The next seven columns (and rows) in tables 6.11–6.14 report the correlations obtained for friends' behavior. These questions and those on friends' ideology and expectations were asked as a group; they were prefaced by the request that the respondent think about his or her five best friends of the same sex and answer all of the questions in terms of those people. These questions asked him or her how many of these persons had engaged in each of the indicated behaviors.

In general, the correlations of friends' behavior and personal ideology

TABLE 6.11. Correlations of peer measures, sexual ideology, and current sexual behavior: student males

	% F PET	% M PET	% F FOND	% M FOND	% F ORAL	% M ORAL	% F INTER	% M INTER	FR NECK	FR FOND B	FR M FOND	FR F FOND	FR F ORAL	FR M ORAL	FR INTER	FR IDEO M	FR IDEO F	FR EXPECT	PER IDEO M	PER IDEO F	CURRENT
% F PET	—																				
% M PET	.856	—																			
% F FOND	.713	.647	—																		
% M FOND	.666	.734	.806	—																	
% F ORAL	.360	.303	.600	.460	—																
% M ORAL	.348	.363	.516	.544	.819	—															
% F INTER	.471	.445	.641	.553	.530	.483	—														
% M INTER	.429	.483	.554	.612	.435	.485	.894	—													
FR NECK	.177	.148	.138	.173	.080	.083	.099	.150	—												
FR FOND B	.356	.336	.296	.337	.175	.221	.229	.267	.715	—											
FR M FOND	.389	.343	.389	.413	.239	.253	.275	.322	.557	.756	—										
FR F FOND	.394	.365	.428	.425	.278	.274	.295	.328	.493	.690	.910	—									
FR F ORAL	.275	.249	.333	.315	.475	.440	.234	.263	.308	.433	.619	.656	—								
FR M ORAL	.223	.178	.267	.249	.389	.455	.193	.209	.299	.414	.592	.594	.854	—							
FR INTER	.344	.336	.410	.410	.302	.293	.520	.553	.384	.542	.710	.738	.604	.576	—						
FR IDEO M	.257	.283	.301	.307	.215	.216	.186	.237	.233	.368	.437	.424	.358	.326	.452	—					
FR IDEO F	.263	.276	.297	.317	.216	.208	.183	.228	.215	.353	.425	.422	.348	.316	.448	.899	—				
FR EXPECT	.290	.306	.310	.307	.202	.200	.232	.277	.263	.392	.496	.478	.357	.325	.488	.784	.757	—			
PER IDEO M	.331	.317	.328	.302	.190	.198	.276	.285	.219	.337	.436	.428	.299	.286	.459	.699	.699	.788	—		
PER IDEO F	.318	.303	.319	.286	.188	.192	.275	.280	.215	.315	.415	.412	.277	.271	.442	.686	.686	.776	.976	—	
CURRENT	.277	.291	.332	.338	.332	.327	.304	.295	.272	.383	.442	.443	.465	.439	.419	.256	.242	.282	.292	.277	—

TABLE 6.12. Correlations of peer measures, sexual ideology, and current sexual behavior: nonstudent males

	% F PET	% M PET	% F FOND	% M FOND	% F ORAL	% M ORAL	% F INTER	% M INTER	FR NECK	FR FOND B	FR M FOND	FR F FOND	FR F ORAL	FR M ORAL	FR INTER	FR IDEO M	FR IDEO F	FR EXPECT	PER IDEO M	PER IDEO F	CURRENT
% F PET	—																				
% M PET	.874	—																			
% F FOND	.713	.631	—																		
% M FOND	.699	.769	.817	—																	
% F ORAL	.402	.386	.643	.601	—																
% M ORAL	.372	.419	.570	.652	.810	—															
% F INTER	.521	.478	.628	.614	.512	.460	—														
% M INTER	.555	.543	.596	.691	.448	.514	.885	—													
FR NECK	.322	.400	.284	.375	.211	.227	.217	.260	—												
FR FOND B	.515	.605	.457	.581	.312	.343	.367	.432	.710	—											
FR M FOND	.407	.481	.472	.569	.321	.386	.363	.459	.582	.791	—										
FR F FOND	.462	.512	.524	.598	.345	.435	.388	.485	.498	.729	.882	—									
FR F ORAL	.346	.401	.426	.527	.467	.555	.292	.377	.334	.493	.642	.697	—								
FR M ORAL	.334	.353	.404	.464	.428	.551	.317	.380	.326	.460	.640	.669	.856	—							
FR INTER	.405	.457	.414	.535	.253	.364	.470	.561	.418	.552	.716	.721	.631	.623	—						
FR IDEO M	.388	.384	.352	.379	.271	.285	.308	.356	.275	.395	.366	.393	.309	.383	.442	—					
FR IDEO F	.399	.364	.362	.357	.271	.308	.273	.332	.261	.392	.396	.430	.336	.400	.407	.882	—				
FR EXPECT	.358	.396	.357	.411	.243	.260	.306	.350	.259	.426	.445	.456	.334	.357	.479	.734	.696	—			
PER IDEO M	.340	.342	.324	.354	.217	.282	.278	.341	.224	.350	.448	.453	.393	.406	.437	.668	.694	.744	—		
PER IDEO F	.335	.322	.327	.342	.221	.269	.252	.305	.197	.322	.413	.425	.383	.390	.405	.652	.697	.731	.972	—	
CURRENT	.383	.384	.371	.408	.201	.243	.249	.285	.258	.416	.484	.487	.454	.390	.433	.278	.297	.356	.360	.351	—

137

TABLE 6.13. Correlations of peer measures, sexual ideology, and current sexual behavior: student females

	% F PET	% M PET	% F FOND	% M FOND	% F ORAL	% M ORAL	% F INTER	% M INTER	FR NECK	FR FOND B	FR M FOND	FR F FOND	FR F ORAL	FR M ORAL	FR INTER	FR IDEO M	FR IDEO F	FR EXPECT	PER IDEO M	PER IDEO F	CURRENT
% F PET	—																				
% M PET	.831	—																			
% F FOND	.737	.620	—																		
% M FOND	.670	.739	.837	—																	
% F ORAL	.437	.381	.634	.555	—																
% M ORAL	.398	.417	.575	.620	.873	—															
% F INTER	.461	.405	.613	.570	.516	.475	—														
% M INTER	.446	.493	.561	.312	.462	.496	.879	—													
FR NECK	.272	.298	.264	.440	.148	.160	.204	.238	—												
FR FOND B	.436	.407	.430	.430	.278	.275	.314	.338	.719	—											
FR M FOND	.395	.337	.453	.407	.329	.297	.344	.343	.514	.809	—										
FR F FOND	.367	.290	.466	.318	.337	.295	.332	.322	.487	.744	.918	—									
FR F ORAL	.324	.255	.395	.316	.477	.402	.269	.256	.291	.480	.637	.678	—								
FR M ORAL	.301	.234	.376	.339	.449	.414	.263	.251	.288	.486	.649	.682	.943	—							
FR INTER	.334	.287	.383	.382	.278	.234	.420	.406	.376	.594	.732	.738	.686	.687	—						
FR IDEO M	.402	.330	.402	.353	.291	.264	.344	.348	.408	.597	.623	.608	.509	.503	.590	—					
FR IDEO F	.368	.291	.386	.376	.262	.229	.332	.314	.398	.582	.601	.626	.531	.532	.609	.938	—				
FR EXPECT	.384	.323	.381	.365	.239	.202	.336	.324	.413	.575	.609	.612	.568	.560	.635	.804	.831	—			
PER IDEO M	.365	.294	.371	.344	.247	.219	.342	.344	.393	.540	.556	.535	.462	.446	.536	.760	.712	.738	—		
PER IDEO F	.329	.271	.344	.279	.230	.201	.312	.304	.364	.540	.557	.543	.486	.475	.565	.759	.751	.775	.936	—	
CURRENT	.198	.175	.290		.242	.240	.238	.265	.276	.457	.507	.500	.526	.515	.487	.366	.374	.427	.388	.424	—

138

TABLE 6.14. Correlations of peer measures, sexual ideology, and current sexual behavior: nonstudent females

	% F PET	% M PET	% F FOND	% M FOND	% F ORAL	% M ORAL	% F INTER	% M INTER	FR NECK	FR FOND B	FR M FOND	FR F FOND	FR F ORAL	FR M ORAL	FR INTER	FR IDEO M	FR IDEO F	FR EXPECT	PER IDEO M	PER IDEO F	CURRENT
% F PET	—																				
% M PET	.857	—																			
% F FOND	.754	.661	—																		
% M FOND	.703	.710	.850	—																	
% F ORAL	.515	.454	.721	.649	—																
% M ORAL	.496	.509	.620	.659	.874	—															
% F INTER	.510	.433	.699	.613	.600	.537	—														
% M INTER	.469	.478	.595	.642	.520	.530	.873	—													
FR NECK	.304	.221	.248	.220	.245	.225	.189	.150	—												
FR FOND B	.447	.374	.428	.437	.338	.315	.348	.334	.727	—											
FR M FOND	.386	.330	.432	.456	.364	.347	.346	.332	.543	.788	—										
FR F FOND	.392	.324	.454	.434	.387	.338	.366	.319	.506	.739	.930	—									
FR F ORAL	.333	.258	.373	.357	.484	.457	.366	.335	.368	.563	.725	.772	—								
FR M ORAL	.338	.277	.363	.360	.437	.465	.366	.334	.364	.574	.732	.740	.922	—							
FR INTER	.350	.282	.390	.398	.315	.312	.339	.493	.389	.597	.753	.746	.673	.662	—						
FR IDEO M	.380	.370	.395	.432	.288	.280	.517	.316	.417	.578	.604	.599	.571	.584	.577	—					
FR IDEO F	.387	.371	.393	.429	.296	.291	.314	.315	.390	.566	.626	.605	.570	.618	.607	.945	—				
FR EXPECT	.340	.297	.372	.380	.250	.247	.300	.281	.351	.510	.615	.605	.570	.603	.553	.825	.549	—			
PER IDEO M	.388	.350	.435	.448	.293	.318	.328	.339	.411	.575	.609	.579	.519	.557	.577	.798	.758	.758	—		
PER IDEO F	.399	.348	.437	.435	.293	.304	.341	.333	.399	.560	.623	.591	.514	.543	.590	.776	.787	.783	.961	—	
CURRENT	.281	.259	.331	.307	.328	.335	.303	.321	.373	.461	.524	.503	.446	.472	.447	.358	.354	.350	.437	.435	—

139

(for both men and women) are sizable, ranging from 0.20 to 0.62. The smallest in each of the four subsamples is consistently between number of friends who neck and personal ideology (0.20 to 0.41); this is primarily because of the small variance on this item; most respondents said all five of their friends had engaged in this activity. The interrelationship of the other six behaviors and personal ideology are larger, ranging from 0.27 to 0.62. There is a consistent difference between males and females; the correlations between one's own ideology and friends' behavior are generally smaller among males (0.20 to 0.46) than among females (0.36 to 0.62).

The correlations of current behavior with friends' activity are equally large. Again, within each subsample, the correlation between number of friends who neck and current behavior is smaller (0.26 to 0.37) than the correlation of the other items concerning peers' activity with the respondent's own behavior (0.38 to 0.53). Again, the association between these is stronger among females (0.28 to 0.53) than among males (0.26 to 0.49). Similarly, Zelnik and Kantner (1973), using a national sample, reported that single women who had ever had intercourse were more likely to report that their friends were nonvirgins.

We can compare the magnitudes of the relationships between context and respondent's attitudes and behavior and between friends' behavior and his or her sexual standards and activity. Within each of the four subsamples, the correlations between friends' behavior and the measures of the respondent's sexuality are larger. This is true of the relationships with both respondent's ideology and current sexual behavior; the difference is particularly large in the female subsamples. Thus, the behavior of one's close friends (or one's perception thereof) is more closely related to one's own attitudes and sexual activity than is a sense of the incidence of behavior among age peers in general. As indicated in Appendix I, we had anticipated that the latter might not be as valid a measure, at least in a large and heterogeneous community.

Friends' Ideology

We also asked each interviewee about his or her five best friends' sexual ideology, using the same format employed to assess personal standards. Thus, the respondent indicated when in a relationship her or his friends felt each of the three behaviors were acceptable; we assessed their ideology for men and women separately. Responses were again combined via Guttman scaling techniques to produce a single measure for males and one for females.

In the preceding section, we were concerned with the respondent's perception of friends' behavior. An objection can be raised to using measures of both friends' behavior and their attitudes on the grounds that these are really two measures of the same thing. Thus, some would argue that since a person rarely witnesses peers' sexual behavior, he or she will merely infer activity from their statements about their attitudes or standards. We assume, however, that the individual has some impression of both others' attitudes and their behavior, and that these items therefore are not two measures of the same phenomenon. Our position is supported by the correlations between reports of friends' behavior and reports of friends' ideologies. Among male respondents, the values range from 0.22 to 0.50; the coefficient of determination, r^2, for the maximum value is 0.25, indicating that only 25 percent of the variance in one is shared by the other. Also, these correlations are similar to those between the respondent's own ideology and behavior, 0.29 and 0.36. The intercorrelations between reports by females of friends' attitudes and behavior are larger, ranging from 0.39 to 0.63; the coefficient of determination for the maximum is 0.39, indicating that about 39 percent of the variance is shared. Also among females the correlations between the respondent's own ideology and behavior are somewhat larger than the equivalent relationships for men. Thus, there is considerable nonoverlap in the reports of friends' attitudes and of their behavior. While respondents who reported that their peers had more permissive standards also reported that more of them were engaging in each of the behaviors, our interviewees indicated that there was a difference between the two.

The correlations between friends' ideologies for men and women and the respondent's standards for the two genders are quite large; in fact, these are the largest bivariate relationships we have considered. Among our male interviewees, these associations range from 0.71 to 0.80. Our respondents thus perceived their own premarital standards to be very similar to those of their peers. These correlations are much larger than those between personal ideology and the context measures or between ideology and friends' behavior.

Similarly, Reiss (1967) found that 89 percent of his student respondents reported that the standards of their "very close friends" were similar to their own. They were less likely to report similarity between their standards and those of "others your own age." Thus, his data also indicate greater correspondence between the individual and his or her friends than between the person and what we refer to as context.

Our respondents reported that their friends had almost identical standards for males and females. The correlations between friends' ideology for men and for women range from 0.88 to 0.95, indicating that the two are almost identical. Thus, our interviewees do not perceive any differential in standards among their peers.

There are substantial relationships between friends' standards and the respondent's current sexual behavior, though these correlations are smaller than those between friends' and respondent's ideologies. Among males, the association ranges from 0.24 to 0.30. It is somewhat larger among females, ranging from 0.35 to 0.37. On the whole, these correlations are smaller than those between the number of friends who engage in the behavior and the individual's current activity.

Friends' Expectations

Our final measure is that of friends' expectations. Whereas the ideology measure concerned peers' general standards for men and women, this one inquired specifically about their standards for the respondent. We felt that an individual may perceive that his or her peers hold different standards for himself or herself than for people in general. In general, however, the correlations between the peer ideology and expectations measures are very high, ranging from 0.70 to 0.85, indicating that they are very similar. Females report more similar ideologies and expectations for their friends (0.80 to 0.85) than males (0.70 to 0.78). Also, in all four subsamples, the relationship between reported peer ideology for persons of the same gender as the respondent and peer expectations is slightly greater than that between ideology for the other gender and expectation. Thus, our respondents reported that their friends' standards in general and for themselves were quite similar.

The correlations between friends' expectations and the individual's ideology range from 0.73 to 0.79; those involving ideology for persons of his or her own gender are slightly larger than those for persons of the opposite gender. Among males, friends' expectations are somewhat more strongly related to the individual's own ideology than was friends' ideology, whereas for females the correlations of the two peer measures are about the same. If one employs the degree of association with the respondents' own attitudes as a criterion, the expectation measure is therefore, slightly better than the ideology one as an indicator of peer attitudes.

The correlations between expectations and the individual's behavior are substantial but smaller; they range from 0.28 to 0.43. In three of the subsamples, the friends' expectation–behavior relationship is stronger than the friends' ideology–behavior one.

On the whole, there was consistency in our respondents' perceptions of the behavior of age peers in the community, the standards and behavior of their best friends of the same sex, and their reports of their own ideology and current behavior. Those whose ideology was more permissive perceived a greater incidence of premarital sexuality among young people their age and reported that their friends had more permissive standards and that a greater number of them engaged in the seven sexual behaviors. In general, the context measures are less strongly associated with the respondent's attitudes and behavior than are the friends' measures; there is a closer correspondence between the individual and his or her best friends. The strongest relationships with one's own ideology are found with the expectation measure, i.e., with the items concerning his or her friends' standards for himself or herself (0.73 to 0.79); however, these correlations are only slightly larger than those involving his or her friends' general standards for persons of that gender (0.67 to 0.79). The strongest relationships with the individual's current behavior involve friends' behavior; these correlations are substantially larger (0.26 to 0.53) than those between friends' ideology and behavior (0.26 to 0.37) or friends' expectations and behavior (0.28 to 0.43). Thus, the closest associations are between peers' and one's own ideology, and peers' and one's own behavior.

Relative Strength

Table 6.15 presents the results of a regression analysis of the peer measures on the respondent's sexual ideology and current behavior. Given the high intercorrelations among these variables (see tables 6.11–6.14), we did not include all of them in the analysis. We dropped the context measures of percentage of males and females who engage in breast fondling and in oral-genital contact and of number of friends who engage in necking because they did not correlate as strongly with respondent ideology and behavior as did the other items in each set. Similarly, we have noted that friends' expectation was a slightly better measure than friends' ideology for men and women, and so the latter were also not included in the regression analysis.

Sexual Ideology

The regression coefficients obtained for ideology follow a consistent pattern across the four subsamples. The coefficients for friends' expectations are very large, ranging from 0.600 to 0.712, and indicate a strong association with the individual's standards. There is a much smaller but significant coefficient for one (and in the NF subsample, two) of the friends' behavior measures. In the two female subsamples, the item concerning number of friends who engage in breast fondling is associated with ideology. Among males, it is items involving more intimate behaviors, female active oral-genital contact (NM) and intercourse (SM). The context measures are generally not significantly associated with ideology; the only exception occurs in the male student subsample, where the coefficient obtained for percent of females who participate in breast fondling is sig-

TABLE 6.15. Stepwise regression of peer measures
on sexual ideology and current sexual behavior

| | MALES | | FEMALES | |
	PER IDEO M	CURRENT	PER IDEO F	CURRENT
		STUDENTS		
% F FOND	.0773^a			
% M FOND		.1021^a		
% F INTER		.1242^b		
% M INTER				
FR FOND B			.1297^d	.2180^d
FR M FOND		.1997^d		
FR F FOND				
FR F ORAL		.2803^d		.3193^d
FR M ORAL				
FR INTER	.0730^a			.1440^b
FR EXPECT	.7095^d		.7017^d	
		NONSTUDENTS		
% F FOND				
% M FOND		.1531^a		
% F INTER				
% M INTER				.1546^c
FR FOND B			.0979^a	
FR M FOND				.3322^d
FR F FOND		.3366^d		
FR F ORAL	.1432^c			
FR M ORAL				.1806^b
FR INTER			.1549^d	
FR EXPECT	.7119^d	.1331^a	.6004^d	

$^a p < .05$
$^b p < .01$
$^c p < .005$
$^d p < .001$

nificant. These results support the conclusion that the primary correlate of sexual ideology is friends' attitudes, specifically their expectations, and that perceptions of behavior, either of age peers in general or of one's five best friends, are only weakly related to the individual's premarital standards. These results are consistent with the assumption in our model (figure 2.2) that peers are a major influence on sexual ideology. The fact that peers' expectations are much more closely related to attitudes than the familial measures were supports our belief that peers replace parents as the primary socializing agents at least by late adolescence.

Current Behavior

In contrast to the pattern for ideology, the significant regression coefficients for current behavior primarily involve behavioral measures. The largest coefficient in all four groups involves one of the measures of friends' behavior. In both student subsamples, it is number of friends who engage in female active oral-genital contact; among the nonstudents it is one of the genital fondling items. These coefficients are all substantial, ranging from 0.280 to 0.337. In three of the subsamples, there is a significant but smaller coefficient associated with a second measure of friends' behavior; among student females, a third friends' behavior item shows a significant association. In three of the groups, there is a significant coefficient for one or more of the context measures; these are generally the smallest of those included in table 6.15 (0.102 to 0.155). There is only one subsample in which friends' expectations are related to current behavior, the NM group; the coefficient is the smallest obtained in this subsample. In general, then, perception of friends' behavior is most closely related to respondent's current behavior. There is a secondary association between perceptions of the incidence of behavior among age peers and one's own behavior in three groups. In three of the subsamples, friends' attitudes are not significantly related to the individual's current behavior. The regression results thus indicate a direct and independent relationship between friends' behavior and one's own behavior, a relationship not anticipated in our conceptual model.

These results indicate that the measures of context, friends' behavior, and friends' expectations are different. Although we found positive correlations between them, they relate differentially to our dependent variables, personal ideology and current sexual activity. At least in the context of a city of 170,000 and a university with 35,000 students, measures concerning age peers in general do not relate as closely to the individual's characteristics as measures involving peers in the specific sense of best friends. In addition, reported *expectations* of one's friends for him or her relate more closely to his or her standards than reported friend's ideology. This has important implications. Past research on peers or reference groups has relied on the latter, whereas our findings suggest the former is a more appropriate measure. Also, we find that there is greater correspondence between peer measures and the individual's characteristics when the object is the same, i.e., behavior or attitudes, than between measures of the attitudes of one and behavior of the other. The fact that peers' behavior measures are more closely related to the individual's behavior leads to the conclusion that one's behavior is more influenced by what others do than by what they say. These conclusions are based on a much more systematic analysis of the interrelations between these measures than has heretofore been conducted. Mirande's (1968) is the only previous research which focused on the behavior-behavior relationship, and his was a nonrandom sample of only 93 persons. Subsequent research has not only neglected this relationship but has used various measures of peer attitudes. Furthermore, we can have greater confidence in our conclusions because they are based on much larger, random samples. Also, we have shown that these findings hold for both students and nonstudents. Thus, our analysis of peer-respondent attitudinal and behavioral measures is much more definitive than past ones. We have accomplished this goal of our research.

SUMMARY

In this chapter we have examined the influence of a number of family-background and peer-group characteristics on current sexuality. Relationship with parents and parental attitudes toward sexuality were related to sexual ideology. The closer the individual is to his or her parents, the less permissive the person's sexual standards. At the same time, there is variation in the attitudes of parents. In general, the more permissive or liberal the parents are, the more permissive the respondent's sexual standards. Thus, parents socialize their children to sexual attitudes and standards similar to their own. Compared to other social influences, however, parental influence acts to decrease permissiveness. The pattern is similar for current behavior, although the regression coefficients are scattered and less substantial.

Several characteristics of the individual are associated with current sexuality. Religious attendance and religiosity are related such that those who are less religious are more permissive in their ideology and engage in more intimate behaviors. Age is related to current behavior among students and marital expectations are correlated with activity in three of the subsamples. Individuals who are older or have plans to marry in the near future are involved in more intimate current behavior. The various measures of lifetime sexual behavior are strongly and consistently related to personal ideology and current behavior. Whether the respondent has ever had intercourse is the best predictor of current sexuality. The characteristics of the individual that are independently related to current sexuality provide evidence for two types of social influence. First, involvement with religious institutions is a conservative influence. Involvement in heterosexual relationships influences the individual toward more permissive sexual ideology and behavior. These findings regarding characteristics of the individual provide additional support for our model.

Finally, we considered the importance of peer influences. Reliance on friends and lovers as sources of information is positively related to current sexuality. In addition, we examined four peer measures: context, friends' ideology, friends' behavior, and friends' expectations for the respondent.

Personal sexual ideology is most strongly related to friends' expectations. Thus, the respondent's attitude is primarily influenced by peer attitudes.

The findings for current behavior reveal that friends' behavior is the primary determinant. To a lesser extent, perceived activity among age peers is related to the individual's sexual activity. These results indicate that close friends are a more appropriate reference group than age peers. Our respondents are able to distinguish the attitudes from the behavior of their peers, and the strongest relationship to their own sexuality is found when the object is the same. In terms of current sexual behavior, respondents are influenced by friends' behavior more than by friends' attitudes.

7

Heterosexual Relationships and Current Behavior

IN THE preceding chapters, we have considered the relationship between several sets of variables and the individual's current sexuality: socio-psychological characteristics of the individual such as self and body image; family and parental factors; the individual's previous or lifetime sexual behavior; and aspects of the peer network of which he or she is a part. As suggested by the perspective presented in Chapter 2, the results indicate that one or more variables from each of these sets is associated with the individual's sexual ideology, the standards he or she applies to a hetero-sexual relationship which define the extent of sexual intimacy which is appropriate or acceptable. We assume that these standards are a major determinant of the person's sexual behavior, and that he or she uses them as a basis for self-control over sexual activity. The other major deter-minant we identified is influence associated with the person's current relationship. With a standard which specifies a level of emotional intimacy, either affection, love, or marriage, the occurrence of the behavior depends upon whether the person is involved in a relationship of that quality and the influence of his or her current partner(s).

This chapter is devoted to consideration of the individual's current heterosexual relationships. Each respondent who had "gone out with a male/female within the last year" (95 to 98 percent of each subsample) was asked a detailed series of questions about one current partner. For those who had dated only one person during that period (30 to 41 percent of each subsample), these questions were asked about that partner. Those who had dated more than one other person were asked to answer the questions based on the person they had most recently been out with. We

148

also asked them how many other persons they had been out with, the quality or intimacy of each of those relationships, and whether or not they had engaged in intercourse with each of the other partners. Thus, all of the data presented refer to persons dated and relationships during the preceding year; the questions, however, systematically concerned the entire period of the relationship and all behavior with the person. For ease of presentation, we refer to the person about whom the questions were answered as *current partner,* and the relationship as *current relationship.*

The first section presents descriptive data concerning social characteristics of partners. The next section focuses on data describing the relationship. These two sets of data are included primarily to allow comparison with earlier research. The third section presents the intercorrelations of partner and relationship variables with current behavior and is followed by the regression results involving them. It is the regression results which are of primary relevance to our conceptual model. The following section, "The Dynamics of Sexual Interactions," looks at behavioral control in dyadic sexual encounters. The last section of this chapter briefly considers additional partners and relationships.

PARTNER'S CHARACTERISTICS

We begin with descriptive data on the characteristics of our respondents' partners. Table 7.1 presents information concerning partner's age, social class, perceived physical attractiveness, and likability.

Age

Virtually all of our respondents were between the ages of 18 and 23 years. We were interested in the age of each person's partner and felt that his or her age relative to the respondent was potentially the most meaningful variable. Accordingly, the partner's age was recorded as the same as or in years older or younger than the interviewee; it is reported in that format in table 7.1. A substantial percentage of partners were of the same age; the range across the four subsamples is from about 30 to 43 percent. For the remainder, however, there is a clear difference between males and females in the distributions of partners' ages. An additional 38 (SM) and 50 (NM) percent of the men reported that their partners were one or more years younger, whereas 52 (SF) and 57 (NF) percent of the women indicated that their partners were older. This differential was even more pronounced in Simon and Gagnon's data collected in 1967; they found that 46 to 60 percent of the males were dating someone younger, whereas 60 to 68 percent of the females were dating someone older.

TABLE 7.1. Current partner characteristics (in percent)

	SM	NM	SF	NF
A. Age of partner compared to age of respondent				
3 or more years younger	5.58	9.10	3.50	0.68
2 years younger	8.37	19.09	1.64	0.68
1 year younger	23.72	21.82	4.91	7.84
The same age	43.02	33.18	35.98	29.69
1 year older	8.60	5.45	18.46	14.67
2 years older	3.72	2.27	12.15	12.96
3 or more years older	2.56	5.46	21.73	29.68
Missing[a]	0.00	0.00	0.00	0.68
No current partner	4.42	3.64	1.64	3.07
B. Social class of partner				
Lower than respondent	14.65	17.27	18.22	13.99
Same as respondent	59.07	55.45	64.25	61.77
Higher than respondent	21.86	23.64	15.65	20.81
Missing[a]	0.00	0.00	0.23	0.34
No current partner	4.42	3.64	1.64	3.07
C. Physical attractiveness of partner				
9	10.47	9.09	19.16	19.45
8	24.88	29.55	28.50	29.35
7	41.14	37.27	31.78	29.01
6	12.56	15.91	10.05	10.92
5 or lower	6.51	4.55	8.88	7.85
Missing[a]	0.00	0.00	0.00	0.34
No current partner	4.42	3.64	1.64	3.07
D. Likability of partner				
9	25.81	26.82	32.48	30.03
8	35.12	30.00	32.71	40.61
7	21.86	24.55	20.33	13.31
6	6.74	8.18	8.18	6.14
5 or lower	6.05	6.81	4.66	6.48
Missing[a]	0.00	0.00	0.00	0.34
No current partner	4.42	3.64	1.64	3.07

[a]Respondent did not answer the item.

The results in Chapter 4 indicated a strong association between age and lifetime behavior. The older a person is within the age range of 15 to 20, the more experienced his or her sexual behavior. The findings here concerning relative age imply that the men we interviewed were frequently dating women who were relatively less sexually experienced, whereas women were dating men with relatively more experience. We anticipate therefore, a relationship between partner's age and respondent's current behavior.

The last line in section A of the table indicates the percentage of respondents who were not currently dating, that is, who had not gone out with a member of the opposite gender in the past year.

Social Class

Ehrmann (1959) found consistent relationships between partner's social class and sexual activity among college students. In general, he found a negative relationship between these variables for males; males were most likely to engage in intimate behavior with females who were relatively lower in social class and least likely to do so with relatively higher class women. Women were most likely to engage in intimate (i.e., "genital") behavior with men of the same class standing, less likely to do so with those of higher status, and least likely to report such behavior with relatively lower class men. Subsequent research (for example, Schofield, 1965; Sorensen, 1972) has not explored this relationship.

Since Ehrmann found that it was relative social class rather than class per se, we asked whether the respondent's partner was of the same, higher, or lower social class. The results in section B of table 7.1 indicate that a majority in all four subsamples (55 to 64 percent) characterized their partner as of the same social class; an additional 14 to 18 percent characterized him or her as lower, and the remaining 6 to 24 percent as higher, in social class. We consider later whether class measured in this manner is associated with the individual's sexual behavior.

Partner's Attractiveness and Likability

We discussed in Chapter 5 the possibility of a relationship between physical attractiveness and sexual activity. Having obtained a rating of self on this dimension from each respondent and a rating of the respondent by the interviewer, we also wanted to obtain a rating of his or her partner. This measure is obviously "subjective," reflecting the respondent's perception and standards; again, however, it is precisely this personal evaluation that might be particularly important to an individual. The question asked the interviewee to rate his or her partner's physical attractiveness on a scale from one to nine, where nine represented extremely attractive. The ratings obtained are presented in section C of table 7.1. Less than 10 percent rated their partner at or below the implied "neutral" point of five on the scale; more than 90 percent gave him or her ratings on the attractive end of the scale. By far the most frequent ratings were seven and eight, which together were given by 58 to 67 percent of the respondents. There is a tendency for women to rate their partners higher; 19 percent of the women compared to about 10 percent of the men rated their partners nine.

We also wanted a measure of the respondent's evaluation of partner's "likability." We asked the question in the same format, substituting "likable" for "physically attractive"; nine again represented extremely likable. This question immediately followed the physical attractiveness item in the interview. The results obtained are presented in section D of table 7.1. Again, relatively few gave their partners a rating of five or less, and the majority rated him or her as seven or eight. Relative to the attractiveness item, more respondents in all four subsamples gave their partners a rating of nine.

Marital Status

We also asked about the current partner's marital status. Virtually all respondents indicated that their partner had never been married (92 to 94 percent). A total of 11 of our 1,376 single respondents reported seeing someone who was currently married; an additional 26 indicated that they were going out with someone who was divorced, and 5 others said their partner was separated from a spouse. It is interesting to note that from 1.5 to 4.5 percent of each subsample was unsure of their partner's marital status; presumably these were persons who had just begun to go out with their partners.

CHARACTERISTICS OF THE CURRENT RELATIONSHIP

Temporal Characteristics

Three aspects of our data concerning current relationships reflect their temporal character: whether or not the respondent was still dating his or her "current" partner at the time of the interview, the length of the relationship, and the total number of times the couple had been together. Table 7.2 presents the distributions obtained for these three questions.

Section A of table 7.2 indicates whether the respondent was still dating the partner. Since the current partner questions referred to that person whom the individual had seen most recently before the interview, those who answered no to this question had terminated the relationship on which they reported in detail and had not begun to see someone else. From 72 to 81 percent of our respondents were still dating their partner; thus, all the information obtained about partners and the relationship from these persons pertained to an ongoing relationship. Fifteen to 24 percent were no longer seeing the "current partner"; these respondents were thus reporting on a person and relationship which had been terminated in the recent past.

Section B of the table indicates the length of the relationship. The most frequent length is more than one year; such duration was reported by 32 to 46 percent of the respondents. The remaining responses are fairly evenly distributed over the categories from "one to four weeks" to "six to twelve months." Less than 7 percent of our respondents reported on dating relationships which had begun within the week prior to the interview. It is worth noting that there are not substantial differences between men and women or between students and nonstudents in reported duration.

Finally, we asked how many times the couple had been together. While this obviously depends in part on the duration of the relationship, it also reflects the intensity of the couple's interaction. Differences on this measure might be especially relevant where two or more relationships are of equal duration. Answers to this question ranged from once to more than 1,000 times (the latter were coded as 999); for section C of table 7.2, responses were categorized as indicated. Between 34 and 48 percent of our respondents reported being with their partner on more than 100 distinct occasions. There is a slight tendency for women to report more frequent interaction. At the same time, 20 to 28 percent of our interviewees report having seen their partner 10 times or less. Thus, on this measure, the relationships represented in our data are distributed fairly evenly over a scale of from few dates to hundreds of them.

TABLE 7.2. Characteristics of the current relationship (in percent)

	SM	NM	SF	NF
A. Still dating current partner				
Yes	71.86	72.27	79.21	81.22
No	23.72	23.64	18.93	14.67
Missing[a]	0.00	0.45	0.23	1.04
No current partner	4.42	3.64	1.64	3.07
B. Length of relationship				
Less than one week	6.28	5.00	3.50	4.44
1–4 weeks	12.09	17.73	13.79	8.87
1–3 months	18.84	17.27	17.06	13.99
3–6 months	12.79	9.55	12.85	10.92
6–12 months	14.65	15.45	14.49	12.62
More than a year	31.63	32.27	36.68	46.42
No current partner[b]	3.71	2.73	1.64	2.73
C. Number of times with current partner				
1–2	10.18	7.73	6.70	5.80
3–10	18.29	19.54	16.20	13.99
11–30	15.51	17.73	13.19	12.62
31–100	15.05	17.27	18.04	13.65
101–400	23.38	19.54	24.10	24.56
401–999	13.17	14.55	20.12	23.54
Missing[a]	0.00	0.00	0.00	2.77
No current partner	4.42	3.64	1.64	3.07
D. Emotional intimacy of current relationship				
Someone you dated only once or twice	15.58	14.09	11.92	9.89
Someone you date(d) often but are/were not emotionally attached to	11.16	12.27	7.94	11.94
Someone you are/were emotionally attached to but not in love with	33.49	29.09	30.14	21.50
Someone you are/were in love with, but are/were not engaged to	20.00	25.45	27.34	22.52
Someone you are/were in love with and expect(ed) to marry	10.93	11.82	14.95	20.47
Someone you are/were engaged to	3.95	3.18	6.07	9.89
Missing[a]	0.46	0.45	0.00	0.68
No current partner	4.42	3.64	1.64	3.07

[a]Respondent did not answer the item.
[b]These percentages differ from those given for "no current partner" in other sections of this table because of variation in the location of this item on the different forms of the schedule.

TABLE 7.3. Partner's sexual ideology (in percent)

Acceptability of behavior	Petting involving breast fondling				Petting involving fondling partner's genitals				Intercourse			
	SM	NM	SF	NF	SM	NM	SF	NF	SM	NM	SF	NF
A. FOR MALES												
Not before marriage	1.63	0.91	1.40	2.05	4.42	4.09	3.26	5.12	11.81	8.64	7.24	7.84
If engaged to be married	2.09	2.27	1.87	1.71	6.51	2.27	2.79	3.41	10.00	7.73	7.48	5.80
If in love and not engaged	15.81	16.82	7.25	8.87	30.35	31.36	21.73	14.67	37.21	39.55	28.97	22.52
If feel affection but not love	40.00	35.45	35.51	29.01	30.35	29.55	30.84	30.71	18.61	15.91	21.96	24.23
If both want it	35.58	36.82	51.63	53.24	23.02	23.64	38.79	40.95	16.98	19.55	31.31	34.12
Missing[a]	0.69	4.09	0.69	2.05	0.92	5.45	0.89	2.06	1.16	5.00	1.38	2.42
No current partner	4.42	3.64	1.64	3.07	4.42	3.64	1.64	3.07	4.42	3.64	1.64	3.07
B. FOR FEMALES												
Not before marriage	2.09	2.73	1.87	2.05	5.35	4.09	3.72	5.12	12.33	9.55	9.81	9.55
If engaged to be married	2.09	0.45	1.64	2.73	6.51	2.73	3.03	4.77	9.77	8.18	7.01	6.48
If in love and not engaged	18.61	18.64	9.35	9.89	31.86	34.09	24.07	15.69	39.31	40.00	31.07	26.96
If feel affection but not love	38.38	33.64	36.68	29.01	28.84	27.73	28.97	31.39	16.98	15.00	20.79	20.47
If both want it	33.95	36.82	47.89	51.19	22.33	22.27	37.15	37.54	15.78	18.64	28.27	31.05
Missing[a]	0.69	4.09	0.93	2.05	1.15	5.45	1.38	2.39	1.61	5.00	1.38	2.42
No current partner	4.42	3.64	1.64	3.07	4.42	3.64	1.64	3.07	4.42	3.64	1.64	3.07

[a] Respondent said that he or she didn't know partner well enough to answer.

Emotional Intimacy

Our measure of the quality or emotional intimacy of a relationship was discussed in Chapter 3. The respondent was given a card which listed seven types of partners or relationships and asked to classify his or her current relationship into one of these. Six were presented exactly as they are listed in table 7.2; the seventh was "paid sexual partner" and was not selected by any of our interviewees. The majority characterized the relationship as involving "emotional attachment" or "love"; 44 to 57 percent of the relationships were so characterized. While only 3 to 10 percent indicated that they were engaged, larger percentages (11 to 20) said they expected to marry their current partner. At the other end of the scale, 20 to 27 percent reported that their relationships were casual, in the sense of involving no emotional attachment, or only one or two dates.

An additional indicator of the intensity of the relationship is whether or not the couple is living together. This information was obtained in a series of questions asked about the person's living situation. We asked whether the respondent shared his or her "room or bedroom" with anyone; if he or she did, we than asked whether the roommate(s) was of the same or opposite sex. By subsample, 4.2 (SM), 6.4 (NM), 7.4 (SF), and 7.8 (NF) percent reported sharing with a member of the opposite sex. Of these 13 of the 18 student males, all 14 of the nonstudent men, 26 of the 32 student females, and 22 of the 23 nonstudent women reported a sexual relationship with their roommate. Incidentally, 11 respondents, 9 of them women, reported a sexual relationship with a roommate of the same gender.

Partner's Sexual Ideology

We assume that a person's sexual standards are the basis of his or her self-control. By implication, these standards should be the basis upon which that person attempts to exercise influence or social control over his or her partner's behavior. Thus, it is particularly important to know partners' standards. Again, we have the respondent's perception of his or her partner's attitudes, but that perception should be based at least partly on the partner's attempts to control the respondent's behavior.

We asked each person about his or her partner's sexual ideology, using the same format and assessing partner's standards separately for men and women. The results are presented in table 7.3. In these data, male respondents (SM, NM) are reporting their partner's (a female) ideology for males (section A of the table) and females (section B). Conversely, women are reporting their male partner's ideology for men (section A) and women (section B). Two comparisons can be made within the table. First, comparing a column in section A with the same column in section B indicates whether our respondents believed that their partners had different standards for men and women. For example, we can look at male students' responses to the question of partner's ideology concerning intercourse (column 9). The percentages in section A of the table indicate that almost 12 percent report that their partners believe that it is not acceptable behavior for males before marraige; 10 percent, that partners believe it is appropriate if engaged; and 37 percent, that it is acceptable if the couple is in love. The comparable figures from section B are 12, 10, and 39 respectively. Thus, these men generally indicate that their women partners have the same premarital standards for both genders. More generally, such comparisons indicate that the differences in reported partner's standards for men and for women are usually small. Our respondents do not perceive their partners as having differential standards. Again, this supports the conclusion that there is no longer a "double standard."

We can also compare reports of males concerning their partners with reports of females about their partners. Thus, we can compare males' responses concerning their female partners' ideology for men, with females' responses about their male partners' ideology for men. Looking again at standards for intercourse for males, males generally attribute less permissive attitudes to their partners than do females; 17 to 20 percent of the men reported that their partners believed coitus to be acceptable if both want it, whereas 31 to 34 percent of the women so characterized their partners' standards for men. A similar gender difference was found in the personal ideology of our respondents (see table 5.1), where females reported less permissive standards for both sexes than did men. Thus, our respondents seem to have accurately perceived that there are gender differences in premarital ideology; males are aware that their female partners are less permissive (for both sexes), while females perceive that their male partners are more permissive (for both sexes).

On the whole, all of our respondents characterized their partners as relatively permissive. The vast majority, 85 to 90 percent, reported that their partners believed intercourse to be acceptable before marriage. Also, our interviewees believed that their partners did differentially evaluate behavior on the basis of the quality of the relationship: as the intimacy of the behavior increases, the quality of the relationship necessary to render the behavior acceptable also increases. In these respects, the findings concerning reported partner's premarital ideology reflect the same patterns as reported personal ideology.

Again, for purposes of analysis, a Guttman scale was constructed for

TABLE 7.4. Characteristics of Guttman scale for partner's sexual ideology

	Partner's ideology for males				Partner's ideology for females			
	SM	NM	SF	NF	SM	NM	SF	NF
Coefficient of reproducibility	0.892	0.914	0.917	0.932	0.902	0.914	0.909	0.916
Minimal marginal reproducibility	0.358	0.359	0.409	0.428	0.365	0.370	0.387	0.399
Percentage of pure cases	96.76	97.27	94.66	94.88	97.45	97.27	93.97	95.54

partner's ideology. Table 7.4 indicates the characteristics of these scales. The differences between the coefficient of reproducibility and the minimal marginal reproducibility are uniformly very large, indicating that there is considerable, underlying unidimensionality in the responses. Again, the percentage of pure cases ranged from 94.0 to 97.4, which indicates that there are very few sets of responses which do not conform to the scale.

CHARACTERISTICS OF PARTNER AND RELATIONSHIP AND CURRENT BEHAVIOR

Our model emphasizes social influence and social control. In this perspective, partner and relationship characteristics would be especially relevant if they were associated with the exercise of control, that is, with differences in the individual's sexual behavior. One might expect partners who were older or of higher social class to be more successful in influencing the individual's activity than those who were younger or of lower relative class standing. Given that partners are relatively permissive, we would expect positive correlations between variables such as relative age and the couple's sexual intimacy.

The measures of current partner and relationship and current sexual behavior are listed in table 7.5; the correlations between them are presented in tables 7.6 through 7.9. In addition to these variables, those involving other partners are included in these tables, but discussion of them is deferred to a later section.

Characteristics of the Partner

There are low to moderate (0.16 to 0.30), significant correlations between partner's age and respondent's current behavior. For both sexes, those whose partners were relatively older were engaging in more intimate behavior with that person. This is not surprising; since our older respondents were relatively more sexually experienced, we expect to find the same relationship between partner's age and behavior. Therefore, relatively older partners are more likely to attempt to engage in intimate behaviors with respondents, and apparently are successful in influencing them to do so. There are no consistent differences between men and women or students and nonstudents in the strength of this association.

There is a significant positive correlation between relative social class of partner and behavior in three of our subsamples; among female students there is no association between the two. The positive correlation in the two male subsamples is a reversal of the relationship Ehrmann (1959) found between relative social class and intimacy among males. It is not clear that these correlations reflect a relationship between social class and behavior per se; there may well be a third factor which varies with both class and current behavior. One such factor is ideology. There are moderate, positive correlations (0.22 to 0.32) between partner's social class and his or her ideology in the same three subsamples. (We shall discuss later the strong association between partner's ideology and respondent's behavior with that person.) Thus, we are particularly interested in the regression of current behavior on these variables, since it indicates whether any relationship remains between partner's social class and current behavior, with controls for other variables.

There is a substantial correlation between rating of the partner's physical attractiveness and current sexual activity. Respondents who considered their partners more attractive were engaging in more intimate behavior with them. There are no consistent differences between males and females or students and nonstudents. Again, we cannot yet conclude that this association is valid; physical attractiveness is highly correlated with the emotional intimacy of the relationship (0.47 to 0.59) in all four subsamples, and it may be primarily the latter which independently relates to the extent of physical intimacy.

The likability and attractiveness ratings are highly interrelated (0.62 to 0.79). Since the latter correlates with current behavior, it is not surprising

TABLE 7.5. Variables pertaining to current partners and relationships

PART AGE—age of current partner
PART SES—social class of partner
ATTR—perceived attractiveness of partner
LIKE—perceived likability of partner
STILL—still dating current partner
LENGTH—length of current relationship
TIMES—number of times with current partner
INTIMACY—emotional intimacy of current relationship
PART IDEO M—partner's sexual ideology for males—Guttman score
PART IDEO F—partner's sexual ideology for females—Guttman score
OTHER—number of other persons dated in last six months
AV INTIMACY—average intimacy of other persons dated
OTHER INT—number of other persons dated with whom respondent had intercourse
CURRENT—Guttman score—current sexual behavior

that respondent's rating of his or partner's likability does also. These correlations are somewhat smaller than those between attractiveness and behavior but still sizable. It should be noted that both ratings of partner are closely associated with the intimacy of the relationship (0.47 to 0.61); the more intimate the relationship, the more highly the respondent evaluates the partner. This probably reflects a selection process in part; we would expect people to develop closer relationships primarily with people they like and find attractive. This may also reflect the operation of a cognitive consistency or dissonance reduction process; having developed a close relationship, one increases his or her evaluation of the partner.

Characteristics of the Relationship

The next group of measures in tables 7.6–7.9 are those concerning the relationship.

All three measures of temporal aspects are positively and substantially related to current sexual behavior. The largest correlations in each subsample are those between length of the relationship and behavior. The reader will recall that these relationships covered the entire range from less than one week to more than one year. Clearly, the longer the relationship, the more intimate the couple's sexual behavior. The number of times the couple has been together is also highly positively related to intimacy of their behavior. In two subsamples (NM and SF), the correlations between these are of almost the same magnitude as the length-behavior associations; in the other two, the times together–behavior correlations are of somewhat lower magnitude. There are no consistent differences in these correlations between genders or between student and nonstudent subsamples.

We indicated earlier that we expect a strong relationship between the quality of current relationship and current behavior. The data support this expectation, with the correlations between these variables ranging from 0.55 to 0.62; the greater the emotional intimacy of the relationship, the more intimate is the couple's sexual behavior. This relationship is among the largest we have found. There is also a very strong association between length of the relationship and its emotional intimacy (0.67 to 0.73); this implies that most of these relationships develop over time, becoming more emotionally intimate only as their duration increases. In terms of our measures, relationships whose duration is relatively short are not emotionally intimate ones.

We noted that the distributions of responses to the partner's ideology questions indicated that partners were reported to have very similar standards for men and women. This is also evident in the correlations between partner's ideology for males and for females which range from 0.96 to 1.00. Partner's ideology is also strongly related to current behavior;

TABLE 7.6. Correlations of characteristics of current relationships and current sexual behavior: student males

	PART AGE	PART SES	ATTR	LIKE	STILL	LENGTH	# TIMES	INTIMACY	PART IDEO M	PART IDEO F	# OTHER	AV INTIMACY	# OTHER INT	CURRENT
PART AGE	—													
PART SES	.293	—												
ATTR	.444	.461	—											
LIKE	.469	.429	.790	—										
STILL	.369	.392	.640	.682	—									
LENGTH	.191	.206	.437	.440	.536	—								
# TIMES	.086	.048	.217	.213	.324	.609	—							
INTIMACY	.268	.303	.590	.608	.624	.728	.526	—						
PART IDEO M	.279	.315	.364	.327	.304	.199	.114	.264	—					
PART IDEO F	.279	.315	.364	.327	.304	.199	.114	.264	1.00	—				
# OTHER	.094	.163	.167	.134	.177	-.110	-.107	-.048	.199	.199	—			
AV INTIMACY	.056	.157	.099	.072	.143	-.104	-.127	-.052	.139	.139	.596	—		
# OTHER INT	.001	.150	.098	.035	.175	-.088	-.023	-.071	.246	.246	.697	.532	—	
CURRENT	.202	.210	.401	.364	.521	.592	.472	.623	.530	.530	.097	.056	.178	—

TABLE 7.7. Correlations of characteristics of current relationships and current sexual behavior: nonstudent males

	PART AGE	PART SES	ATTR	LIKE	STILL	LENGTH	# TIMES	INTIMACY	PART IDEO M	PART IDEO F	# OTHER	AV INTIMACY	# OTHER INT	CURRENT
PART AGE	—													
PART SES	.216	—												
ATTR	.303	.470	—											
LIKE	.340	.365	.734	—										
STILL	.253	.417	.567	.645	—									
LENGTH	.157	.232	.311	.373	.403	—								
# TIMES	.097	.103	.203	.231	.283	.609	—							
INTIMACY	.173	.255	.528	.558	.538	.673	.545	—						
PART IDEO M	.228	.223	.349	.258	.288	.133	.111	.328	—					
PART IDEO F	.246	.222	.351	.256	.272	.141	.118	.324	.989	—				
# OTHER	.113	.124	.278	.216	.124	-.115	-.141	-.048	.280	.275	—			
AV INTIMACY	.134	.076	.177	.164	.042	-.204	-.173	-.075	.141	.145	.505	—		
# OTHER INT	.050	.064	.180	.150	.142	-.166	-.120	-.092	.315	.306	.756	.416	—	
CURRENT	.156	.148	.354	.351	.359	.436	.418	.554	.591	.608	.254	.037	.221	—

TABLE 7.8. Correlations of characteristics of current relationships and current sexual behavior: student females

	PART AGE	PART SES	ATTR	LIKE	STILL	LENGTH	# TIMES	INTIMACY	PART IDEO M	PART IDEO F	# OTHER	AV INTIMACY	# OTHER INT	CURRENT
PART AGE	—													
PART SES	.153	—												
ATTR	.213	.214	—											
LIKE	.288	.302	.619	—										
STILL	.254	.230	.447	.559	—									
LENGTH	.053	.077	.333	.330	.437	—								
# TIMES	.002	.033	.217	.208	.297	.658	—							
INTIMACY	.181	.130	.470	.500	.560	.706	.558	—						
PART IDEO M	.133	.077	.256	.211	.207	.087	.109	.173	—					
PART IDEO F	.143	.063	.269	.210	.210	.081	.106	.167	.974	—				
# OTHER	.085	.001	.075	.037	.002	−.215	−.268	−.209	.160	.158	—			
AV INTIMACY	−.010	.016	.053	.071	.019	−.247	−.316	−.220	.146	.150	.508	—		
# OTHER INT	−.104	−.031	.048	.016	.015	−.197	−.200	−.161	.278	.285	.589	.572	—	
CURRENT	.175	−.004	.348	.288	.365	.505	.498	.611	.467	.460	−.096	−.080	.106	—

TABLE 7.9. Correlations of characteristics of current relationships and current sexual behavior: nonstudent females

	PART AGE	PART SES	ATTR	LIKE	STILL	LENGTH	# TIMES	INTIMACY	PART IDEO M	PART IDEO F	# OTHER	AV INTIMACY	# OTHER INT	CURRENT
PART AGE	—													
PART SES	.313	—												
ATTR	.388	.423	—											
LIKE	.391	.372	.709	—										
STILL	.475	.318	.620	.613	—									
LENGTH	.158	.137	.353	.347	.430	—								
# TIMES	.033	−.020	.252	.204	.246	.636	—							
INTIMACY	.260	.178	.515	.531	.583	.734	.606	—						
PART IDEO M	.324	.246	.395	.317	.392	.272	.220	.297	—					
PART IDEO F	.332	.252	.374	.300	.400	.313	.174	.260	.963	—				
# OTHER	.266	.154	.127	.113	.167	−.132	−.135	−.120	.207	.180	—			
AV INTIMACY	.136	.196	.111	.024	.067	−.189	−.146	−.216	.204	.207	.522	—		
# OTHER INT	.169	.124	.120	.047	.085	−.126	−.103	−.173	.266	.271	.686	.618	—	
CURRENT	.297	.203	.464	.368	.414	.524	.455	.586	.613	.589	.004	.042	.175	—

the magnitude of the association ranges from 0.46 to 0.61. There is a tendency for the correlation to be larger among nonstudents (0.59 to 0.61) than students (0.46 to 0.53), which suggests that partner's standards are a more important aspect of current behavior among nonstudents.

It should be noted that while both length of the relationship and its intimacy are associated with reported partner's ideology, these correlations are much smaller than those we have considered so far. In particular, length of relationship is only weakly related to ideology (0.08 to 0.31); the correlation between these is larger than 0.20 in only one subsample. Thus, there is not a strong tendency for respondents to report more permissive partner's ideology as the duration of the relationship increases. This provides some evidence that reports of partner's premarital standards do not simply reflect a tendency on the part of respondents to perceive partners as more permissive as a function of length of the relationship and the associated level of physical intimacy in which the couple has engaged. The correlation between emotional intimacy and partner's ideology is somewhat larger, ranging from 0.17 to 0.33; this indicates that at most 10 percent of the variance in each is accounted for by the other.

Relative Influence

Table 7.10 presents the results of the regression analysis of partner and relationship characteristics on current behavior.

Characteristics of Partner

The regression coefficients of the four partner characteristics do not indicate any consistent relationship between them and the individual's current sexual activity. The coefficient of partner's relative age is significant only in the nonstudent female subsample. In this group, those whose partners were older reported more intimate behavior; however, this coefficient is relatively small.

The results also indicate that there is no systematic, independent relationship between relative social class of partner and current activity. Again, the coefficient is statistically significant in only one of the four subsamples and quite small. It indicates a negative relationship, that is, that student women engage in somewhat more intimate behavior with men whom they report as relatively lower in class standing than themselves. In contrast, Ehrmann (1959), in data collected 25 years ago, found a positive relationship between intimacy and social class of companion among females.

We noted earlier the high correlations between ratings of partner's physical attractiveness and likability, and we could not conclude that either was independently related to other variables. The regression results indicate that neither is consistently related to sexual behavior. The coefficients associated with each are significant in only one subsample. Rated likability is negatively associated with sexual intimacy among student males; physical attractiveness is positively associated with sexual behavior among nonstudent females.

The fact that none of the four partner measures is significantly associated with current behavior in more than one subsample indicates the absence of any general relationship between these variables. In addition, it makes it difficult to assess the meaningfulness of the isolated relationships which were found. It is possible, for example, that partner's physical attractiveness is an aspect of women's sexual behavior, but that it is less significant in a college environment. On the other hand, it is also possible that attractiveness is not generally important to women, and that its association with behavior in the NF subsample is unique to that group.

In general, then, these partner variables are not associated with variation in effective control over sexual intimacy. Our model did not anticipate that they would be; the partner variables were included because some associations involving them had been found in previous studies.

Characteristics of Relationship

Of the three temporal measures, length of relationship is significantly and consistently associated with behavior. Thus, the longer the relationship, the more intimate the behavior in which the couple engages. The regression coefficient is particularly large in the student male group. When duration is controlled, as it is in this analysis, there is no significant relationship between number of times together or frequency of interaction and behavior.

TABLE 7.10. Stepwise regression of characteristics
of current partners and relationships on current sexual behavior

	SM	NM	SF	NF
PART AGE				.1094[a]
PART SES			−.0741[a]	
ATTR				.1395[b]
LIKE	−.1277[b]			
STILL	.1675[c]			
LENGTH	.2809[d]	.1730[a]	.1694[d]	.1939[c]
# TIMES				
INTIMACY	.4063[d]	.4606[d]	.5213[d]	.3831[d]
PART IDEO M				
PART IDEO F				
# OTHER		.1750[a]	−.1153[b]	−.2436[d]
AV INTIMACY				
# OTHER INT	.2071[d]	.1598[a]	.2914[d]	.3978[d]

[a] $p < .05$
[b] $p < .01$
[c] $p < .005$
[d] $p < .001$

The correlations with frequency reported earlier occurred because of the strong relationship between duration and intensity. The third temporal variable, whether the respondent was still seeing his or her partner, is significantly related to behavior in only one subsample. Among student males, continuing relationships were associated with more intimate behavior than terminated ones were. The smallest percentage of continuing relationships (71.9 percent) was reported by this group; however, the figure for nonstudent males is only slightly larger (72.3 percent) and the regression coefficient is not significant in this group.

In general, the strongest association is found between intimacy of the relationship and current behavior. The coefficients range from 0.383 to 0.521; all are substantial and highly significant. Thus, our expectation that this variable would be closely related to behavior is borne out by the regression analysis. The magnitude of these coefficients indicates that a substantial amount of the variance in current sexual behavior is accounted for by the emotional quality of the relationship, which is what we would expect if the latter is a primary basis for exercising control over the former.

Finally, the coefficients indicate that partner's ideology is not independently associated with current sexual activity. We noted earlier that there were moderate correlations between reported ideology and emotional intimacy (0.17 to 0.33); these correlations apparently produced the significant bivariate correlations reported in tables 7.6–7.9 between partner's ideology and behavior. When we control for intimacy in the regression framework, this relationship is no longer significant. More generally, we have seen that several variables are related to both intimacy and behavior; the results in table 7.10 indicate that in such cases the primary independent association is between intimacy and behavior and that the other correlations are spurious.

We will discuss the relationships between the last three variables listed in table 7.10 and current behavior in a later section.

THE DYNAMICS OF SEXUAL INTERACTIONS

To our knowledge, Ehrmann (1959) is the only researcher who has inquired into the dynamics of premarital sexual interactions. For each occurrence of a sexual activity reported by the individual, he asked (1) whether the male or female initiated it (which he termed "positive control"), and (2) if the couple did not engage in more intimate activity on that occasion, was it because there was no opportunity, or because the male, female, or both would not ("negative control"). Ehrmann found that both men and women consistently identified the male as the initiator; this was true for the substantial majority (66 to 87 percent) of all dates involving male active behaviors, e.g., breast and genital fondling and intercourse, as well as for a majority (53 to 76 percent) of those involving female active genital fondling (though the total number of such dates was relatively small). For dates on which the couple stopped with a given behavior, he found that "neither tried to go further" and "female would not go further" were the reasons given for about seven out of ten occasions by females. For breast and genital fondling, the reason given most frequently by both sexes was that the female would not go further. Ehrmann concluded that, in general, males were the initiators of premarital sexual activity, and females or both controlled whether the couple went further than a particular behavior.

Given the perspective of this research, we wanted to obtain data about interactional dynamics. Such information allows us to study directly the exercise of influence and control. We employed a format similar to Ehrmann's. Each respondent who reported engaging in a given behavior on one or more occasions with the current partner was asked a series of questions about those occasions. We asked first who "generally" initiated the behavior; we could not obtain precise figures since some couples had engaged in a behavior hundreds of times over several years. In addition, we were interested in our respondents' perceptions of motivation and so we asked two additional questions: "Who wanted to do this the most?" and "Why do you think you engaged in this behavior?" We then inquired whether there had been occasions on which the couple did not engage in more intimate behavior; if there were, we asked Ehrmann's "negative control" question, whether they stopped because of situational factors or because the male, female, or neither wanted to go further.

In considering Ehrmann's question, we were struck by the fact that he did not consider the achievement of orgasm as a possible reason for not progressing to more intimate behavior. He did so indirectly with respect to female active genital fondling and intercourse, since he did not ask the negative control items for these behaviors, but he did ask these questions for male active genital fondling. We felt that it was important to consider orgasm as a possible reason for not going further than genital fondling, apposition, or oral-genital activity (Ehrmann did not include this last behavior in his scale). Accordingly, we coded "stopped because of orgasm" as a separate answer; we also asked on what percentage of the time the male, female, or both (for apposition and intercourse) experienced an orgasm.

The patterns of responses to these items are very similar across the nine behaviors included in our scale. Accordingly, we will not present the results for each behavior. Table 7.11 presents the distribution of responses for male and female active genital fondling; since there were no substantial differences between students and nonstudents, we present only the responses of our student subsamples. We selected these behaviors (1) because they are fairly intimate and yet substantial numbers of our respondents had engaged in them (compared to oral-genital contact, for example, which less than half reported on the current behavior measure), and (2) because Ehrmann presents comparable data. The percentages in the table are based on the number who reported engaging in the behavior, not on the total sample size.

Our results indicate that most male active genital fondling is initiated by men, whereas female active behavior is initiated by women. While this may seem obvious, it contrasts sharply with Ehrmann's results in which men were the primary initiators regardless of which sex was active. Another finding in our data is congruent with Ehrmann's results; relative to men, females are somewhat more likely to report that the male initiates behavior. About 6 percent more women reported male initiation of male active fondling; the difference increases to 13 percent in reports of female

TABLE 7.11. Responses to detailed questions on genital fondling: students (in percent)

	Male active		Female active	
	SM (N = 271)	SF (N = 278)	SM (N = 257)	SF (N = 273)
Who initiated it				
Male	78.23	84.17	8.56	21.24
Female	5.53	1.44	78.21	64.47
Both	16.23	14.38	13.23	14.29
Who wanted it the most				
Male	35.05	33.81	14.78	24.18
Female	13.65	6.12	35.80	12.45
Both	51.29	60.07	49.41	63.37
Reason for engaging in genital fondling				
Respondent oriented (I)	18.82	18.70	19.84	10.99
Partner oriented	9.23	6.84	7.00	19.41
Couple oriented (we)	61.99	64.71	63.04	61.91
Other	9.96	9.75	10.12	7.69
Reason for stopping with this behavior				
Situation	28.04	24.10	30.47	27.84
Male	3.69	0.36	3.91	1.09
Female	12.91	17.62	6.64	11.72
Neither wanted to go further	24.72	28.06	26.95	29.30
Because of orgasm	1.11	0.00	1.56	1.46
Didn't stop	29.52	29.86	30.47	28.57
Percentage of times orgasm experienced				
0	17.62	29.64	26.07	24.18
1–35	39.84	34.99	41.24	33.33
36–75	24.14	24.29	17.89	17.22
76–100	18.39	11.05	14.78	25.27

active genital contact. Relatively few respondents indicated that the behavior was jointly initiated; across all behaviors, only 5 to 15 percent answered "both" to this question, except for intercourse where 50 to 60 percent gave this response.

Responses to the question "who wanted it most" were quite different. Here, "both" was the most frequent answer given by both men and women for both male and female active behaviors. Our respondents thus attributed equal motivation or desire to the two participants; the initiator is seen as acting in a context of shared motivation rather than out of personal desire. Secondarily, about one-third of both sexes indicated that the male wanted male active genital fondling the most; while men similarly perceived the female as wanting female active activity, women are much less likely to perceive themselves as having the primary motivation.

In our pre-test interviews, we did not specify categories for responses to the question "Why do you think you engaged in this behavior?" Answers were recorded as completely as possible. On the basis of these spontaneous replies, we developed a number of categories which seemed to include the vast majority of specific answers given. Five of these reflected respondent-centered reasons: I was curious, wanted to, wanted to prove my love, to prove I am a man/woman, and I enjoyed it/it felt good. Four additional categories were partner-centered: partner wanted it, wanted me to prove love, convinced me it was appropriate, and enjoyed it. Finally, four were couple-centered: mutual curiosity, because we're in love, because we like each other, and mutual physical desire. During the interviewing, the interviewer recorded the response to this question and selected the most appropriate category; during coding, the coders verified the interviewer's categorization of the response. For purposes of presentation, table 7.11 reports the percentage in each of the three general categories instead of the distributions across the 13 specific ones.

About 60 percent of our respondents reported couple-oriented reasons for the behavior. More specifically, about 35 percent indicated mutual desires and 25 percent gave mutual liking (15 percent) or love (10 percent) as the reason. Smaller percentages (11 to 20 percent) gave personally oriented reasons, and fewer gave partner-centered ones.

Regarding what Ehrmann refers to as "negative control," two reasons for not going further predominate in our respondents' answers; "neither wanted to go further" and situational factors which prevented it are given almost equally often. Female control is not as important in our data as it was in Ehrmann's; he found that when couples did not go beyond male active genital fondling, "female would not" was the reason given in almost half of these instances. He also found that situational factors were relatively infrequently cited by his interviewees, whereas ours gave this response a substantial portion of the time. Thus, the availability of appropriate physical settings seems to be relatively more important to our respondents, and the exercise of control by women less frequently responsible, for limiting physical intimacy. This is quite consistent with our findings discussed earlier, particularly that our female respondents had much more permissive premarital ideologies and were much more sexually experienced than the women who participated in Ehrmann's research.

The last section in table 7.11 presents the frequency of orgasm experienced as a result of genital fondling. We have summarized the specific percentages given by respondents into the four categories included in the table. Relatively few couples consistently engaged in genital fondling to orgasm. Eleven to 15 percent reported that the passive partner (male in female active and female in male active) experienced orgasm on more than 5 percent of the occasions on which this activity occurred. It is interesting to note that the passive partner was less likely to report orgasms as frequently as the active partner. More than half of our respondents reported orgasm 35 percent of the time or less, and 18 to 30 percent had not experienced orgasm from this activity with their current partner. Finally, it should be noted that orgasm was rarely given as a primary reason for stopping.

Table 7.12 presents the same data for intercourse with the exception of the reason for stopping. Our student respondents were much more likely to indicate that both initiated this behavior; over half of them gave this response. Most of the others reported that the male generally initiated it. We cannot compare these results with Ehrmann's, since he did not provide "both" as an alternative in his initiation question. Also, three-quarters of both sexes responded "both" to the question of who wanted coitus most, a larger percentage than did to this question for genital fondling. The same emphasis on the shared or joint nature of intercourse occurs in the reasons given for engaging in the behavior, where more than three-quarters of the responses were couple oriented; 40 percent gave mutual physical desire as the reason and 30 percent cited mutual affection or love. Relatively few gave person-centered reasons, and only 6 out of 212 women gave partner-centered replies.

Immediately following these questions in the interview, we asked each respondent what percentage of the time he or she and his or her partner experienced orgasm. For presentation here, the responses were summarized into the four categories used earlier; these results appear at the bottom of table 7.12. The data indicate that both males and females reported that the vast majority of males (87 percent) experienced orgasm on more than 75 percent of the occasions that they had intercourse. More than half of both sexes reported that the male had an orgasm at least 95 percent of the time. At the other extreme, virtually none of our respondents reported that the male had never had an orgasm on these occasions. The data concerning females indicate much greater variability in frequency of orgasm. Between 39 and 52 percent reported that the female experienced orgasm more than 75 percent of the time; more than 35 percent reported frequencies between 36 and 75 percent; and 10 to 25 percent reported frequencies of less than 35 percent. There is a consistent difference between men's and women's reports of female orgasmic frequency, with men giving larger estimates than women.

In summary, our data on sexual interactions indicate that our respondents perceived their sexual activity in terms of the couple rather than in terms of themselves or their partners. Although they usually identified the male or female as initiating male and female active behaviors respectively, they characterized the various sexual behaviors as jointly wanted, and gave mutual physical desire, affection, or love as the reasons for engaging in them. Similarly, control in the sense of not engaging in more intimate behavior was perceived as due to situational factors or mutual desire not to go further. Comparisons with Ehrmann's results indicate that this emphasis on mutuality is greater now than it was at the time of his research, particularly in the area of negative control, where he found

TABLE 7.12. Responses to detailed questions on intercourse: students (in percent)

	SM (N = 228)	SF (N = 212)
Who initiated it		
Male	42.10	37.74
Female	4.39	2.36
Both	53.51	59.91
Who wanted it the most		
Male	17.54	14.15
Female	6.14	1.89
Both	76.32	83.96
Reason for engaging in intercourse		
Respondent oriented (I)	14.91	13.21
Partner oriented	0.00	2.83
Couple oriented (we)	77.63	79.72
Other	7.45	4.24
Percentage of times orgasm experienced		
Male		
0	0.00	0.47
1–35	2.19	2.83
36–75	10.53	8.96
76–100	87.28	87.74
Female		
0	1.32	10.85
1–35	9.25	14.62
36–75	37.00	35.38
76–100	52.42	39.15

that the female played a much more significant role. Mutual physical desire was the single most frequent reason given for engaging in the more intimate sexual behaviors, which indicates that this is perceived as a legitimate or valid motivation by our respondents. The other most frequent reason, that they engaged in the behavior because of joint affection or love, reflects the importance of sexual ideology; substantial numbers of respondents believed that it is appropriate to engage in intercourse when two people are in love, and this in itself perhaps becomes one reason why they engage in this behavior when they find themselves in such a relationship. Thus, there is little evidence in our data on interactional dynamics that sexual behavior is the result of unilateral attempts at influence and control. In general, it is both initiated and stopped in a context of shared motivation.

OTHER PARTNERS

Questions Employed

Following the detailed questions on current partner, relationship, and the couple's sexual interactions, we asked each respondent whether he or she had been out with anyone else in the past six months. From 59 to 72 percent of the interviewees had dated one or more other persons; of these respondents, about 60 percent had been out with one, two, or three other persons. Thus, of the total number interviewed, approximately one-third had dated only one person, an additional 40 percent had been out with two to four persons in the preceding six months, and the remainder had dated more than four people.

We asked the respondents to characterize the nature of each of these other relationships using the emotional intimacy scale. In general, most of these other relationships were relatively casual. Only 1 or 2 percent reported that one of these partners was someone to whom the respondent was engaged; an additional 2 to 3 percent indicated that one of these was someone the respondent expected to marry. About 10 percent reported that they were in love with one or more of their other partners. The remainder were characterized as persons to whom the respondent was emotionally attached, or had dated without emotional attachment. Thus, the decision to ask detailed questions about the person most recently seen before the interview did result in our not obtaining detailed information about the most intimate relationship the respondent had been involved in from, at most, approximately 100 of our respondents (out of 1,376; about 7 percent). We were cognizant of this potential loss of information but felt that focusing on the partner most recently seen would facilitate accuracy of recall on the part of respondents and more reasonably represent the range of relationships in which they were engaged.

For purposes of analyses, we wanted a summary measure of the quality of these other relationships. Accordingly, we computed the average intimacy for the respondents' other partners. If a respondent reported only one other, it received the appropriate score; if there was more than one, we added the scores for the relationship category of each (from one to seven, with seven being someone to whom the respondent had been engaged) and divided by the total number of relationships.

Finally, we asked whether the interviewee had had coitus with any of these other partners. Of the total sample, 22 to 31 percent reported that they had; half of these had had intercourse with only one of these other persons. Thus, only 10 to 15 percent reported that they had engaged in intercourse with more than one or two persons in the six months prior to the interview.

Correlations with Current Behavior

We included three measures in our analysis of the respondent's current behavior: number of other persons dated, average intimacy of these relationships, and number of others with whom respondent had had intercourse. The correlations are included in tables 7.6–7.9. In general, neither number of other persons dated nor the average intimacy of those relationships is correlated significantly with current behavior. The only exception occurs among the nonstudent males, where number of other dates is positively associated with current behavior. The lack of significant correlations between average intimacy and behavior reflects the fact that most other relationships reported were relatively casual, as previously mentioned.

The number of other persons with whom the respondent had had intercourse in the six months before the interview is significantly related to current behavior. Those who reported relatively more intimate behavior with their "current partner" more frequently had engaged in intercourse with one or more other persons. These correlations are relatively small in magnitude (0.11 to 0.22), so this association is not substantial.

Relative Influence

These variables were included in the regression analyses reported in table 7.10, to determine whether they were independently related to current behavior.

The regression coefficients indicate that the number of other persons dated in the past six months is significantly associated with current behavior in three of the four subsamples. In both female groups, the coefficients are negative (−0.115 and −0.244), indicating that those who were dating one or more others were engaging in less intimate behavior with their "current partner." Thus, women who are involved in one physically intimate relationship (as measured by current behavior) are less likely to be going out with other men. Among males, the coefficient is significant for only one of the two groups (NM) and is positive; in this subsample, men who were engaging in more intimate current behavior were more likely to be dating other women.

The coefficients for average intimacy of respondents' other relationships are not significant. However, the number of other persons with whom the person had had intercourse is consistently and positively associated with current sexual behavior. Such an association seems to indicate consistency in sexual behavior across relationships, so that those persons reporting more intimate behavior with current partner are more likely to report having had intercourse with one or more other persons in the past six months. This seems to be inconsistent with our earlier results; note that average intimacy of those other relationships is not related to behavior, in contrast to the substantial association between intimacy of relationship and sexual activity with current partner. This finding also seems in conflict with the finding of a negative association between number of others dated and current behavior for women.

OTHER BEHAVIORS

Our interest in behavior was primarily in heterosexual activity in dyadic relationships. Since we hoped to obtain representative samples of young people, both students and nonstudents, we did want to use the opportunity to estimate the frequency of two other activities, homosexual behavior and group experiences, specifically sexual activities involving three or more persons. Accordingly, we included two questions toward the end of the interview, immediately after the questions on current partner and behavior and on other partners and relationships.

The question regarding homosexual experience asked whether the respondent had ever participated in genital fondling, apposition, oral-genital contact, or intercourse with a person of the same sex. The percentages responding "yes" were 7.7 percent of the student and 17.3 percent of the nonstudent males, and 4.0 percent of the student and 7.5 percent of the nonstudent females. With the exception of the nonstudent male percentage, the lifetime incidence of these homosexual activities is small. Generally, these frequencies are too small to allow any substantive analysis of differences between respondents who did and did not report these behaviors. It is possible, of course, that these percentages are biased, that some who had engaged in these behaviors were unwilling to report them. This seems relatively unlikely since (1) there was no evidence of differential reporting of heterosexual behavior (see Appendix II) and (2) these questions came at the very end of the interview, when rapport was presumably high.

The group experience question asked whether the respondent had ever participated in activities involving three or more persons "simultaneously providing sexual stimulation for each other." The reported frequencies by subsample are 6.1 (SM), 16.8 (NM), 3.7 (SF), and 3.4 (NF) percent. Here, the incidence reported by females is smaller than that reported by males. As in the case of reported homosexual activity, the frequency among nonstudent males is about 10 percent larger than among the other three groups. On both of these measures, these men were more sexually experienced. The results presented in Chapter 4 for lifetime intercourse also indicated somewhat greater experience in this group; there we noted that male nonstudents reported relatively larger numbers of intercourse experiences and coital partners than did the student males. With the exception of this group, reported incidence of group sexual activity is quite low.

We analyzed the data to determine the extent to which those who had engaged in homosexual activity had also engaged in group activities. The results indicate virtually no overlap; of the 200 respondents who reported either activity, only 29 said they had participated in both.

Thus, under the assumption that their reports are accurate, very few of our respondents had ever engaged in sexual activities with a member of the same sex or in groups. In contrast to the relatively high incidence of various dyadic heterosexual activities, the incidence of these variant expressions of sexuality is quite low.

SUMMARY

The data in this chapter indicate a pattern in heterosexual dating. Most respondents in these samples were dating an attractive, likable, never-married partner of the same age and social class. There is relatively little variance on these characteristics of the partner. The length of the relationship and emotional intimacy varied, although the majority of relationships had been ongoing for at least six months and were characterized by emotional attachment or love.

While most respondents were involved in long-term, emotionally intimate relationships, these relationships were not characterized by exclusivity. Most respondents had dated someone else during the preceding six months. These additional relationships were generally casual and about one-quarter involved sexual intercourse.

The relationship variables are more strongly and independently related to current sexual behavior than are characteristics of the partner. The length of the relationship and its emotional intimacy are related to sexual activity in all subsamples. Additionally, for those having had coitus in other relationships, current behavior was more intimate. Thus, there seems to be a subsample of individuals who are sexually active with a number of people.

The results in this chapter support our assumption that one important aspect of premarital sexual activity is the emotional quality of the relationship. We noted in Chapter 2 that the logic of extant measures of individual standards implied that the quality or emotional intimacy of the relationship is an important determinant of behavior. The individual's rating of intimacy has one of the strongest associations with current behavior, both in correlation and regression analyses, of any variable we have considered. This is a major finding, partly because this association has often been neglected in past work. We also found that the longer a relationship has existed, the more intimate the behavior. This indicates that sexual expression is more likely in long-term than in more casual relationships. Finally, in contrast to some earlier studies, we found no independent association between partner's social characteristics, especially class, and individual behavior. Again, the finding that all of these results apply to nonstudents as well as students substantially broadens our knowledge about premarital sexuality.

8

The Determinants
of Current Sexuality

IN CHAPTERS 5, 6, and 7, we presented data concerning the relationships between several sets of variables and the individual's personal ideology and current sexual behavior. We have seen that various aspects of parental attitudes, sexual experience, respondent's characteristics, and peer and partner influence are associated with sexual attitudes and behavior. In general, these results support the conceptual model discussed in Chapter 2 and summarized in figure 2.2. In those chapters, we considered each set by itself; it remains to consider them simultaneously to determine which of these aspects are independently related to current sexuality. We again employ regression analysis and include all of the variables which earlier regression analyses have shown to be associated with either ideology or behavior or both. The results of this analysis also serve as a convenient summary of the material in the last three chapters. The first half of the chapter discusses the variables which were found to be independently related to sexual ideology; the second half focuses on the variables associated with current behavior.

IDEOLOGY

Table 8.1 presents the results of the regressions of the variables discussed earlier on sexual ideology. We did not include current partner and relationship variables in this analysis. We assume that the individual brings an ideology to his or her current relationships. The omission of partner and relationship measures is certainly justified for those respondents whose relationships had begun shortly before the interview; it is more problematic

177

for respondents whose "curent" relationship had existed for the preceding year or more.

In table 8.1, we have included only those variables which were associated with significant regression coefficients in one or more of the subsamples. Thus, a variable which appears in an earlier regression table but is not included here was not associated with ideology in this final analysis.

Parental Characteristics

Of the various parental attitude variables, only parental ideology is consistently related to the respondent's sexual standards (see table 6.3). In this overall analysis, it is the perceptions of the attitudes of the same-sex parent that are significantly and independently associated with the

TABLE 8.1. Final regression model of personal sexual ideology

	Standardized regression coefficients			
	SM	NM	SF	NF
Background and parental characteristics				
Parental attitudes				
Father's understanding of respondent			$-.0939^b$	
Evaluation of sex education from mother				$-.1727^d$
Father's sexual ideology	$.1816^d$	$.2167^c$		
Mother's sexual ideology			$.1842^d$	$.1431^c$
Sources of standards				
Mother as source of moral attitudes		$-.2113^c$	$-.1203^c$	
Female friends as source of moral attitudes		$.2346^d$	$.0842^a$	
Self-generated moral attitudes	$.1101^a$			
Sexual experience				
Ever lifetime intercourse	$.3872^d$			
Relationship with first partner	$-.1932^a$			
Number of lifetime intercourse partners		$.2374^d$		
Number of lifetime intercourse experiences			$.1275^c$	
Respondent characteristics				
Religious attendance	$-.2454^d$	$-.2234^c$	$-.2387^c$	$-.1340^d$
Religiosity				$-.1626^c$
Role behavior scale			$.1816^d$	
Peer influences				
Percentage of females engaging in fondling a male's genitals	$.1575^c$			$.1411^b$
Number of friends engaging in breast fondling			$.3066^d$	$.2358^d$
Number of friends engaging in intercourse				$.2404^d$
Multiple correlation coefficient	.5918	.5833	.7429	.7383
Corrected coefficient of determination	.3411	.3248	.5434	.5339

$^a p < .01$
$^b p < .005$
$^c p < .001$
$^d p < .0001$

respondent's sexual ideology. All four coefficients are positive, indicating that more permissive standards among young people are associated with fathers and mothers having more permissive attitudes. The results discussed in Chapter 6 indicated that the value of sex education received from parents was related to ideology in three of the subsamples. The present analysis indicates that when all of these variables are included simultaneously, there is an independent association between these measures in only one, the nonstudent female group. It is negative, which indicates that more adequate parental instruction is related to less permissive ideologies among these women.

Most of the measures of the quality of the relationship with parents do not seem to be independently associated with the respondent's attitudes. The one exception is the father's understanding, which is negatively associated with ideology only among student females.

Sources

Table 6.3 indicated a number of relationships between various persons as primary sources of moral information and the respondent's sexual ideology. Table 8.1 indicates that when all of the variables are included, the measures of the importance of sources are less consistently related to standards. Mother as a source is associated with attitudes in two groups (NM and SF); both coefficients are negative, indicating that respondents who rated maternal influence as more important had less permissive ideologies. The generality of this relationship is limited, however, since it is not found in the other two subsamples.

The earlier results also indicated a substantial relationship between peers (both friends and lovers) as sources and permissive premarital standards. The present analysis indicates that the importance of neither male friends nor lovers is associated with ideology. There are significant positive coefficients for female friends as sources in two subsamples, indicating that those who rated them more important as sources had more permissive attitudes. The coefficient is substantial and highly significant among nonstudent males and smaller among student females.

A final relationship involving sources appeared for the first time in this analysis. We included "self-generated" as a source of moral attitudes in our list of potential sources. It was not related to ideology in our earlier analyses but is associated with sexual standards among student males in the present one.

Thus, there are no consistent relationships between the importance of various sources and respondent's premarital standards. Those associations which are found may reflect genuine differences in experience between the four subsamples, but it is not obvious what these differences may be. Alternatively, the character of the data may vary enough to cause some of these relationships to appear in some subsamples but not others.

Sexual Experience

The earlier analyses (see table 6.9) indicated a substantial relationship between whether the respondent had ever had intercourse and his or her ideology. The regression coefficients ranged from 0.25 to 0.89; they were substantially larger than the coefficients associated with number of coital experiences and number of coital partners. The present results are quite different. Here, a different measure of experience is associated with premarital standards in each of three subsamples.

The "ever intercourse" measure is associated with ideology only among student males. Its coefficient is the largest of those for ideology in this group and indicates that this is the variable which is most highly associated with standards. Among nonstudent males, it is number of partners which is associated with attitudes. This group reported larger numbers of partners than the other three subsamples. Thus, there was greater variation on this measure for this group. Since the number of partners was highly correlated with the other measures of experience (see tables 6.5–6.8), it is not surprising that this variable is significantly associated with standards in the present analysis, instead of the other experience variables. Among student females, it is the number of intercourse experiences which is significantly related to sexual attitudes. All of these coefficients are positive, meaning that those with more sexual experience had more permissive ideologies. It is interesting to note that none of the experience measures are related to standards among nonstudent females.

There is also one new relationship in this set of variables. The nature of the relationship with the first coital partner, which was not significantly associated with standards in earlier analyses, is significantly related to ideology among student males. The coefficient is negative, indicating that the more intimate that relationship, the less permissive one's premarital standards. In effect, this indicates that the less permissive these men had been with respect to their first partner, the less permissive they were at the time of the interview. This is a logical relationship; again, its generality is limited by the fact that it occurs in only one subsample.

Respondent Characteristics

The substantial relationship between religion and sexual ideology reported in Chapter 6 is confirmed by the present regression analysis. In all four subsamples, there are substantial, negative coefficients for religious attendance: those who attended religious services more frequently had less permissive premarital standards. While the coefficients are smaller in magnitude for both student samples compared to those reported in table 6.9, they are larger in both nonstudent groups than those reported earlier. The respondent's self-rating of religiosity is associated with ideology in only one of the four subsamples, nonstudent females. This coefficient is also negative, meaning that those who considered themselves more religious had less permissive standards.

We included in this analysis all of the sociopsychological measures discussed in Chapter 5. The results reported there indicated relatively few and inconsistent associations between ideology and perceived morality and social desirability, self-esteem, body image, internal-external control, and the role definition measure (see table 5.10). Only one of these measures, definition of gender roles, is associated with premarital standards in this analysis, and the coefficient is significant in only one subsample (SF). In this group, women with more egalitarian attitudes toward gender roles also had a more permissive ideology.

Peer Influences

In the discussion of peer influences in Chapter 6, we found that the various measures of perceived behavior, both of age peers in general and of one's five best friends, were not substantially nor consistently associated with ideology (see table 6.15). That conclusion is supported by the present analysis. Of the four measures of perception of behavior of age peers, only the perceived incidence of female fondling of male genitals is significantly associated with standards in the analysis reported in table 8.1. This association is found in two of the four subsamples (SM and NF) and is positive in both. Perceptions of the number out of the five best friends of the same sex who engage in various behaviors are also inconsistently related to premarital attitudes. In both female groups, the number of friends who engage in breast fondling is positively associated with permissiveness; in the nonstudent female subsample, the number of friends who engage in intercourse is also significantly related to standards. These results indicate that the ideology of nonstudent women is associated with their perception of peers' behavior and thus, is possibly influenced by their friends' activities. The relationship between peer behavior measures and standards is much less consistent for the other three subsamples.

The regression analyses in table 6.15 identified friends' expectations for the individual's behavior as the major variable associated with ideology. This variable is not included in table 8.1. When we included it in the present analyses, we again obtained regression coefficients of 0.60 to 0.71 for friends' expectations; this relationship was so strong that it eliminated most or all of the other significant associations indicated in table 8.1. This reflects the fact that those other variables, e.g., parents' ideology, religious attendance, and the measures of lifetime sexual experiences, are all highly related to both personal ideology and friends' expectations. When the latter is included, it is so strong that it eliminates the association of ideology with the other variables. Thus, friends' expectations are highly associated with one's own ideology, in addition to the variables discussed above.

The last two rows in table 8.1 indicate two statistics which reflect the overall strength of the associations found in the regression analyses. The first is the multiple correlation coefficient, which is the correlation between all of the various "independent" variables and the dependent variable, in this case sexual ideology. The second is the corrected coefficient of determination; as is true in the two-variable situations discussed earlier, this is the square of the correlation and indicates the amount of variance in the dependent variable which is accounted for or explained by the independent variables. These coefficients are of different magnitudes for the male and female subsamples. For males, the coefficients are 0.34 and 0.32, indicating that about one-third of the variation in men's personal ideology is accounted for by the variables included in the analysis. For women, the coefficients are substantially larger and indicate that 53 or 54 percent of the variation in their standards is accounted for by these variables. Thus, we have identified some of the major factors which are associated with premarital ideology or permissiveness, particularly for women.

When we included friends' expectations in these analyses, while the other relationships generally became nonsignificant, the coefficients of determination increased substantially, especially among men. The values obtained ranged from 0.59 to 0.68.

In summary, there are four factors which are strongly and consistently related to the respondents' premarital sexual standards. By far the most substantial association is between the expectations of their best friends and their own ideology. More permissive expectations by friends are highly associated with more permissive personal standards. Secondarily, and to a considerable extent associated with the first, there are three other relationships. The ideology of the same-sex parent is also positively associated with the individual's attitudes. Similarly, greater sexual experience is associated with more permissive standards in three of the four subsamples. Finally, those who attended church more frequently had less permissive premarital attitudes. It is impossible to definitively identify cause and effect in these data, since all our measures were obtained at the same point in time. But we can say that these five factors are highly inter-related. Those persons with more permissive sexual standards came from families with more permissive attitudes toward premarital sex, had relatively more previous sexual experience, attended church less often, and interacted with peers who had more permissive expectations for them.

These results are quite consistent with our conceptual model. In particular, they provide strong support for our expectation that peer influence and prior sexual experience were important factors vis-à-vis one's premarital standards. Also, we had expected that, by the time young people were 18 or older, the influence of parents would be relatively weaker than the influence of peers and of partners. The lack of association of parental variables with ideology found here is consistent with this aspect of our developmental model.

SEXUAL BEHAVIOR

Table 8.2 presents the results of regression analyses including all the variables which earlier analyses identified as related to current behavior. Again, only those for which a significant regression coefficient was obtained are listed in the table.

The results in Chapter 6 indicated that the various measures of parental attitudes and relationship with the respondent were not consistently related to current behavior. In the analyses reported in table 8.2, when all of the other variables are included, none of these measures of parental characteristics are significantly associated with current sexual activity.

Sexual Experience

Of the three sexual experience measures, only whether or not the person had ever had intercourse is consistently associated with current behavior. In both male and in the nonstudent female subsamples, there are substantial regression coefficients. In the student female group, it is the coefficient for age of first intercourse which attains statistical significance; this is the only subsample in which this measure is associated with behavior. The number of lifetime coital experiences is also significantly related to current activity in one group, nonstudent males. All these coefficients are positive, indicating that greater lifetime experience is associated with more intimate current behavior.

One additional variable is related to current behavior for the first time in the present analysis. The "pregnancy scale" is based on answers to two questions: the first inquired whether the respondent had ever been

TABLE 8.2. Final regression model of current sexual behavior

| | Standardized regression coefficients | | | |
	SM	NM	SF	NF
Sexual experience				
Ever lifetime intercourse	.2480^d	.3060^d		.4217^d
Age at first intercourse			.1534^c	
Number of lifetime intercourse experiences		.1947^d		
Pregnancy scale			.1576^c	
Respondent characteristics				
Perceived social desirability	.0890^b	.1709^c		
Personal sexual ideology for females			.1116^b	
Peer influences				
Number of friends engaging in breast fondling			.0950^a	
Number of friends engaging in male fondling of female genitals	.1158^b			
Number of friends engaging in female fondling of male genitals		.1531^a		
Number of friends engaging in female active oral-genital contact		.1899^d		
Number of friends engaging in male active oral-genital contact				.2255^d
Current relationship				
Hours alone in living quarters			.0799^b	
Intimacy of current relationship	.2980^d	.2255^c	.3602^d	.3349^d
Length of relationship	.2504^d	.1518^a	.1382^c	.1411^b
Multiple correlation coefficient	.7959	.7599	.8202	.8127
Corrected coefficient of determination	.6283	.5655	.6666	.6558

$^a p < .01$
$^b p < .005$
$^c p < .001$
$^d p < .0001$

pregnant/gotten a girl pregnant, and the second asked whether the individual had ever thought she was pregnant/thought he had gotten a girl pregnant. The pregnancy scale was created by giving a score of three to respondents who reported an actual pregnancy, two to respondents who had been concerned about a pregnancy, and one to all others. As discussed in Chapter 9, this scale is highly correlated with whether the person had ever had intercourse. In the regression analysis considered here, this scale is associated with current behavior for student women. This is the subsample in which the "ever intercourse" measure was not associated with current activity, which suggests that the pregnancy scale in this instance is a substitute for the other measure.

Respondent Characteristics

Of all the sociopsychological measures considered in Chapter 5, only one is related to current behavior in the present analysis. Perceived social desirability is positively associated with sexual activity in both male subsamples: those who rated themselves higher on traits such as social desirability and physical attractiveness were engaging in more intimate behavior.

Personal ideology is the only other measure in this group which attains a significant regression coefficient, and it does so in only one subsample. This does not mean that ideology is unimportant in relation to behavior. As indicated earlier in this chapter, ideology is highly correlated with the intimacy of the current relationship. Generally, in the present analysis the latter is most closely related to behavior; this association indirectly reflects the association discussed earlier between ideology and current activity. Thus, the fact that the regression coefficient for personal standards is significant only among student women indicates that this is the only group in which there is an association between these which is independent of the relationship between emotional intimacy and behavior.

Peer Influences

Of the various measures of peer influence, none of the measures involving perceived behavior of age peers are significantly related to current behavior. By contrast, several of the measures involving the number of friends who participate in various activities are associated with present sexual activity. The number out of the five best friends who engage in breast fondling is associated with current behavior in the female student group. The number of friends engaging in male fondling of female genitals is so related among male students. The coefficient for female active genital fondling is significant among male nonstudents. Female active oral-genital activity is significantly associated with current behavior in the male nonstudent subsample. Finally, male active oral-genital activity is related to the respondent's own behavior in the female nonstudent sample. Thus, at least one of the friends' behavior measures is related to the respondent's current sexual activity in each of the four subsamples. As indicated in tables 6.11–6.14, all of these are highly intercorrelated. Thus, which one is associated with current behavior in the present analysis is partly determined by its variation relative to the others; the one with the greatest variance is most likely to attain a significant regression coefficient. In all cases, the association is positive; those who reported a larger incidence of activity among their best friends reported more intimate current behavior.

Partner Characteristics

Table 7.10 indicated some associations between partner characteristics and current behavior. In the analysis reported here, none of these (age, relative social class, physical attractiveness, and likability) are significantly related to behavior.

Current Relationship

The substantial relationship between the quality of the current relationship and current behavior indicated in table 7.10 is also found in the present analysis. In all four subsamples, there are sizable, positive coefficients which indicate that the more emotionally intimate the respondent's current relationship, the more intimate was his or her sexual behavior. In the two student groups, these coefficients are the largest of all those found; in the nonstudent subsamples, these are smaller than coefficients associated with sexual experience. In addition, there is an independent association between length of the relationship and current behavior; the longer the duration of the relationship, the more intimate the activity in which the couple was engaged. Neither times together nor the measures of other relationships (number of other persons dated, average intimacy, and number with whom the respondent had had coitus) are related to current behavior in the present analysis.

One variable is significantly associated with current activity for the first time in the present analysis. We asked, as part of a set of questions concerning living situation, how many hours per week the respondent could have exclusive use of his or her living quarters. This is a measure of the availability of privacy, which we thought might be related to sexual activity. In general it was not, though the coefficient is significant for one subsample in this analysis, the student women. The coefficient is negative; thus, the more hours they could be alone, the less intimate their current behavior.

Again, the multiple correlation coefficients and coefficients of determination are included at the bottom of the table. These coefficients are quite large, indicating that the variables included in the analyses are highly related to the dependent variable, current sexual behavior. The coefficients of determination range from 0.57 to 0.67, which means that from 57 to 67 percent of the variance in behavior is accounted for by the "independent" variables.

In summary, four factors are consistently associated with current behavior. More extensive past sexual experience, particularly having previously engaged in intercourse, is strongly associated with relatively more intimate current sexual activity. Of the various peer measures, the number of friends who engage in various sexual activities is also positively related to the individual's current activity; these coefficients are smaller in magnitude than those associated with prior experience. The quality of one's current heterosexual relationship is strongly related to the extent of physical intimacy in that relationship; this is somewhat more closely associated with current behavior than past experience among men. Finally, there is an independent association between length of current relationship and current sexual activity. This indicates that, within a set of relationships at the same level of emotional intimacy, those of longer duration are likely to be characterized by more intimate sexual behavior.

It is important to note that the regression analyses reported in tables 8.1 and 8.2 generally included the same variables. Thus, the differences in the results reflect differences in the phenomena being analyzed. In considering personal ideology, we are dealing with attitudinal phenomena, the person's beliefs about the acceptability of various sexual activities before marriage. The results shown in table 8.1 indicate that the variables most closely associated with the individual's standards are his or her parents' standards, his or her involvement in organized religion, and friends' expectations regarding his or her behavior. The parental ideology and peer expectation measures clearly reflect, at least in part, these other persons' attitudes. Furthermore, we assume that the importance of church attendance lies in the values, both sexual and others, to which the individual is exposed in this setting. Thus, we interpret these results as indicating that sexual standards are primarily influenced by the standards to which the individual is exposed at home, in church, and in his or her peer groups.

The results in table 8.2, by contrast, indicate that the important associations with current sexual behavior involve perception of one's best friends' behavior and the quality of the present relationship. These results indicate that peers' expectations, parents' ideology, and church attendance are *not* associated with current activity. The only set of variables associated with both ideology and behavior is the individual's past sexual experience. Ideology influences behavior by determining what kind of relationship must exist in order for a particular behavior to be acceptable. But our results indicate that, in addition to the relationship itself, other factors are associated with the extent of physical intimacy; physical intimacy is not simply a function of whether or not the person is involved in the appropriate relationship. Thus, we are dealing with two related phenomena, ideology and behavior; but the variables associated with each in our data differ in ways which give us some faith in the validity of both our attitudinal and behavioral measures and in the validity of our other measures as well.

Our findings concerning the determinants of current sexual behavior are summarized in figure 8.1.

A comparison of figure 8.1 with figure 2.2 indicates the extent to which the results support the conceptual model upon which this research

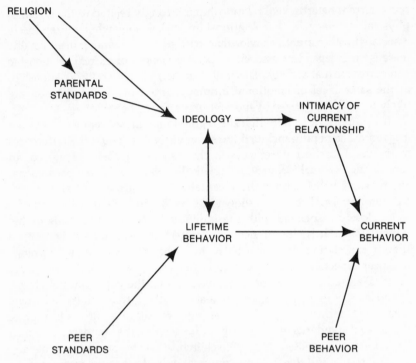

FIGURE 8.1. Social Factors and Current Sexual Behavior

was based. In general, the data indicate that the variables identified in the model are the primary correlates of current sexual behavior. The only set of factors included in figure 2.2 which are not significantly related to sexuality are the sociopsychological characteristics. Our findings involving these measures were the focus of Chapter 5. Some of the interrelationships of the other variables are different than anticipated. As discussed in Chapter 2, we expected various social influences and lifetime sexual experience to affect the individual's sexual ideology and only indirectly affect his or her current behavior. Figure 8.1, summarizing the results of the regression analyses, indicates that reported lifetime behavior and perception of peers' behavior each directly affect current activity. Current sexual behavior is also affected by the quality or intimacy of the current relationship, as expected. Finally, we had anticipated direct relationships between both ideology and quality of relationship and behavior; however, our results indicate that either, but not both, is independently related to sexual activity.

9

Sexual Behavior
and Contraception

SEXUAL ACTIVITY is a necessary, though not sufficient, condition for contraceptive use. On the other hand, the use of contraceptives is a product of the process of sexual development. We believe that our model of sexual development also applies to contraceptive use. First, the individual learns particular attitudes toward and information about contraceptives from socialization agents. Second, as the individual participates in sexual behavior, contraceptive use may become more salient, and the individual may seek out more information or contraceptive devices. Within particular relationships, as sexual behavior becomes more intimate, the couple may discuss contraception and make some decisions about its use. In long-term sexual relationships, it seems likely that contraception would be an integral part of the sexual behavior of the couple. In terms of our developmental model, contraceptive use would seem particularly likely by persons who are well into Stage III (see Chapter 2). Thus, an examination of contraceptive use with our framework seems appropriate.

In recent years, there has been greater acceptance and availability of contraceptives. Social control of contraceptive behavior is exercised primarily through the particular attitudes toward contraceptives which are taught and secondarily, through laws regulating access to contraception. Therefore, as with sexual behavior, we are interested in the sources of knowledge about contraceptive methods and attitudes acquired through socialization. Since this learning requires a certain amount of sexual knowledge, it occurs later in sexual development, and we expect friends and sexual partners to be particularly important as sources. In the first section of this chapter, we consider contraceptive knowledge, particularly the social context which includes sources of information and sources of contraception. Second, we examine attitudes toward contraceptives. This section is primarily descriptive.

Since contraceptive use occurs in the context of a particular relationship, it is influenced by characteristics and experiences of the sexual partners and the characteristics of the relationship. In terms of the former, we anticipate that sociopsychological characteristics of the individual, insofar as they serve as a basis of self-control, are related to contraceptive use. Internal locus of control and egalitarian role definitions, in particular, are expected to be related to use.

In addition, since contraceptive use emerges from the development of sexuality, it should be related to the sexual attitudes and sexual behavior that also developed in this process. Atitudes favorable to contraceptive use are expected to be related to other attitudes about sexuality, such as sexual ideology. Previous sexual experience should be related to contraception as well. We also believe that previous experience with pregnancy or fear of pregnancy might influence individuals to use more contraception.

In terms of the particular relationship, those characteristics that reflect long-term involvement are expected to be related to contraceptive use. Since contraceptive use implies the expectation of sexual intercourse, we anticipate that use is related to the sexual and emotional intimacy of the relationship. Thus, in analyzing the frequency of contraceptive use, we apply our developmental model of sexuality. Particular attention is paid to the social influences on contraceptive attitudes, characteristics and previous sexual experiences of the individual, and the nature of the particular relationship. We conclude the chapter with a section on nonusers that focuses on their reasons for not using contraceptives.

CONTRACEPTIVE KNOWLEDGE

Along with other types of sexual information, individuals learn about various kinds of contraceptives. They acquire this information relatively late in the developmental process, since information about sexual behavior and an understanding of conception are prerequisites to understanding particular devices.

Familiarity with Methods

In order to choose whether to use a particular method of contraception, a person must have enough familiarity with that technique to evaluate it. Other factors can enter into the choice after some degree of familiarity exists. To put respondents in this frame of reference, we first asked them to assume that they wanted to choose a birth control method. The respondent was asked to indicate which of the birth control devices or techniques he or she was familiar enough with to evaluate whether he or she would want to use it. Familiarity did not imply that the person would actually use the method. A list of contraceptive methods was shown to the respondent to avoid underestimates of knowledge about contraceptives because the respondent forgot particular ones. The results, as shown in table 9.1, indicate that most respondents were familiar with the principal contraceptive devices. The largest of the percentages is the percentage of the respondents who had some familiarity with birth control, that is, who had knowledge of at least one technique. These figures are 95 to 96 percent for the males and 98 to 99 percent for the females. Our respondents had a higher overall familiarity than those in Sorensen's study (1972), where 84 percent of the males and 82 percent of the females claimed to have some knowledge of contraception. This is no doubt because of the fact that our respondents were older (18–23) than his (15–19). Our results show that males were more familiar with the male device, condoms, while females were more familiar with the female birth control methods, pills and IUDs. Coitus interruptus or withdrawal is the only exception to this pattern, where among the students, more females reported familiarity with it than males.

TABLE 9.1. Familiarity with contraceptives (in percent)

Contraceptive	SM	NM	SF	NF
Condoms or rubbers	94.18	96.36	85.3	88.73
Spermicidal foam, jelly, or cream	50.47	65.91	57.1	68.94
Douches	40.20	48.18	56.4	63.82
Birth control pills	95.11	96.36	97.9	98.63
Diaphragm	66.90	73.18	78.1	76.45
Intrauterine device	56.70	59.55	75.1	74.06
Rhythm method	71.40	75.00	81.8	77.81
Coitus interruptus or withdrawal	69.10	78.64	76.9	75.42

Birth control pills are the device with which the most respondents were familiar. The second most widely known was condoms. These rank orders are the same as those found by Zelnik and Kantner (1973).[1] A major

1. Kantner and Zelnik's sample differs from the one in this study in two significant ways. First, their respondents were adolescent women (ages 15–19) and hence younger than ours. Thus, some of the differences in findings can be attributed to age. Second, about 32 percent of their sample was black. In most cases, the data they present are controlled for race. Thus, wherever possible, we have compared our data to their data on white adolescents. In spite of these differences in sample composition, Kantner and Zelnik's work is cited because it is based on a random sample and covers a large number of similar aspects of contraception.

contrast to Zelnik and Kantner's data occurs with douches, where knowledge was widespread in their study yet was lowest in our study. In general, all the contraceptives are well known to the majority of the respondents, and nearly all respondents knew of at least one contraceptive device.

Sources of Information

Information and knowledge about contraception may come from several sources. Parents are not expected to be an important source of contraceptive knowledge. As discussed in Chapter 4, parents were rated a primary source of moral attitudes toward sex but not of information about anatomy and physiology and mechanics of sexual behavior. Contraceptive information may be similar to these topics in that parents may be embarrassed to discuss it. In addition, providing information about contraceptives implies recognition that the recipient may be engaging in intercourse, and parents may be concerned that their children will interpret such discussions as encouraging or accepting premarital sexual intercourse. Grinder and Schmitt (1966) concluded that information about socially disapproved sexual practices is more likely to be obtained from peers or from reading material than from parents or other adults. Reiss's (1967) data indicated that adults disapprove of premarital intercourse and presumably, therefore, of contraceptive use. Thus, we expect peers and partners to be more important sources of information than parents.

As with the questions on the sources of other kinds of sexual knowledge discussed in Chapter 4, the respondents were asked to rate each of several sources as very, quite, slightly, or not at all important. Parents were the least important of all the sources. For males, both parents were rated not important at all by 61 percent of the samples. For those men for whom parents were an important source, fathers were slightly more important than mothers; 9 to 15 percent rated fathers very or quite important compared to 7 to 11 percent who gave those ratings to mothers.

The reverse was true for females; female respondents reported that their mothers were a much more important source of contraceptive knowledge than their fathers. Fathers were not at all important for 77 to 80 percent of the females, while the corresponding figures for mothers were 46 to 51 percent. At the other end of the scale, only 5 percent of the females rated father as very or quite important, while mothers were considered this important by 20 percent.

As expected, peers were a more important source of contraceptive information. As sources of other sexual information, peers of the opposite gender were rated as particularly important, implying that young adults learn this information in dating situations. With contraceptive information, this relationship is reversed: peers of the same gender are the more important sources. Male friends were a source of information primarily for male respondents; over 41 percent of the men rated these friends as at least quite important. Less than 35 percent gave comparable ratings to female friends. Among the female respondents, same-gender friends were much more important than opposite-gender friends. About 60 percent of the females rated female friends as an influential source, compared to the 10 to 15 percent who rated male friends as important. Some information about contraception is learned through participation in the dating or courtship institution. Lover as a source is rated high by all groups and is the most important source for males. The percentages rating lover as very important were 19 (SM), 26 (NM), 10 (SF), and 16 (NF) percent. Therefore, peers of both sexes are generally more important sources of contraceptive information than parents.

Other adults who might be sources of contraceptive information include doctors, clergy, and teachers. These professionals were particularly important for female respondents and were their most important source. Thirty-five to 46 percent of the females rated professionals as very important. Doctors may have provided contraceptive knowledge to females when giving advice on choice of a contraceptive device or providing the device or prescription itself. Information may have been provided more frequently to women for whom the topic may be more salient than for men. Professionals may generally have been more likely to have had sexually related discussions with women about menstruation or pregnancy in anticipation of these events.

In contrast to the results concerning sources of other types of information, sex education courses and literature were an important source, second in importance for all respondents. These were rated very important by 16 (SM), 21 (NM), 24 (SF), and 30 (NF) percent of the subsamples. Sixty percent of the student males and 65 percent of each other subsample had taken a course in school which dealt at least in part with sexual behavior. The majority of the respondents reported that less than one-quarter of the course concerned sexuality. In addition, the overall quality of the course was low; about one-third reported that the course contained little new information, and more than an additional third said an equal amount of new and old information. Ehrmann (1959) found that over half of his respondents had had inadequate or no sex education. For our respondents, however, sex education courses and literature were important sources of information about anatomy and physiology and contraception.

The final source presented to the respondent was the media, including movies, magazines, and other literature. This source was fourth in over-all importance of the seven sources for all samples. About 10 percent rated it very important with an additional 20 to 25 percent ranking it quite important. Therefore, media was more important than parents for all groups, and more so than lovers for females. A detailed question was asked of those who rated media very or quite important to ascertain which specific medium was involved. In 89 to 95 percent of these cases, the source was nonfictional: for 35 to 60 percent, it was scientific materials, and for 35 to 54 percent, popular nonfiction sources.

In summary, sex education courses, media, and same-gender peers are important sources of information about contraception for young adults. In addition, professionals are the most important source for females, while lovers were the most important source for males.

Accuracy of Information

It should be noted that the answers to these questions about knowledge of contraceptives are reports of the respondent's perception of his or her knowledge. Whether the respondent actually had accurate information may be a different matter. While no attempt was made to assess the validity of respondents' information about contraception, on some occasions, spontaneous responses indicated misinformation. For example, one female respondent reported using a diaphragm because she thought it provided protection against venereal disease. Zelnik and Kantner (1973) in their study of 15-to-19-year-old women asked at what time during the menstrual cycle a girl can become pregnant. Correct information on this topic is necessary for effective use of the rhythm method. Forty-two percent of the white respondents correctly identified the time of greatest risk within the menstrual cycle. This percentage increased with age of respondent, so it could be expected that the respondents in our study would have more accurate information, since they were older. Questions concerning accurate information about the rhythm method, condoms, diaphragms, and douches were asked in Grinder and Schmitt's study (1966). Their sample of single, white, female students is more comparable to ours. Their results indicated that only 14 percent had no correct information about any of the contraceptive devices. Fifty-four percent knew of one or two methods, and 32 percent knew of three or more. The results of these studies of accurate contraceptive information suggest that a majority of the women who were familiar with a particular device probably had correct information about its use. However, a respondent's perception of his or her knowledge does not correspond perfectly to accurate information.

CONTRACEPTIVE ATTITUDES

Besides information about various techniques, attitudes toward contraception are also important in influencing use. One such attitude focuses on the responsibility for using contraceptives. As gender role definitions have changed, attitudes about contraceptive responsibility have been affected. Schofield (1965) found that most girls considered birth control a man's business, although only a third always insisted that her partner use contraception. Zelnik and Kantner (1973) found that the overwhelming majority of women felt that the responsibility for using contraception should be shared jointly by both partners. Of those who felt the responsibility should be primarily that of one partner, more respondents favored the female partner over the male.

In our study, the respondent was asked to think about an unmarried couple who wanted to have intercourse but wanted to avoid pregnancy. The respondent was asked which partner should make sure that a contraceptive method was used. Over half of the respondents felt that both partners should make sure a birth control method was used. Slightly more of the male respondents chose both than did the females (55 percent compared to 50 percent). Of those respondents who felt the responsibility rested primarily with one partner, most chose the female. Among the female respondents, 45 percent chose the female partner, while the remaining 5 percent chose the male. This tendency to choose the female partner was somewhat weaker among males, of whom 27 percent chose the female partner and 18 percent the male partner.

We were also interested in which partner the respondent felt should actually use the contraceptive. There are more methods that can be used by females, and some of these methods are the most effective; because we did not want this differential availability to influence the responses, the question was stated in terms of equal availability. The respondent was to assume that equally effective methods were available for both sexes, e.g., pills for both men and women, and indicate who should use a birth control method. An even larger percentage felt that under these circumstances, the responsibility for use should be shared. Among males, 57 to 60 percent answered both; the comparable percentages for females were 49 to 53 percent. Among those interviewees who chose one partner, males were more frequently chosen than in the earlier question. Approximately 18 percent of the males and 20 percent of the females felt that the male partner should use birth control. It is interesting that although women are the ones who would get pregnant, there is not a tendency for our respondents to think that females should have the responsibility of using contraception.

Generally, egalitarian attitudes are prevalent in attitudes about who should make sure contraception is used as well as who should use birth control. Egalitarian attitudes were also found in sexual motivation, where a majority of respondents gave answers that included both partners in reasons for engaging in the various sexual behaviors. When the assumption is made that equally effective methods were available for both sexes, the tendency to choose the female partner was reduced, particularly among female respondents. This difference seems to indicate that attitudes about responsibility are influenced by the fact that the most effective methods are female linked. Since an egalitarian approach is predominant, one would expect actual choice to be influenced by other attitudes toward birth control and by particular aspects of each type of device, including effectiveness, side effects, and differential availability by gender. Even for those persons who feel that birth control is primarily the responsibility of one partner, these attitudes must be communicated to the other partner in order for them to be of any effect. Since there are such intermediate factors, one would not expect a direct relation between attitudes about differential responsibility and actual use.

Parental attitudes could also be of importance in determining a respondent's attitudes. The results discussed above indicated that parents were relatively unimportant as sources of information. It was believed, however, that even if parents were not influential through conveying information to their children, their own contraceptive behavior might have an effect. Accordingly, respondents were asked if they knew whether their parents had ever used a birth control method. Over 45 percent of the male respondents and 30 percent of the female respondents did not know if their parents had ever used birth control. Of those respondents who knew whether their parents had used contraceptives, 79 to 84 percent responded that they had.

Parental attitudes about premarital pregnancy could also influence the respondents to use birth control; for example, respondents anticipating negative parental reaction might be more likely to use contraception to avoid the situation. However, perceived parental attitudes toward premarital pregnancy varied so little that they could have very little effect. Over half of the females responded that both their father and mother would feel "very negative" if she were to tell them she were unwed and pregnant. About 90 percent of the females placed their fathers on the negative end of the scale (slightly negative, quite negative or very negative) and 90 to 95 percent said their mothers would react similarly.

For males, the question was phrased in terms of telling parents that he "had impregnated a girl out of wedlock." Males reported that their fathers would not react as strongly to this situation, compared to the female's perceptions of their fathers. Only 42 percent of the males felt that their fathers would react very negatively, although 86 percent gave responses in the negative range. Men and women gave similar responses to the question about mother's reaction. Fifty-one to 55 percent of the males anticipated a very negative reaction from their mothers, which is a somewhat stronger reaction than that anticipated by females. Nearly the same percentage of men and women felt that their mothers would react negatively to some degree.

Respondents were also asked what their parents would want the respondent to do if a premarital pregnancy occurred. Between 40 and 62 percent indicated that marriage would be the parental preference. For females and male students, abortion was the second most frequently chosen preference; it was third for male nonstudents. The second preference of male nonstudents and third for male students was finding one's own solution without involving the parents. For females, the third choice was staying at home, having the baby, and putting it up for adoption.

Because of their lack of importance as a source of contraceptive information and the little variance in reported parental attitudes, parents do not seem to be an important influence on contraceptive information or attitudes. Even with factors that might indirectly affect the respondent's attitudes, such as parental use of contraceptives or parents' attitudes toward premarital pregnancy, our results do not show a strong association between parental variables and the individual's attitudes.

CONTRACEPTIVE USE

Most respondents knew about at least one method of contraception. Every respondent was asked whether he or she had ever used any birth control method. Over half of the respondents had; 60 percent of the males, 53 percent of the student females, and 61 percent of the female nonstudents had used birth control. It will be recalled from Chapter 4 that 75 and 79 percent of the male students and nonstudents respectively had ever had intercourse; thus, only 20 and 24 percent of the sexually active men had never used contraception. For females, the corresponding figures are 12 percent for students and 15 percent for the nonstudents. It seems then that most young people who engage in intercourse personally use birth control at some time.

Methods Used

The respondents who reported having used a birth control method were presented with a card listing all the gender-appropriate techniques and asked which of these methods they had ever used. Of the males who

TABLE 9.2. Age at first use of contraceptive methods: males

Age	Condoms		Rhythm method		Coitus interruptus	
	SM	NM	SM	NM	SM	NM
12 or under	0.00	1.87	0.00	0.00	0.00	0.00
13	0.95	1.87	0.00	1.37	0.00	1.12
14	0.95	1.87	0.00	4.11	1.46	3.37
15	4.28	9.34	0.89	6.85	0.00	8.99
16	15.24	14.02	14.28	9.59	23.35	15.73
17	27.62	32.71	24.10	28.77	21.16	24.72
18	29.04	20.56	28.57	21.92	29.19	24.72
19	14.28	5.60	19.75	9.59	14.59	6.74
20	3.81	4.67	8.03	10.96	7.29	8.99
21	2.38	5.60	4.46	4.11	1.46	5.62
22	0.47	1.87	0.00	2.74	1.46	0.00
23 or over	0.94	0.00	0.00	0.00	0.00	0.00
N	210	107	112	73	137	89
Ever used contraceptive	48.61%	48.64%	25.93%	33.18%	31.71%	40.45%

had used a contraceptive, 82 percent of the students and 80 percent of the nonstudents had used condoms and 43 percent of the students and 55 percent of the nonstudents had used rhythm. The use of coitus interruptus also varied by educational status, with 53 percent of the students and two-thirds of the nonstudents who had used a contraceptive reporting its use. The respondents were also asked at what age they had first used each particular contraceptive. The results are shown in tables 9.2 and 9.3. Most of the males first used contraceptives when they were 17.5 years old, which corresponds to the average age for having first engaged in intercourse of 17.5 for student males and 17.2 for nonstudent males. Coitus interruptus seems to be first used at the average ages of 17.8 and 17.4 years for students and nonstudents respectively. The first use of rhythm occurs later, at 18.0 and 17.6 years for students and nonstudents. Condoms, which are the most effective contraceptive method available to males, had been used by most of our respondents, and these men had begun to use this method early in their contraceptive history.

Among the females, birth control pills were the most widely used technique; they had been used by 43 to 52 percent of all respondents and by over 80 percent of all women who had ever used contraceptives. Coitus interruptus and rhythm were used by the next largest groups, between 35 and 49 percent of the female contraceptive users. Spermicides follow as the fourth most commonly used method. This use pattern differs from that found by Schofield (1965), where girls relied on male use of the condom, coitus interruptus, and withdrawal. Kantner and Zelnik (1973) found that withdrawal, condoms, and birth control pills in that order were the most widely employed contraceptives for whites. Sorensen

TABLE 9.3. Age at first use of contraceptive methods: females

Age	Spermicides		Douches		Pills		Diaphragm		IUD		Rhythm method		Coitus interruptus	
	SF	NF	SF	NF	SF	NF	SF	NF	SF	NF	SF	NF	SF	NF
12 or under	0.00	0.00	0.00	0.00	0.55	0.00	0.00	0.00	0.00	0.00	0.00	0.00	0.00	0.00
13	0.00	0.00	0.00	0.00	0.00	0.00	0.00	0.00	0.00	0.00	0.00	0.00	0.90	0.00
14	3.03	3.45	0.00	0.00	0.55	0.65	0.00	0.00	0.00	0.00	0.97	1.61	1.80	0.00
15	0.00	0.00	0.00	7.69	0.00	1.31	0.00	0.00	0.00	0.00	4.85	3.22	7.20	2.63
16	6.06	24.14	0.00	0.00	2.73	3.92	0.00	0.00	0.00	0.00	7.76	19.35	10.81	14.47
17	27.27	20.69	54.54	38.46	12.02	11.11	21.05	5.00	5.88	0.00	28.15	16.13	26.12	23.68
18	33.33	27.59	27.27	7.69	34.42	22.87	21.05	10.00	5.88	25.00	31.06	20.97	23.42	25.00
19	15.15	13.79	9.09	30.77	27.32	24.18	31.57	25.00	35.29	12.50	11.65	24.19	14.41	22.37
20	3.03	0.00	0.00	15.38	15.30	17.65	5.26	35.00	35.29	18.75	10.67	8.06	9.00	2.63
21	6.06	10.34	0.00	0.00	6.55	13.72	10.52	15.00	17.64	25.00	1.94	4.84	3.60	6.58
22	6.06	0.00	0.00	0.00	0.55	3.27	5.26	10.00	0.00	12.50	0.97	1.61	2.70	1.31
23 or over	0.00		0.00	0.00	0.00	1.31	5.26	0.00	0.00	6.25	1.94	0.00	0.00	1.31
N	34	29	11	13	185	153	19	20	17	16	103	62	111	76
Ever used contraceptive	7.89%	9.89%	2.55%	4.44%	42.92%	52.22%	4.41%	6.83%	3.94%	5.46%	23.90%	21.16%	25.75%	25.94%

(1972) found that the same three contraceptives were used most frequently, although the order was different, with pills being moved to the first position. Thus, it seems that the pill is widely and increasingly used in America. Since Kantner and Zelnik (1973) reported increasing reliance on the pill with age, it is understandable that use of the pill would be more common in our sample, which is relatively older.

Examining the ages at first use of each of the contraceptive devices presented in tables 9.2 and 9.3, there seems to be a shift to use of the more effective contraceptives at older ages. The less effective devices tend to have average ages at first use that are similar to the average age of first intercourse. The youngest average ages are associated with coitus interruptus, rhythm, douches, and spermicides among student women. For the nonstudents, the techniques used earliest are rhythm, coitus interruptus, douches, and spermicides. The average age at first use of the more effective devices is later than the age at first intercourse, with pills being used seven to nine months later and diaphragms and intrauterine devices more than one year after first coitus. Caution should be used in looking at these age figures as they are based on one-year intervals and thus are not highly specific. But with this cautionary note, two factors could account for the difference between ages for first use of the more effective and less effective contraceptives. The differences could reflect a shift by individuals to the more effective contraceptives as they grow older. Also, the more effective contraceptives require a visit to a doctor in order to obtain them. Younger women may be reluctant to visit doctors, and doctors may be unwilling to provide these contraceptive devices to them.

Kantner and Zelnik (1973) found that women living in college dormitories were the most consistent users of contraception and women living alone were the most likely to have used contraceptives at last intercourse. They argued that not only do the opportunities for engaging in sexual activities increase in these types of residence as compared to living with parents or other adult household heads, but privacy for contraceptive use is also greater. There is, however, a confounding factor of age and education, since only those oldest women in their sample could have lived in dormitories or, to a lesser degree, alone. Since our results indicate that, on the average, older respondents use more effective contraceptives, in both student and nonstudent samples, the decline in parental control associated with moving away from home may be the most important factor. The importance of leaving home vis-à-vis sexuality is also suggested by our finding of a marked increase in the incidence of more intimate behaviors at age 18. Thus, it seems that use of the more effective contraceptive devices and perhaps spermicides as well is increased at later ages when the females are more likely to be living away from home and, therefore, less likely to fear discovery of the evidence of their contraceptive use. At any rate, average age at first use of the pill, diaphragm, and intrauterine device is higher.

Sources of Techniques

Contraceptive devices or information about the use of the technique in the case of rhythm and coitus interruptus can be obtained from a variety of sources. For each method that a respondent had personally used, he or she was asked where or from whom the device or technique had been obtained. It was expected that to a certain extent the sources of obtaining the device should parallel the sources of information about contraception insofar as information is provided with the device.

As can be seen in table 9.4, friends and drug stores are the primary sources of condoms. Kantner and Zelnik (1973) also found that drug stores were the major source of condoms, although their responses were from females reporting on their partners. Males in our study learned about the rhythm method from a large variety of sources with "other" being the most important category. This category included reading and other types of media and siblings. Lover, friends, and sex education courses or birth control clinics were about equally important as the other sources. Coitus interruptus was learned about primarily from the "other" sources and friends. These results parallel those of Kantner and Zelnik, who also found that information about coitus interruptus and rhythm did not come from doctors, clinics, or drug stores; it was expected that parents would not be sources of devices, since they are not important as sources of information about contraception.

As mentioned earlier, the primary source of pills, diaphragms, and intrauterine devices is doctors. Kantner and Zelnik (1973) found that clinics were an important source for these devices, particularly among blacks. For student females, "other" sources, sex education courses or birth control clinics, and friends were the most often mentioned sources for information on rhythm. For nonstudent females, lovers were cited instead of friends. Females learned about coitus interruptus from their partners and friends. Overall, these patterns for methods used by both genders are the same as those reported by males.

In summary, doctors are the important source for pills, diaphragms, and intrauterine devices, and drug stores for condoms and spermicides. Friends and lovers are important for conveying information about rhythm and coitus interruptus, and friends supply condoms to males. The media and siblings are important as "other" sources for information about rhythm and coitus interruptus.

TABLE 9.4. Sources of contraceptive devices or information about contraceptive methods (in percent)

MALES WHO HAD EVER USED CONTRACEPTIVE
(N = SM, 257; NM, 133)

Source	Condoms		Rhythm method		Coitus interruptus	
	SM	NM	SM	NM	SM	NM
Lover	0.39	0.75	7.84	11.28	3.92	8.27
Friends	33.86	36.09	9.02	14.28	20.78	19.55
Parents	3.15	5.26	0.78	2.25	0.39	0.00
Doctor	0.00	0.00	0.00	0.00	0.78	0.00
Sex ed course or birth control clinic	0.39	0.75	7.44	11.28	4.70	7.52
Drug store	38.98	30.07	0.00	0.00	0.00	0.00
Other	5.91	6.01	15.29	15.04	21.56	32.33
Never used	17.32	21.05	59.61	45.86	47.84	32.33

FEMALES WHO HAD EVER USED CONTRACEPTIVE
(N = SF, 229; NF, 179)

Source	Spermicides		Douches		Pills		Diaphragm		IUD		Rhythm method		Coitus interruptus	
	SF	NF	SF	NF	SF	NF	SF	NF	SF	NF	SF	NF	SF	NF
Lover	1.33	3.37	0.88	0.56	0.00	0.00	0.00	0.00	0.00	0.00	2.64	8.43	21.14	21.35
Friends	1.33	1.68	1.32	0.56	2.21	0.56	0.00	0.00	0.00	0.00	8.81	5.06	11.45	6.74
Parents	0.00	1.12	0.44	0.00	0.00	1.69	0.00	0.00	0.00	0.00	4.40	1.12	0.88	0.00
Doctor	1.33	1.68	0.44	1.13	70.36	73.60	6.64	8.43	7.08	7.87	1.32	2.25	1.32	0.00
Sex ed course or birth control clinic	2.21	0.00	0.44	0.00	7.96	8.99	1.33	2.81	0.44	1.12	12.33	6.18	4.85	3.37
Drug store	7.96	8.42	1.32	2.26	0.44	0.00	0.00	0.00	0.00	0.00	0.00	0.00	0.00	0.00
Other	0.44	0.00	0.00	2.81	0.44	0.56	0.44	0.00	0.00	0.00	15.42	11.24	8.81	10.11
Never used	85.40	83.71	95.16	92.69	18.58	14.61	91.56	88.76	92.48	91.01	55.06	65.73	51.54	58.43

FEAR OF PREGNANCY

Fear of pregnancy could provide motivation to use contraception. For those women who had gotten pregnant, the notion that they could not get pregnant would be dispelled. All of the females who reported ever engaging in apposition or intercourse were asked if they had ever been pregnant. About 6 percent of the students and 15 percent of the nonstudents reported that they had. Those who had never been pregnant were asked if there had ever been a time when they thought they might be pregnant, when it was a serious possibility for at least one week. An additional 32 percent of the students and 35 percent of the nonstudents said they had thought they were pregnant.

Males were asked a parallel set of questions about having gotten a female pregnant or thinking they might have gotten a female pregnant. The experiences are not as distinct for males because if the female partner gets pregnant, there may still be some doubt in the respondent's mind as to his paternity. Six percent of the student and 15 percent of the nonstudent men reported that they had gotten a girl pregnant. Thirty-nine percent of the student males and 32 percent of the nonstudent males had thought they had gotten a girl pregnant. Throughout this discussion, the phrase *pregnancy experience* will be used to refer to both pregnancy and thinking she was pregnant for females, and getting or thinking he has gotten a female pregnant for males.

The figures computed only for the respondents who had had intercourse or engaged in apposition provide a basis of comparison with other studies. Eight percent of the student males and females, 10 percent of nonstudent males, and 12 percent of nonstudent females who were sexually active had actually experienced pregnancy. An additional 47 to 56 percent of the sexually active had thought they were pregnant or thought they had gotten a female pregnant. These rates are comparable to those found in other studies. Kantner and Zelnik (1973) found that 10 percent of the white respondents had been pregnant; Sorensen (1972) found higher rates (11 percent of the younger girls and 28 percent of the older girls had been pregnant), but it has been suggested that his sample was more sexually experienced (DeLamater, 1974b).

The question arises whether the experience of pregnancy has any effect on subsequent use of contraception. MacCorquodale (1974) found that while those who indicated that they had been pregnant reported that the experience led to more contraceptive use, their actual contraceptive behavior did not differ from those who had never been pregnant or had never thought they were pregnant. It could be, however, that individuals who experienced a pregnancy had previously used the less effective contraceptives or were less frequent users of contraceptives, and that the experience improved the quality or frequency of use to levels comparable to other respondents. Kantner and Zelnik (1973) examined the methods profile of women who had been pregnant compared to those who had not been pregnant. They found some evidence of a shift to greater use of pills and intrauterine devices among the previously pregnant, although the effect was not as strong among whites as among blacks.

In order to look at the effect of the pregnancy experience on contraceptive use, the individuals studied cannot currently be pregnant, and the pregnancy experience needs to have occurred sometime in the past. In our study, less than 2 percent of those who had experienced pregnancy or had thought they were pregnant or had gotten females pregnant reported that the experience was currently occurring. For the students, about 30 percent of such experiences were within the preceding six months, 20 percent between six months and a year, and 25 percent between one and two years before the interview. The remaining 25 percent of the experiences had been more than two years prior to the interview. Among the non-students, 20 to 25 percent had had the experience within the previous six months, 20 percent in six months to a year, and nearly 30 percent between one to two years. Thus, for nonstudents, the experience of pregnancy had been in the more distant past than for students. For both groups, hardly any were currently experiencing pregnancy and only a quarter to a third had had the experience recently—within six months.

We can also look at the alternatives young people would prefer in the event of a premarital pregnancy. Using a hypothetical question, Schofield (1965) found that for all respondents, getting married was the most widely chosen alternative, followed by telling parents. Secondarily, nearly 40 percent of his males responded that they had not considered the possibility enough to make a hypothetical choice. Women, in addition to these responses, said that they would have the baby and keep it. Sorensen (1972) found that marriage, and having and keeping the baby were the preferred solutions for both the whole sample and those who had actually been pregnant. Abortion was more frequently chosen by his respondents than by those in Schofield's study; it was chosen by 18 percent of the females and 30 percent of the males.

In the present study, respondents who had experienced or fathered a pregnancy or were concerned about pregnancy were asked what alternatives they had actually considered. Abortion was mentioned by 65 to 85 percent of these respondents. Marriage was considered by 40 percent of the males and 25 percent of the females. Ten to 20 percent of the respondents thought about having the child and keeping it or having the child and giving it away. These four are the alternatives that received serious consideration. We also inquired about to whom they had talked at the time and the extent to which these persons influenced them. In trying to decide what to do, women reported that only partners and female friends had had very much influence. The other possible influences, including parents, relatives, male friends, clergymen, doctors, and formal and informal social agencies, had had little effect; most respondents had not communicated with any of these.

Between a third and a half of the respondents had not actually reached a decision; the majority of these did not have to decide because they found out that the female was not pregnant. Legal abortion was the decision reported by 26 percent of the males and 35 percent of the females. The other decisions, in order, were to have child and keep it, illegal abortion, and marriage.

We also asked a series of questions to determine what effects the experience had had on them. Changes in contraceptive use was the effect reported by the largest number of respondents. Sixty percent of the males and 70 percent of the females said that they currently used more effective contraceptives. In addition, 65 percent of the males and 75 percent of the females reported that they were now using contraceptives more frequently or carefully. Asked whether they were more likely to make sure their partner was using contraceptives, 75 percent of the men but only 40 percent of the women said that they were. Respondents do, then, perceive a change in their contraceptive behavior toward both increased frequency of use and choice of more effective techniques.

The experience did not seem to effect heterosexual relationships. Between 55 and 70 percent of the respondents reported that the experience had had no effect on their relationships. When there was an effect, the change was in the direction of being less trusting of persons of the opposite sex (16 to 30 percent). About 20 percent reported having intercourse less frequently as a result of the pregnancy experience. Both Schofield (1965) and Sorensen (1972) found that adolescents feared becoming pregnant and over a third reported that they had stopped engaging in sexual activities or avoided intercourse because of this fear. While we do not know how much these fears pervaded our sample, it seems that people who have experienced seriously thinking about pregnancy and its consequences report that they have changed their contraceptive use. This increased use and effectiveness could serve to reduce the fear of pregnancy without interfering with sexual activities.

FREQUENCY OF CONTRACEPTIVE USE

In order to assess how frequently respondents used contraceptives when they had intercourse, the sexually active respondents were asked on what percentage of these occasions either the respondent or the partner used any birth control method. The respondent was handed a card that listed all methods. The focus of this question is upon the dyad as a unit rather than just the respondent's personal use. Only 4 percent of the students and 7 percent of the nonstudents never used contraception when they had intercourse. Less than one-quarter of the respondents used contraception on 50 percent or less of the occasions when they had intercourse (12%, SM; 26 %, NM; 8 %, SF; 13 %, NF). Use more than half but less than 99 percent of the time was reported by 40 percent of the females. The remaining respondents always used contraception (50 %, SM; 28 %, NM; and 44 %, both SF and NF).

Kantner and Zelnik (1973) found that as age increases, the proportion of persons who have never used and who have always used contraceptives diminishes. Of all white respondents in their study, 20 percent always used, 16 percent never used, and 61 percent sometimes used birth control techniques. Schofield (1965) found that 43 percent of the males always used, 25 percent never used and the remaining 30 percent occasionally used them. The females in Schofield's study apparently relied primarily on males for use of contraceptives, as 60 percent said they had never used them, but it was unclear whether the referent of this use question was the respondent personally or either partner in the relationship. Thus, the respondents in our study seem to be more consistent users of contraception than the respondents in the other studies, who were younger.

Additionally, we were interested in whether the use of birth control was discussed before our respondents had intercourse with someone for the first time. Attitudes about the responsibility for using contraception as well as preferences for use of particular contraceptives need to be communicated before they can have an effect. One-quarter of the students and one-third of the nonstudents had never discussed the use of birth control in advance of first intercourse with a partner. Thus, for a sizable portion of the respondents, communication about birth control did not precede the first intercourse experience with a particular partner. The percentage who always discussed it in advance are 37 and 26 for the student and nonstudent males and 47 and 36 for the female students and nonstudents. It is not obvious why there is such a gender difference; perhaps discussing birth control is more important to the females and thus, they remember the discussion better.

Determinants of Contraceptive Use

We conducted several analyses in order to identify the correlates of contraceptive use. As our primary measure, we employed the percentage of time that the respondent had used birth control when having intercourse; this variable constitutes a measure of the consistency of contraceptive use. A correlation matrix was computed using the measures considered in earlier chapters of background variables, parental attitudes, lifetime sexual experience, respondent characteristics, peer influences, and current relationships. All of the respondents were included in this analysis. The results of the regression analysis performed to find the independent effects of these variables are presented in table 9.5. Because of the strong correlation between whether the respondent had ever had intercourse and consistency of contraceptive use, which ranged from 0.67 to 0.89 among the subsamples, the multiple correlation coefficient is very high and the effects of the other variables are markedly reduced. As expected, none of the background or parental characteristics were significantly associated with use. Of the measures of quality of the relationship between parent and respondent, mother's affection toward the respondent was related to use among nonstudent males only. Since this association was not found in the other subsamples, its significance seems limited.

Since contraceptive use is part of sexual development, it was expected that sexual experience would be related to use. Amount of sexual activity,

TABLE 9.5. Final regression model of contraceptive use: all respondents

	Standardized regression coefficients			
	SM	NM	SF	NF
Background and parental characteristics				
Mother's display of affection toward respondent		.1398[b]		
Sexual experience				
Ever lifetime intercourse	.8014[d]	.6182[d]	.4037[b]	.4144[d]
Age at first intercourse			.3885[b]	
Relationship with first intercourse partner				.2364[b]
Number of lifetime intercourse experiences		.1488[b]	.1079[d]	.1250[c]
Respondent characteristics				
Perceived social desirability			.0543[a]	
Peer influences				
Number of friends engaging in male fondling of female genitals				.1485[c]
Number of friends engaging in intercourse			.0876[c]	
Current relationship characteristics				
Intimacy of current relationship	.0801[b]			.0963[a]
Multiple correlation coefficient	.8296	.7029	.9052	.8224
Corrected coefficient of determination	.6868	.4870	.8172	.6706

[a] $p < .01$
[b] $p < .005$
[c] $p < .001$
[d] $p < .0001$

as measured by number of lifetime sexual experiences, was in fact significantly associated in three of the four subsamples.

Age at first intercourse is related only among student females. This relationship may reflect the fact that those who begin to have intercourse at later ages may be more likely to use those contraceptives that also have later age at first use, pills, diaphragms, and intrauterine devices, two of which require consistent use. Those who first have intercourse at later ages may be living away from home so that contraceptives are discussed more readily with peers, and fear of their discovery is reduced. Kantner and Zelnik (1973) found that women living alone or in dormitories reported better contraceptive use. They also found that as age increased, the numbers who always used and never used contraceptives decreased. Those in our sample who had begun to have intercourse recently may thus not have "regressed" to less consistent use, as women apparently did in their study. However, since this variable was significant for only one sample, only tentative conclusions can be drawn about its importance.

It was expected that sociopsychological factors would serve as a basis for evaluating and regulating one's behavior with regard to contraceptives. Internal locus of control and egalitarian role definitions, which were expected to be particularly relevant, were not related. Perceived social desirability was significantly associated with contraceptive use for student females. Similarly, Reiss, Banewart, and Foreman (1975) found that college women attending a birth control clinic rated themselves higher on self-confidence, attractiveness, looks, and popularity. Such variables probably operate through sexual behavior insofar as those persons who are or see themselves as more socially desirable may have more dates and more exposure to sexual experiences and thus come to accept contraceptive use or view use as important. The correlation between perceived social desirability and other partners with whom the respondent had had intercourse is 0.10; the correlation with lifetime and current Guttman scores are 0.19 and 0.12 respectively. These results are only tentative as the relationships are not consistent across the subsamples.

Peers are particularly important in providing information and in influencing sexual attitudes and behavior. We have seen that friends' sexual behavior was associated with the individual's activity. Perceived friends' behavior as measured by the number of friends engaging in genital fondling and intercouse was also related to contraceptive use. This relationship may be related to Rains's (1971) idea of coming to accept contraceptive use when one perceives more sexual activity among one's peers. It may well be that those who perceive more sexual activity among their friends are more inclined to accept the likelihood of the continuance of their own sexual behavior and thus use contraceptives.

Since contraceptive behavior occurs late in sexual development, in the context of a particular relationship, it was expected that the dyad would be particularly important in determining use. Consistency of use was related to the intimacy of the current relationship and the relationship with first partner for nonstudent females. These two variables lend support to Rains's (1971) model of "becoming a contraceptive user." Basically, she has argued that one has to be in a relationship in which intercourse comes to be expected in the future and in which a relatively high commitment to the partner exists for the norms proscribing contraceptive use to shift to norms supporting use. Reiss, Banewart, and Foreman (1975) found that three factors were related to attendance at a birth control clinic by college student women, including "dyadic commitment"; the two measures of commitment were having definite plans to marry, and going steady or being engaged. In the present study, intimacy of the current relationship is related to marriage plans, in that the more intimate end of the scale corresponds to a person one expects to marry or a fiancé. These results contrast with Kantner and Zelnik's (1973) finding that marriage plans were negatively related to contraceptive use. They found some evidence that white women who had plans to marry a year or more in the future were better contraceptive users. In our study, length of time until respondent planned to marry was not related to use. Degree of intimacy thus did not inhibit contraceptive use as it might if the couple viewed conception as less problematic since they planned to get married. Our results indicate that increased intimacy led to greater consistency of contraceptive use; this was also found by MacCorquodale (1974).

Both the multiple correlation coefficients and the coefficients of determination are extremely high. In a comparison across the subsamples, more of the variance can be explained for women than for men. This difference would be expected, since one would expect the females' reports of contraceptive use to be more accurate, because most of the methods are used by women. Second, one would not necessarily expect the characteristics of the males to relate to contraceptive use by the female partner. It should also be noted that most of the multiple correlation is due to one variable—lifetime intercourse experience. While this relationship is understandably strong, it is not particularly informative. Therefore, we decided to look only at those respondents who had ever had intercourse, the sexually active. Since the variation in the responses to the other questions will be reduced because of the more homogeneous nature of this sample, one would expect the significant relationships to be weaker.

Examination of the correlations with percentage of intercourse occasions on which contraceptives were used for the sexually active only shows that the magnitude of the coefficients is reduced as expected. Few of the correlations are above 0.20. Also, the gender difference observed above remains with a larger number of significant correlations found in the female samples. Looking first at student males, we find that many of the relationships are consistent with Rains's (1971) model. The largest correlations are positive ones with the Guttman score for current behavior and current intercourse. The next largest positive correlations are with intimacy of current relationship. Contraceptive use was also positively related to other characteristics of the dyad—partner's ideology, percent of time engaging in intercourse, and length of relationship. In addition, use was positively related to previous sexual experience as measured by age at first intercourse. Thus, given that intercourse had occurred at some point in the respondent's life, the more physically and emotionally intimate the relationship with his current partner, the more likely he was to have permissive attitudes toward sexual behavior and contraception and to be a consistent user. Contraceptive use was negatively correlated with "truthfulness," a rating of the frequency with which he or she told the truth during the interview, which was obtained from each respondent at the end of the interview (see Appendix I); this association may reflect the fact that males were likely to be estimating use by their partners, and therefore, the more contraceptive use they reported, the less they were sure that they were telling the truth.

For nonstudent males, the same pattern of relationships between contraceptive use and the sexual experience variables is evident. More contraceptive use was positively associated with number of friends engaging in intercourse, times with current partner, current intercourse, percentage of time engaging in intercourse, still dating partner, age of partner, and length of relationship. In addition, it was correlated with three of the sociopsychological scales, perceived social desirability, the face and genitals body-image factor, and the gender role score. Those with more positive images of themselves and more liberal attitudes about sex roles are more likely to be consistent users. The perceived probability of getting venereal disease was related to more consistent contraceptive use. It could be that this reflects the use of condoms, which serve both as a contraceptive device and VD preventative, or that more consistent use is associated with more emotionally intimate, long-term relationships, where the probability of getting VD is perceived as lower.

Family influences are also important for nonstudent males. More consistent use is related to socioeconomic status through less work outside the home by the respondent's mother, greater estimated family income, higher perceived familial social class, and higher educational achievement of the father. Kantner and Zelnik (1973) also found that socioeconomic status was positively associated with contraceptive use. More contraceptive use is also related to more affection shown to the respondent by both parents and by the father placing greater value on sex in his own life. It could be that for males from higher socioeconomic classes, the fear of pregnancy is greater, as marriage or other alternatives are potential disruptions of the respondent's education and career. Alternatively, the greater affection shown by parents toward the respondent may produce caring in his heterosexual relationships which may lead to greater use of contraception.

For student females, the strongest correlations are between contraceptive use and the number of friends having intercourse, number of lifetime intercourse experiences, and whether the respondent was still dating her current partner. Contraceptive use is also related to several measures of sexual behavior, including peer and context measures, current intercourse, percentage of time engaging in current intercourse, and lifetime Guttman score. Use is also positively associated with age of partner. Consistency of use is also related to more liberal ideologies of self and partner, more permissive expectations of friends, and more liberal orientation to sex roles and participation in civil disobedience. These correlations suggest that attitudes toward and use of contraception are related to more general attitudes about sexuality and sex roles. These variables are again suggestive of Rains's (1971) developmental model in which certain conditions lead the person to view himself or herself as engaging in intercourse and subsequently use contraception. Perceived social desirability and the face and genitals factor of body image are associated with use as they were for nonstudent males. We did not find any correlation between self-esteem or any of the internal-external control scores and use; Lundy (1972), with a sample of sexually active female students, found no relation between esteem and use but reported a positive association between internal control and contraceptive use.

Several background and family variables are related. Larger home town and high-school size correlate positively with contraceptive use. This association may indicate that greater availability or less fear of discovery characterize larger towns, or that attitudes toward contraception are more favorable in more urban environments. Kantner and Zelnik (1973) found that suburban dwellers were below average in sexual experience but very high in levels of contraceptive use, while farm residents were low on both. Contraceptive use correlated negatively with religious attendance in high school; this was also found by Kantner and Zelnik. They explained this finding by stating that for whites, the prohibition against sexual intercourse extends to the use of contraceptives, which would show a more blatant and planned violation of the first norm. Contraceptive use is positively associated with closeness to mother and negatively with adequacy of sex education from father.

For the nonstudent females, the relationships found for the student females are replicated although they are stronger and there are additional correlations. Among the sexual experience variables, there are larger correlations with the peer and context measures and with the relationship with first partner, emotional intimacy of the current relationship, attractiveness of partner, length of relationship, and current Guttman score. The sociopsychological scales are associated with use, including perceived morality and body build as well as those already mentioned. Finally, there is a positive correlation with physical attractiveness as rated by the interviewer but a negative correlation with the interviewer rating of grooming.

The respondent's age and income are related to consistency of use. The other background variables have the same relationship as among student females. In addition, there are positive correlations with lover and self as source of moral attitudes, probability of VD, and favorable attitudes of both parents toward cohabitation. Father and mother as sources of moral attitudes were negatively correlated, indicating that they were less important sources for those who were more consistent users of contraception.

The results of the regression analyses are presented in table 9.6. For males, it should be noted, first of all, that the multiple correlation coefficients are very low as are the amounts of variance explained. For student males, age at first intercourse, current intercourse, and truthfulness are significantly associated with use. For nonstudent males, affection from mother and number of lifetime intercourse experiences are related. Because of the small coefficients of determination, not much can be said about the determinants of contraceptive use in relationships where the male partner was the respondent.

For females, emotional and physical intimacy are important, as evidenced by the significant coefficients for number of lifetime intercourse experiences, current intercourse, still dating current partner, and number of friends having intercourse. Egalitarian role definitions and high perceived social desirability are also influential. The pregnancy scale is negatively related; this scale is a rough approximation of the pregnancy experience questions with the responses never pregnant nor thought pregnant, thought pregnant, and pregnant scored one, two, and three respectively. Those who had never had either experience were the more consistent users of contraception. Size of town is significant for student females. In general, a small amount of the variance is explained for women, and the more important variables are those concerned with sexual experience. It seems thus, that the data in general support our model; increasing intimacy in a continuing relationship (i.e., movement into Stage III in our developmental model) leads to increased acceptance of and more consistent use of contraception.

Preferences for Contraception

Respondents were asked which of the contraceptive methods would be or are most acceptable to them. They were asked to rank them in order of preference, giving first, second, and third choice. Birth control pills were the first choice of over 70 percent of both men and women, followed by intrauterine devices and diaphragms for women, and by intrauterine devices and condoms for men. The respondent was given a list of reasons including easy to obtain, easy to use, easy to conceal, highly effective, morally acceptable, and spontaneous use; he or she was asked to choose the first and second most important reasons for each preference. Pills

TABLE 9.6. Final regression model of contraceptive use: sexually active respondents

	Standardized regression coefficients			
	SM (N = 324)	NM (N = 174)	SF (N = 257)	NF (N = 211)
Background and parental characteristics				
Size of town where respondent lived in high school			.1625[a]	
Mother's display of affection toward respondent		.2092[b]		
Sexual experience				
Age at first intercourse	.1353[a]			
Number of lifetime intercourse experiences		.1907[a]	.1486[a]	
Pregnancy scale				−.1533[a]
Respondent characteristics				
Perceived social desirability			.1573[a]	.1929[b]
Role behavior scale				.2008[b]
Truthfulness	−.1318[a]			
Peer influences				
Number of friends engaging in male fondling of female genitals			−.1983[a]	.1744[a]
Number of friends engaging in intercourse			.2698[c]	
Current relationship characteristics				
Current intercourse	.2227[d]			.3096[d]
Still dating current partner			.2050[c]	
Multiple correlation coefficient	.2863	.2863	.4369	.4939
Corrected coefficient of determination	.0734	.0712	.1715	.2255

[a] $p < .01$
[b] $p < .005$
[c] $p < .001$
[d] $p < .0001$

were chosen primarily because of their effectiveness and secondarily because they were easy to use. Intrauterine devices and diaphragms were chosen for the same reasons, although many people mentioned the fact that they preferred diaphragms, since other methods, particularly pills, might have undesirable side effects. Kantner and Zelnik (1973) found that one-quarter of their respondents felt the pill was unsafe, although many of them continued to take it. Condoms were chosen by our respondents because they were effective and easy to obtain. Since pills and intrauterine devices require continuous use, it is not surprising that so many respondents always used contraception. Additionally, it is interesting that efficacy is such an important factor in determining contraceptive preferences.

Reasons for Not Using Contraception

Another issue involved in contraceptive use is the reason that respondents do not use contraceptives. In light of the possibility of pregnancy, and the fact that for our respondents, efficacy was a primary consideration in choosing contraceptives, and that nearly everyone was familiar with some method of birth control they could use, why then were some of our sexually active respondents nonusers?

Kantner and Zelnik (1972) found that two factors seemed to account for nonuse. The first was the woman's evaluation of her own fecundity. Many of their respondents did not use contraception because they did not think unprotected intercourse a risk. Nearly 43 percent of the white respondents did not use contraceptives on some occasions because they believed it was not the time of the month when they could get pregnant. This belief may be based on misinformation, in consideration of the lack of knowledge about the timing of ovulation that they found. The extent to which this belief actually enters into the decision not to use contraceptives, or is a rationalization post hoc, cannot, of course, be determined from survey data. The second reason given was the episodic nature of sex. Some respondents believed that they could not get pregnant if they had intercourse infrequently. High frequency of intercourse is related to the use of contraception, as we have seen. Kantner and Zelnik (1972) argued that contraception becomes more necessary as the perceived risk is increased and that use becomes routinized as frequency increases.

Schofield (1965) found that many girls left contraception to their male partners. Additionally, girls said that they did not like birth control devices, did not have any, did not care, and that devices were not necessary, as reasons for not using contraceptives, in that order. Boys responded that they did not have any, did not care, and did not like them, as the most important reasons, in that order. The adolescents in Sorensen's study (1972) said that they did not know where to get reliable contraceptives and were afraid that their parents might find them. Nearly three-quarters of his sexually active female respondents agreed that "if a girl uses birth control pills or the other methods of contraception, it makes it seem as if she were planning to have sex." Half of the sexually active girls who were nonusers believed that a girl who does not want a baby will not have one even in the absence of birth control. Younger adolescents seem to be nonusers because of lack of availability of contraceptives, lack of concern about pregnancy, and negative connotations associated with being a user and ready for sex. Since some of these reasons are based on misinformation and others seem related to age and living situation of younger adolescents, one would not expect them to be as prevalent among young adults.

In our study, a questionnaire was given to sexually active respondents who were not currently using birth control. Twenty-five reasons were listed; the respondent was to indicate whether the reason applied and if so, whether it was slightly, quite, or very important. Because there were few people not using birth control and some confusion among interviewers as to who should get the questionnaire, responses were obtained from 37 student and 45 nonstudent males and 25 student and 48 nonstudent females. Because of the small numbers involved, the reasons given most often can only be considered suggestive of the reasons in the population studied. From the five reasons that were rated most important by each sex, three reasons were the same for both groups; these were that they did not have intercourse often, did not think that the female partner would get pregnant, and that female partner was afraid to take the pill because it was bad for her health. Males also indicated as important the reasons that contraceptives take the excitement out of sex and that they "just don't get around to using any contraceptive." These reasons are particularly applicable to contraceptives used by males, primarily condoms and withdrawal. Females said that they wanted to be able to say "no" to their partner(s)'s sexual demands in order to control when they would have intercourse and that they were too afraid, shy, or embarrassed to go to a doctor for contraceptive help. These reasons would be more important for females, since the more effective female contraceptives require seeing a doctor, and males are more active than females in initiating intercourse. It is interesting that many of these reasons are the same as those found in earlier research. Primarily, it seems that nonusers do not feel that the female will get pregnant, second, that contraception will have negative side effects (on health or excitement) or is unavailable. Additionally, women use lack of contraception as a means of controlling intercourse.

SUMMARY

Contraceptive knowledge is widespread, and preferences for particular contraceptive methods were shared by a majority of the respondents. The attitudinal data indicate that respondents felt that the responsibility for contraception should be shared by both members of the dyad. Actual use of contraceptives, however, is heavily influenced by the relative effectiveness of the currently available methods; effectiveness was the primary reason for choosing a particular method. Overall, use was more frequent than had been reported in other studies, and there was only a small percentage who reported never using birth control. Between 30 and 50 percent always used contraception. Consistency of use seems to be primarily related to sexual experience and longevity and intimacy of relationships. These relationships indicate that increasing sexual experience and an intimate, continuing relationship bring about acceptance of contraception and plans for its use, thereby acknowledging future intercourse. These findings support our model and indicate that contraceptive use may be an outcome of the same process of sexual development and socialization. The reason for not using contraceptives is primarily the low perceived risk of pregnancy. Increased frequency of intercourse may increase the perceived risk, as could pregnancy experience. The consequences of "pregnancy experience" as defined here cannot be evaluated post hoc, although most respondents reported more effective and more frequent use of contraceptives as a result of the experience. The decision to use contraceptives seems to be related to sexual experience and sexual attitudes and guided by perceived fecundity.

10

Contemporary Premarital Sexuality

THIS CHAPTER summarizes some of the major findings and develops their implications. The discussion is more general and to some extent more speculative than the presentation in earlier chapters. It is oriented toward the themes developed in Chapters 1 and 2.

In Chapter 1, we described the purposes of the research. At the most general level, the object was to develop and test empirically an integrated model of the major aspects of premarital sexuality. The data presented in Chapters 4-9 provide considerable support for this model. The variables in our model, taken together, explain a relatively large amount of the variance in sexual attitudes and behavior.

More specifically, we have suggested three ways in which this research goes beyond previous work. Our interviews include measures of several sociopsychological characteristics, aspects of the person which we expected to be related to his or her sexuality. With one exception, none of these have been studied before in this context. Thus, the data indicating the interrelations between these variables and sexual attitudes and behavior are unique and therefore an important contribution. We also studied the characteristics of heterosexual relationships and partners in some detail; these have also been relatively ignored in past research. Finally, we obtained for the first time a large random sample of 18-to-23-year-old nonstudents, which enabled us to analyze the data systematically to determine whether there are subgroup differences between men and women and between students and nonstudents. We discuss our findings in these three areas below.

217

INDIVIDUAL CHARACTERISTICS AND SEXUAL EXPRESSION

In this section we discuss the interrelationship between sexuality and four characteristics of the individual. The first two were identified in Chapter 2 as subjects of controversy or issues within the literature on premarital sexual behavior. These are whether sexual behavior undergoes or is the result of a developmental process, and the nature of the relationship between attitudes and behavior. We begin by discussing these issues and then turn to the characteristics of the relationship and the sociopsychological variables as they relate to sexuality. All are aspects of the individual. The second section focuses on differences between men and women and students and nonstudents.

The Developmental Nature of Sexual Behavior

A major difference among authors in this area has been whether they discuss a developmental process vis-à-vis sexual behavior. As we noted in Chapter 2, while some authors have proposed developmental models, no one has collected behavioral data in the forms necessary to determine whether and how such a process occurs.

We reviewed in Chapter 2 the findings of past research which suggested that premarital sexual behavior undergoes a process of sociosexual development. This process begins with the young person's involvement in the least intimate heterosexual behaviors, such as holding hands and kissing; it progresses relatively slowly to involvement in more intimate sexual behaviors. Hardy (1964) emphasized the behavioral aspects of this process. He asserted that the person must learn a given behavior and the associated sociosexual skills and find participation in it rewarding before he or she will advance to a more intimate behavior. Reiss (1967) emphasized another aspect, a change in the person's premarital standards toward accepting his or her own participation in the behavior. While these authors differ in the relative emphasis placed on behavioral and attitudinal components, both have recognized the importance of heterosexual and peer interactions in producing changes in sexuality. It seems justified,therefore, to consider this a sociosexual process.

Many of the findings of this research support our assumption that such a process occurs. Most directly relevant are the data on lifetime behavior in Chapter 4. Using a measure composed of nine distinct behaviors, we found that participation in these behaviors was sequential over time for almost all of the young people we studied. The best evidence was the excellent fit of a Guttman scale to the individual's lifetime activity, which indicates that participation in each of the behaviors precedes one's first experience with more intimate behavior. The behavioral sequence begins with kissing, procedes through french kissing and breast and genital fondling to intercourse and oral-genital contact. The high percentage of "pure cases" and the coefficients of reliability and validity for the scale reported in table 4.2 indicate that virtually everyone who had ever participated in a given behavior had engaged in all of the less intimate ones, and that those who had not experienced the behavior had never participated in more intimate activities.

The findings concerning age of first participation in each behavior are also important evidence of a developmental process in sexuality. The data in table 4.1 indicate that each of the nine behaviors, on the average, occurs at a later age than preceding behaviors in the scale, i.e., than less intimate ones. In general, these averages indicate that this process occurs over a period of at least four years from first participation in kissing to first coital experience. We pointed out in Chapter 4 that when all of those who will engage in the more intimate activities before marriage have done so, the average age of first participation for these behaviors will be somewhat older. Thus, for many young people the progression from least to most intimate sexual behavior may involve as much as five years.

The cumulative incidence figures in tables 4.3–4.6 indicate that there is tremendous variability in when young people begin this process. Relatively few first engage in necking at ages younger than 11. From 10 to 20 percent of our respondents began to participate in this behavior at ages 12, 13, 14, 15, or 16. The cumulative percentages for the other behaviors show similar variation in the age of first experience with each activity. Thus, the average ages in table 4.1 are just averages; underlying each is a considerable range from the youngest to the oldest ages at which young persons first participate in a particular behavior.

We noted in Chapter 2 that both Schofield (1965) and Sorensen (1972) reported positive relationships between age of first date or intercourse and current behavior. We indicated that this was consistent with a developmental interpretation. We did not find a substantial relationship between these variables, however. The difference is most likely due to the different ages of the samples involved. Their studies involved adolescents, about half of whom had not engaged in the most intimate behaviors. With such samples, the developmental model would predict that the earlier one begins the process, the further he or she will have progressed. Our respondents were all 18 or older, and two-thirds to three-fourths of them had engaged in intercourse at least once. It appears that age of first experience is less important in such a group, since most have completed the process. For these persons, factors in their more immediate social environment are more strongly related to current sexual behavior.

Thus, our results provide strong support for the conclusion that the expression of sexuality is the result of a developmental process which occurs during adolescence.

The Importance of Sexual Ideology

In Chapter 2, it was noted that while previous research has assumed that sexual standards are a major influence on behavior, the empirical evidence is meager. The relative importance of attitudes in relation to behavior is thus a major issue. Accordingly, one of the primary objectives of this study was to explore that relationship systematically and in detail. The analyses in earlier chapters have consistently identified the individual's ideology as one of the major factors associated with his or her sexual behavior. Both correlation and regression coefficients for the relationship between ideology and behavior are consistently large, both absolutely and relative to the size of the coefficients associated with other relationships. The results in Chapters 5 and 6 are especially relevant; they demonstrate, with much larger samples and more extensive measures of behavior than those utilized heretofore, the high correspondence between the person's sexual ideology or standards and current sexual behavior.

These results provide strong support for the work of persons such as Reiss (1967), Clayton (1972), and Walsh, Ferrell, and Tolone (1976), who have assumed that attitudes regarding premarital sexual activity are an important determinant of behavior. In the overall regression analyses reported in Chapter 8, different groups of antecedents were related to ideology and behavior respectively. Thus, the interrelation of ideology and behavior does not merely reflect a common set of determinants. This view contrasts with the work of those such as Rains (1971) and Sorensen (1972), which has deemphasized or ignored premarital sexual ideology.

We have argued that the importance of ideology lies in the fact that it is the basis for self-control. The individual's standards specify the type of relationship, in terms of the extent of emotional and psychological intimacy, which is necessary before particular sexual activities are appropriate or acceptable.

In consideration of the importance of ideology, the next question is, what influences the individual's premarital standards? Ira Reiss has been particularly concerned with this question. We drew on his propositional model, and on subsequent research based thereon, of the relative influence of parents and peers on "premarital standards" in developing our own model, presented in Chapter 2. In general, many of our results are consistent with our model.

Reiss (1967) argued that standards are first learned from one's family.

His data from a national survey of adults showed that adults in general and parents in particular are generally conservative in their premarital standards. More recent data from Roper and Gallup polls in the early 1970s indicate that more than half of the adult population believe that intercourse before marriage is wrong. We asked each respondent what standards his or her parents held for him or her. Sixty-one to 70 percent of them reported that their mothers would not accept their having intercourse before they were married. Thirty-nine to 47 percent of the men and two-thirds of the women reported that their fathers would disapprove of premarital coitus. Thus, our interviewees perceived their parents as relatively nonpermissive. We found negative relationships between a variety of measures of perceptions of parental attitudes and parent-respondent relationships, and the person's ideology. These findings, discussed in Chapter 6, indicate that the more influenced by and the closer to their parents respondents were, the less permissive their current standards. Against this background of generally conservative parental attitudes, some parents were more permissive. The consistently positive association we found between perceived parental ideology per se and the respondent's standards indicate that relatively more permissive parents socialize their children to a more permissive premarital ideology.

Reiss has stated that other sources of less permissive standards include organized religion, both indirectly through its influence on parental attitudes and directly through its influence on the person. We did not consistently find significant relationships between denominational background or affiliation and ideology or behavior. We did find negative relationships between frequency of attendance at services and the individual's standards and accordingly, between attendance and the person's sexual activity. This relationship was found both between participation in services during the high-school years and lifetime behavior and between attendance prior to the interview and current ideology and behavior. Thus, our results indicate that how frequently one attends services, that is, is exposed directly to the influence of the church, is more important than whether the church is Catholic, Protestant, Jewish, or of some other denomination. The absence of an influence of denomination per se perhaps reflects the variation in the values and norms found within a single denomination, which may be as great as the differences between denominations.

Reiss has proposed that the primary source of increased permissiveness in one's standards is participation in the courtship institution. A large number of our findings empirically verify this proposition; this verification constitutes another of the contributions of this research to the area. On questions concerning sources of knowledge, especially moral and contraceptive information, we find that lovers and same-sex friends are consistently rated among the most important. The rated importance of dating partners and peers is positively associated with permissive standards in the individual. Lifetime sexual behavior, a measure of participation in the sexual aspects of courtship, is consistently related to the individual's ideology; in particular, the results in Chapter 6 indicate that whether the person had ever had intercourse is strongly associated with his or her standards. Again, we find high correlations between a variety of peer measures (the respondent's perception of the behavior of young people in the community, perceived behavior of his or her best friends of the same gender, best friends' ideology, and their specific expectations for him or her) on the one hand, and the respondent's standards and current behavior on the other. The regression analyses reported in Chapter 7 indicate that peers' expectations, their beliefs about the acceptability of behaviors for the individual, are most closely related to his or her ideology. Thus, the expectation measure seems to be preferable to the more commonly used scale, which asks about one's friends' general attitudes about premarital activity. With respect to current behavior, it is perceptions of whether his or her best friends are engaging in various behaviors which are most closely associated with the respondent's own heterosexual activity.

Thus, many of our results support the model presented in Chapter 2. Our results indicate that the young person's premarital standards are the result of the differential impact of two sets of influences. Early influences, especially parental and religious, are associated with conservative standards. To the extent that these influences decline in importance relative to close friends and dating partners, the individual on the average will come to hold more permissive standards. Again, there is considerable variation. Some learn relatively more permissive standards from their parents; others learn less permissive attitudes at home, and thereafter are less permissive relative to their age peers. So the changes in ideology associated with participation in the courtship institution are changes relative to the individual's initial standards. Peer and partner influences apparently lead our respondents to greater acceptance of various sexual activities prior to marriage. But these influences by no means lead to uniformity in ideology, as evidenced by the variation in our respondents' standards reported in tables 5.1 and 5.2.

The Nature of the Relationship

A third issue was discussed in both Chapters 1 and 2. In general, past research on sexual activity before marriage has ignored the quality of the relationship between partners and the characteristics of the partner. The implicit assumption seems to be that "opportunity" or the availability of appropriate partners is not problematic. It was pointed out, however, that the logic of measures of standards or "permissiveness" suggests that the emotional intimacy of one's relationships is a critical determinant of current activity. Ideology or standards, we have argued, are the basis of self-control. Thus, a person will engage in a particular sexual behavior when the relationship is of the type specified in his or her standard.

Because of the importance we ascribe to relationships and because of their relative neglect in the literature, we devoted an entire chapter (7) to results involving characteristics of the partner and the relationship. In general, we found that characteristics of the partner, including age, relative socioeconomic class, and his or her perceived likability and attractiveness, were not related to the respondent's sexual behavior. At the same time, various aspects of the relationship were consistently associated with sexual activity. Indeed, the results in Chapter 7 indicate that the variable most closely related to current behavior is the emotional quality of the relationship. In fact, in the regression analysis of behavior reported in Chapter 8, we did not find a substantial association between ideology and behavior when we controlled for emotional intimacy. Thus, the person brings his or her ideology to particular relationships; it provides a decision rule indicating what behavior is appropriate with the partner. Once the relationship develops, it is its quality which, given the person's standards, determines the behavior.

Thus, our results strongly support our assertion that the relationship is an important aspect of premarital sexual behavior.

Sociopsychological Characteristics and Premarital Sexuality

One of the unique aspects of this research is the inclusion of measures of several sociopsychological characteristics of individuals. We used measures of self-image, self-esteem, body image, internal-external control, and gender role definitions. The interrelations of these with ideology and with current sexual behavior are one of the foci of Chapter 5. The results of the correlational analyses (tables 5.6–5.9) indicated some significant, albeit relatively small, associations. Our more stringent analyses, the regressions which control for the correlation between variables, indicated that there are no consistent, substantial relationships between these characteristics and ideology (table 5.10, section A). There are significant regression coefficients for the relationship between perceived social desirability and sexual behavior among men. The comparable coefficients for women are not significant, which is consistent with the findings of Reiss, Banewart, and Foreman (1975). They found that several self-ratings were unrelated to virgin/nonvirgin status but were related to contraceptive use for females.

Among students, there are significant positive associations between satisfaction with their physical characteristics and intimacy of behavior. The self-esteem, role definition, and internal-external control measures were not related to behavior.

Thus, the sociopsychological variables are not consistently or substantially related to premarital sexuality. In view of the care with which these scales were developed (see Appendix I), we do not believe that this lack of association reflects poor measures. It may be that our hypothesis was basically wrong, that sexual attitudes and behavior are relatively isolated from one's view of self as a social and physical object. Alternatively, the relationships may be more complex than we envisioned, and it may require more sophisticated research and analytic methods to specify them.

SUBGROUP DIFFERENCES

The last major concern in our research was to explore systematically the possibility that single university students differ from single nonstudents of the same age in the same community and that men differ from women. The former concern has never been addressed empirically. Our data and findings with respect to this comparison are thus a major addition to the literature on premarital sexuality. On the other hand, male-female differences have been frequently reported in research on student samples. It is thus important to determine the extent to which such differences are found in our results. This section summarizes our findings with respect to these concerns.

Similarity of Student and Nonstudent Populations

Past research on premarital sexuality has involved either adolescents or college students. There are virtually no published data on sizable samples of young people aged 18 to 23 who are not attending college. Since nonstudents comprise more than one-half of the population within this age group in the United States, there has often been speculation about whether one could generalize the results of research on students to those who are not in post-secondary educational institutions. As indicated in Chapter 1, the study of such persons was another objective of this research, and one which was reasonably well accomplished. While the rate of completed interviews with nonstudents was lower (62.8 percent) than we preferred, it is apparently comparable to completion rates of other surveys in the recent past. There is no reason to believe that those persons we did not interview differed in ways which would affect their sexual attitudes and experience from those for whom we obtained data. Certainly the comparisons in tables 3.2 and 3.4 do not indicate substantial differences between our nonstudent respondents and those we did not interview (table 3.2) or between these interviewees and the population as characterized by 1970 census figures (table 3.4).

In general, we found few differences between our university student respondents and young people of the same ages residing in the same community. Comparisons of both lifetime and current incidences of behavior showed no substantial difference in sexual experience. The nonstudent men did report a somewhat larger number of lifetime coital experiences and partners and were somewhat more likely to have participated in group and homosexual activities. These differences were all relative, however, and in some cases not very large. Similarly, we found no major differences in attitudes toward premarital sexuality, as measured by our ideology scale.

There were a relatively small number of differences between students and nonstudents in the strength of relationships. In Chapter 5, we noted that there was a tendency for the sociopsychological measures—self-esteem, perceived social desirability, and body image—to be related to sexual attitudes and behavior among students but not nonstudents. We also found that current behavior is more closely related to personal ideology among nonstudents than students (see the regression coefficients in table 5.10). At the same time, the coefficients for current religious attendance (table 6.9) and lover as a source of information (table 6.3) regressed on current behavior are much larger for students.

These differences, while limited relative to the large number of similarities between the groups, suggest that the dynamics of influence on an individual's sexuality differ somewhat in these two groups. Among students, sexual attitudes and behavior relate to self-perceptions, religion, and the importance of lovers, whereas among nonstudents, sexual behavior is more closely related to one's own standards. The sexuality of university students may be more subject to social influences. These young people inhabit a relatively homogeneous student subculture, where peer and partner influences are especially strong and the criteria for self-evaluation apparently include sexual ones. Nonstudents may be subject to more diverse influences. They much more frequently live at home (36 percent of the males and 43 percent of the females, compared to 10 percent of the student men and women) which enhances parental influence; they are exposed to influence by co-workers; and they may retain friendship ties from institutions such as high school and church. To the extent that they are subject to such multiple and less homogeneous influences, we would expect the relationship between any one source and the individual's own sexuality to be weaker. In addition, to the extent that nonstudents are exposed to more diverse influences, they may rely more heavily on their personal ideology to provide cross-situational consistency.

More important, the patterns of relationships between variables were generally very similar. All the generalizations discussed earlier in this chapter apply equally to students and nonstudents. Most of the correlational and regression analyses we performed yielded coefficients of similar magnitude, and virtually all of these were in the same direction (positive or negative).

Earlier research on adult sexuality has found marked differences in both attitudes and behavior between college-educated and non–college-educated people. Kinsey et al. (1948, 1953) systematically compared educational groups and found differences in the incidence of most of the aspects of behavior they studied. As a result, such differences have been major emphases in both popular and scientific discussions of sexuality. For example, Kinsey reported a higher incidence of oral-genital contact among college-educated persons; we did not find such a difference in our research. This implies that differences in sexual activity do not exist or develop while college-educated people are in the educational institution. It may be that such differences will develop after those now in school complete their education, that social influences will operate in ways which will eventually produce attitudinal or behavioral differences.

Alternatively, differences in sexuality as a function of differences in education may be disappearing in our society. Whereas Kinsey and some subsequent researchers found differences in extent and types of premarital activity as a function of education, we find few differences between groups. If Kinsey's retrospective data are valid, it may be that there were differences in the sociosexual development and experience of those who went to college in the 1940's and earlier. More recently, developmental experiences may have become more homogeneous in our society, and the lack of differences between our student and nonstudent respondents at ages 18 to 23 may persist into adulthood. Hunt (1974), in his analysis of data concerning the sexual behavior of a national sample of adults, found that differences between educational groups were smaller and less pervasive than those found by Kinsey et al. He has argued that sexual attitudes and behavior are becoming more homogeneous in American society.

Similarity of Men and Women: The Decline of the Double Standard

We have noted at various points that previous research has consistently found gender differences in premarital standards and behavior. Because of this, we analyzed separately the data from men and women. It was partially for this reason that we systematically varied interviewer gender, since we were concerned that gender differences might lead our respondents to be differentially honest depending upon whether the interviewer was of the same or opposite sex.

The gender differences identified in past research have in general related to the traditional "double standard," the acceptance of premarital sexual experience, particularly intercourse, for men but not for women. Studies of standards found that both single men and single women tended to accept coitus before marriage for men but believed that it was wrong for women. Presumably as a consequence, the incidence of coitus was quite different. Ehrmann (1959) reported that 64 percent of his male respondents had engaged in intercourse, compared to only 14 percent of the females. Ehrmann found a related difference in the intimacy of relationships within which coitus occurred; men were most likely to engage in it with casual acquaintances, while the few women who had participated in it had done so with men they expected to marry. Such differences were explained by both Ehrmann and Reiss (1967) as reflecting the socialization of men and women to different standards, and subsequent exposure to differential social influences.

Our results indicate that, in the strict sense of accepting premarital coitus for men but not for women, the double standard has disappeared. The ideologies of our respondents for males and females were essentially the same; their standards did not differ as a function of gender. Furthermore, they reported that both their best friends and their current partners held the same standards for men and women. In general, our interviewees reported a personal standard which accepts premarital intercourse, though they varied in whether they believed persons who engage in it should be in love, feel mutual affection, or both desire it. The dominant ideology among our respondents, irrespective of gender or educational status, was what Reiss has termed permissiveness with affection; a substantial minority believed intercourse to be acceptable "if both want it," which he termed "permissiveness without affection."

While men and women have the same standards for both sexes, women are somewhat less permissive than men. Given the strong relationship between personal ideology and sexual behavior, it is not surprising that there are only small differences in behavior. On the whole, our male and female respondents were equally likely to have ever engaged in breast and genital fondling and to have engaged in these behaviors with their current partner. Student females were somewhat less likely than the other three subgroups to have engaged in sexual intercourse and oral-genital contact both in terms of lifetime and current experience.

A number of studies over the past two decades have measured sexual standards. Thus, to some extent, the decline in differences can be documented empirically. Ehrmann (1959) collected data from 841 college students between 1947 and 1951. Reiss (1967) conducted his empirical studies about 12 years later in 1959. His data included both high-school and college students. Simon and Gagnon surveyed college students in 1967. Our data on college students and nonstudents was collected in 1973. Thus we can compare across studies spanning 26 years. The relevant data are summarized in table 10.1.

A comparison of the ideologies of respondents in Ehrmann's and Reiss's data reveals few differences. A majority of the men accepted premarital intercourse for themselves while a majority of the women did not. The comparison with Simon and Gagnon's results is somewhat limited because they only asked respondents about their standards for individuals of their own gender. Thus, there is no measure of the double standard in their study. In Simon and Gagnon's data, there is no decline in the percentage of males and females holding a standard of abstinence and a slight shift to the more permissive standards. This shift toward greater permissive-

TABLE 10.1. Change in sexual ideology

CHANGE IN PREMARITAL STANDARDS, 1959 TO 1973

Standard	Reiss 1959[a]		Simon & Gagnon, 1968		DeLamater & MacCorquodale, 1973			
	M	F	M	F	SM	NM	SF	NF
Abstinence	28	58	28	55	5	5	11	13
Double standard	30	24	[b]	[b]	0	0	2	1
Permissive with affection (If feel affection, love)	26	16	45	40	55	50	64	54
Permissive without affection (If both want it)	14	2	25	5	40	45	22	31
N	386	435	593	584	432	220	429	293

CHANGE IN PERCENT ACCEPTING PREMARITAL INTERCOURSE
FOR THEIR OWN GENDER, 1947 TO 1973

Ehrmann, 1947–51		Reiss 1959		Simon & Gagnon, 1968		DeLamater & MacCorquodale, 1973	
M	F	M	F	M	F	M	F
50–75	14	73	17	70	45	95	86–87

[a]The data presented here are from Reiss (1967, page 26, Table 2.6). The respondents holding a reverse double standard, i.e., coitus accepted for women but not men, are omitted from this table, as interpretation of this standard and comparison to other studies are not clear cut.
[b]Respondents asked only standards for their own gender.

ness is most marked among women, where the percentage accepting intercourse for members of their own gender increased from 18 to 45 percent.

Our data provide additional evidence of a shift toward increased permissiveness. First, in our sample, few young people adhered to an abstinence standard. Consequently, the vast majority were accepting of intercourse for their own gender. Second, the double standard has virtually disappeared. Third, the shift into the more permissive standards, especially permissiveness without affection, is particularly evident.

In terms of gender differences, the more striking changes in standards have occurred among women. While in the period 1947-51 most women held a standard of abstinence, over time women have increasingly come to accept premarital intercourse. The gender differences at each level of permissiveness become smaller over time. However, while women have become more like men, the differences have not disappeared. In 1973, more men than women accepted a standard of permissiveness without affection. Thus, women seem to require somewhat greater emotional involvement before they are accepting of premarital intercourse. Carns (1973) has reported the same difference based on the data collected by Simon and Gagnon. These differences may be of substantial importance in particular relationships where the negotiation over appropriate behavior and definitions of intimacy is accomplished. Insofar as the particular man and woman involved differ in the requisite intimacy specified by their standard, the potential for conflict exists. The issue may have shifted from whether to abstain to whether the emotional intimacy of the relationship is of the appropriate degree. This shift in standards underscores the importance of emotional intimacy in determining current behavior, as previously discussed.

Corresponding changes are evident in the behavioral data. Virgins constituted 33 percent of the men and 86 percent of the women in Ehrmann's samples, about 43 percent of the males and 67 percent of the females in Simon and Gagnon's research; they constituted 25 and 21 percent of our male respondents and 40 and 28 percent of our females. Each of these studies involved students from different colleges and universities which complicates comparisons of the results. A more direct comparison for our purposes is available in the data from research conducted by David Heise and briefly discussed by Adams (1975). Heise surveyed 800 University of Wisconsin–Madison undergraduates in 1966; his results indicate that about 54 percent of the men and 75 percent of the women were virgins at the time of the interview. Thus, there is evidence of a marked increase in the incidence of premarital intercourse, especially among females, which parallels the increase in permissiveness of women's premarital standards.

Simon, Berger, and Gagnon (1972) also concluded that the primary change in premarital sexuality is an increased frequency of intercourse among women.

A great deal has appeared in the mass media in recent years about the "sexual revolution"; various commentators have pointed to college campuses as the locale where the revolution is in full swing. Accordingly, there has been considerable interest in statistics on the frequency of various sexual activities and relationships—of intercourse, cohabitation, etc.—and on related events such as pregnancy, abortion, and venereal disease. What is often lacking in such commentaries is historical perspective. To the extent that one can compare the disparate studies discussed above, that comparison indicates that the major changes have been in the sexual standards and behavior of single women; in essence, they seem to have been gradually moving toward the permissive standards and frequencies of intercourse which have characterized male college students for the last three decades. Such changes are also evident in the findings reported by Bell and Chaskes (1970), who compared the standards and behavior of female students in 1958 with those of co-eds in 1968. In addition, some of the results reported by Ferrell, Tolone, and Walsh (1977) and by Vener and Stewart (1974) show smaller male-female differences in the more recently collected of the two data sets reported by each. Whether such changes are revolutionary depends on one's values. If one adheres to the double standard, such changes in female attitudes and behavior perhaps do qualify as a revolution and are cause for concern. From a more egalitarian viewpoint, women are becoming more like men, which is a promising sign. We have discussed the possibility that differences in sexuality associated with education are declining, that our society is becoming more homogeneous in sexual norms and behavior. The available data indicate that the gender differences are disappearing as well.

It should be repeated that we found very low incidences of premarital pregnancy (6 percent of the students and 15 percent of the nonstudents), cohabitation (4 to 8 percent), homosexual experience (4 to 18 percent), and group sexual activities (4 to 17 percent). Thus, changes have occurred primarily in heterosexual activities, in which women have come to accept and engage in intercourse with men for whom they feel affection or love.

Reiss (1967) asserted that the relative influence of peers is a function of the autonomy of the "courtship group" from other social influences and institutions. This suggests that the source of the increase in the permissiveness of standards of and for women is an increase in the autonomy of young people or a decline in the relative influence of parents, religion, and other social institutions. One of the major contributors to increased autonomy may be age-segregation, which seems to have been increasing in American society. During adolescence, young people probably spend relatively more time with peers now than they did 30 years ago. Whether dating, participating in activities sponsored by schools and churches, or just "hanging around," an adolescent spends much of his or her time with age peers, with minimal or no parental influence. The age-segregation becomes much greater at age 18, when many young people go away to college or get jobs and establish separate residences. The influence of this seems to be evident in our findings that the lifetime frequencies of most of the behaviors we studied increased from 20 to 30 percent between the ages of 17 and 18. Similarly, 18 is the average age at which our respondents first engaged in the most intimate sexual activities: intercourse and oral-genital contact.

Other social factors may also contribute to increasing the autonomy of the peer group. Increasing access to automobiles provides young people with greater mobility, enabling them to temporarily remove themselves from surveillance by adults. Similarly, if child-rearing in our society has become more "permissive," as some analysts have suggested, one aspect of this change would be less attempt by parents to exercise control over their children's behavior. Finally, the influence of religion has declined generally in our society, at least as evidenced by the declining membership which many denominations have experienced. All of these would reduce the influence of those institutions—family and church—which Reiss identified as the source of less permissive premarital standards.

In addition to these factors which support increased permissiveness, the women's liberation movement has emphasized equality between the sexes. To the extent that individuals have been made aware of expectations and standards that are differentiated by gender, holding a double standard is more problematic than it was previously.

MICRO AND MACRO INFLUENCES

We began this volume by indicating the existence of two disparate orientations to the study of premarital sexuality. The orientation which we termed "micro" emphasizes the importance of the individual's immediate social environment—parents, peers, partners—and his or her own characteristics in explaining sexual activity. The "macro" perspective, by contrast, emphasizes the importance of sociological variables such as social class, religion, and educational attainment. Since both types of variables were measured in our interviews and included in our analyses, we can assess their relative importance as measured by the strength of relationships between them and sexual ideology and behavior.

Our findings have repeatedly demonstrated the importance of aspects of the person's immediate environment in relation to his or her premarital sexual behavior. Sociopsychological factors such as the individual's standards, perceptions of the quality of heterosexual relationships, and perceptions of parental attitudes and of the ideology and behavior of peers were all found to be associated with the individual's premarital activity. These variables had substantial coefficients in our regression analyses of current behavior; in some cases, taken together they accounted for two-thirds of the total variation in our behavioral measures.

The logic of the ideology measure, which specifies degrees of emotional intimacy in a relationship, argued for examining the influence of characteristics of the partner and the relationship on sexual behavior. The results support our model by indicating the importance of the nature of the relationship for sexuality. Thus, a dyadic or couple-oriented perspective is needed to explain sexual behavior, particularly for individuals involved in long, ongoing relationships, or in Stage III of our developmental model. Research should focus on the interaction between individuals, particularly their attempts to influence or control each other. Insofar as past research has focused on partners at all, it has examined characteristics of the partner such as age, and socioeconomic status rather than the relationship. These characteristics per se were included and found not to be related to premarital activity.

We generally did not find strong relationships between more sociological variables, such as indices of family social class, and the individual's ideology or behavior. We also did not find substantial differences in sexuality as a function of religious denominational affiliation. While our samples are somewhat limited, in that most of our respondents were white, middle-class, young people from midwestern backgrounds, they are probably no more so than the college student samples employed in past studies. Some of these earlier studies found differences in premarital sexuality which were related to differences in parental income, education, and the individual's or family's religious affiliation. The fact that these macro variables are not associated with premarital sexuality is consistent with our suggestion that the sexual experiences of adolescents in American society are becoming more homogeneous. Future research may find that gender, educational achievement, religion, and social class are less and less associated with differences in sexual attitudes and behavior, whether premarital, marital, or extramarital.

As sexual socialization and development become more homogeneous, as there are no longer systematic differences associated with societal variables, we would expect differences to be primarily related to influences in the immediate social environment, in the nature of relationships with family, friends, and partners, and in the standards one learns from such persons. In general, these are the variables which we found to be most closely associated with the premarital ideology and behavior of our respondents.

DIRECTIONS FOR FUTURE RESEARCH

We have noted in several places the major limitation which results from our use of data obtained from interviews conducted at one point in time. While such cross-sectional information allows us to determine the pattern of relationships between variables, we often cannot draw conclusions about the causal nature of these relationships. At times, the variables are such that we can assume that one preceded the other. Thus, the lifetime behavior of our respondents, in general, occurred before their current relationships and behavior. Therefore, we can infer that associations between these reflect the influence of the former on the latter. Such instances are relatively infrequent in our data.

We have systematically related our results to those from other research on premarital sexuality. One of the objectives of this study was to collect the data necessary to allow a fairly definitive analysis of some of the relationships found by or implied in earlier research. Thus, we assessed as systematically as possible the developmental nature of premarital sexuality, the relationships between the person's premarital standards and his or her sexual behavior, and the interrelationships of characteristics of current relationships and current activity. The findings presented here, in conjunction with that literature, provide a broad and fairly coherent picture of contemporary premarital sexuality as reflected in surveys of single persons.

Longitudinal studies, research which follows the same people over a period of time, still need to be done. The major questions which remain unanswered concern the sequences of events over time and the relative influence of potential causes on these events. On the basis of the conceptual model and the results presented here, four questions seem particularly important.

First, we need longitudinal data on the nature of the interaction between attitudinal and behavioral components in the development of sexuality. Hardy (1964) stressed behavioral learning; his model suggests that engaging in the behavior and the consequent reinforcement for it and reduction of fear and inhibitions is the primary process. This view implies that attitudinal components are relatively unimportant, that changes in attitudes will follow changes in behavior. By contrast, we, Ehrmann (1959), Reiss (1967), and others believe that the individual regulates his or her behavior on the basis of personal standards; in this view, one's standards change because of social influence, and the corresponding changes in behavior follow. Reiss (1967) discussed the interaction of standards and behavior and pointed out that cross-sectional data cannot definitively identify the causal sequence involved. Therefore, we need research which involves measures of standards and behavior collected from the same persons over a substantial period of time, to see whether changes in one generally precede changes in the other.

Second, we need research on the closely related process of peer influence over time. Our findings show high correspondence between personal and friends' ideologies, and between one's own and one's friends' behavior. But as noted in Chapter 6, we do not know whether these similarities are due to selection or socialization. It may be that young people choose as friends those who have similar attitudes and values, including sexual ones. In this case, attitudinal and behavioral congruence is a result of the selective process of friendship formation. Alternatively, friendship patterns may be determined by factors such as propinquity due to residence, employment, or course selection in schools. In this case, as friendships develop, there would be influence by peers on the individual which operates over time to make them more similar in their attitudes and behavior. In reality, it is likely that both occur; it is highly desirable to obtain information on these processes over time, to ascertain the relative influence of the two and the nature of the socialization process, to the extent that one takes place.

Third, we need longitudinal studies of the development of heterosexual relationships. There is a large amount of literature reporting experimental studies of interpersonal attraction. This research, summarized by Berscheid and Walster (1978), identifies a number of variables which affect attraction between relative strangers in laboratory situations; these include propinquity, physical attractiveness, and real or perceived similarity in attitudes, values, or personality. There have also been some studies of naturally occurring relationships, often of couples who were going steady or engaged. The results of these studies have been somewhat contradictory regarding the importance of factors such as propinquity, physical attractiveness, and similarity. As Berscheid and Walster have indicated, we need research on the development of relationships over time in order to integrate the findings from these two types of studies. Such research should include measures of the occurrence of sexual intimacy and dynamics. Only with such data can we assess the extent to which behavior reflects the preexisting standards of the two partners, compared to the extent to which one partner influences the other to engage or not engage in particular behaviors, to act in ways which are inconsistent with personal standards.

Finally, we need studies which assess contraceptive use over time. The data from our own and other studies indicate that older persons use more effective methods and are more consistent users of contraceptives. Longitudinal studies are necessary to identify the causes of these changes, to learn whether they occur because the older individual is more likely to know about effective techniques, because one's attitudes and identity change in the directions indicated by Rains (1971), or because of increasing availability. Again, all of these factors may be at work; but if one influence can be identified as most important, such knowledge has important implications for sex education and pregnancy and family planning programs.

Thus, much remains to be studied in the area of premarital sexuality. It is hoped that the present research will provide both a foundation and stimulus for subsequent efforts.

Appendices
References
Index

Appendix I

Measures of Principal Variables

This appendix discusses in detail our basic measures. They are discussed in the same order in which the variables were considered in Chapters 2 and 3. For each, we discuss the measures utilized in past work, present the rationale for the measures we employed, and describe the actual questions or scales which we designed.

SEXUAL BEHAVIOR

As discussed in Chapter 2, Ehrmann (1959) was the first researcher to employ a measure of heterosexual behavior which distinguished between a variety of specific activities. His rationale was that heterosexual behavior is perceived by young people as consisting of distinct or "compartmentalized stages," and that such a measure is therefore necessary to reflect accurately their orientation to sexuality. The inclusion of only a few behaviors, such as breast fondling, genital fondling, and intercourse, ignores the fact that other behaviors can and do occur (for example, oral-genital activity) and does not allow the person to indicate whether he or she engages in them. Alternatively, the use of broad categories such as "petting" as used by Reiss (1967), which included both breast and genital fondling, may inappropriately equate those who have done the former with those who have done the latter. By employing a detailed measure, we can obtain more complete and meaningful results. This rationale is empirically supported by the often marked differences in reported frequency of the various behaviors, even when the behavior is identical (e.g., genital fondling) and the differentiation is between male and female active. In addition to increasing validity, the use of such a scale increases the likelihood of finding relationships with other measures because of the greater variance in summary measures derived from multiple items or questions.

Ehrmann (1959) employed an eight-stage scale, ranging from no contact, through breast fondling, sexual intercourse (Stage 7), to female fondling of male genitals

(Stage 8). Some of his stages involve the same behavior (e.g., genital fondling) but distinguish between male and female active. He also distinguished between breast fondling over and under clothing, and the female fondling of male genitals over and under clothing. Schofield (1965) also included eight behaviors, retaining distinctions between male and female active "genital stimulation" and "breast stimulation" over and under clothes. He introduced genital apposition, contact between genitals without penetration, as a distinct behavior but did not include "no physical contact or only holding of hands" which was Ehrmann's first stage. Gagnon and Simon conducted a survey in 1967; some of their results are reported by Simon, Berger, and Gagnon (1972). They were the first to include oral-genital contact. They distinguished seven behaviors: french kissing, breast fondling, male and female active genital fondling, male and female active oral-genital contact, and intercourse. Thus, they dropped distinctions between over and under clothing. Having considered these various measures, we adopted a scale composed of the seven behaviors included by Gagnon and Simon, and genital apposition. We did not distinguish breast and genital fondling over and under clothing, in the belief that it would not be meaningful for the young people aged 18 to 23 years whom we planned to study. This distinction might be worth including with high-school age respondents, although Sorensen (1972) did not include it in his survey of this age group. It should be noted that the changes over time in the behaviors comprising the behavioral measure undoubtedly reflect, in part, changes in the nature of premarital sexuality.

Having selected the behaviors to be included, we faced the problem of selecting the words to describe them. This is one of the issues in this area of research. Schofield (1965) and Sorensen (1972) used vernacular or slang terms, such as feeling or touching a girl's breast, feeling "a girl's sex organ with your hand," and "have sex" (quoted phrases were used by Sorensen). Schofield suggested that use of the vernacular facilitates communication with respondents and enhances rapport; he argued that high rapport is essential to obtaining honest answers. Thus, "heavy petting" may seem more natural to respondents than "fondling genitals." But it cannot be assumed that the use of the vernacular results in accurate communication; the imprecise and at times euphemistic nature of phrases such as "sleeping together" create the possibility that the meaning of the terms will vary across respondents. For example, while some people use "heavy petting" to refer to genital fondling, for others this phrase means a long and intensive session of bodily contact, with high sexual arousal but not necessarily any genital contact. At the other extreme, "scientific" terms are likely to be unknown to many respondents, who may be too embarrassed to admit it. Thus, we decided not to use, for example, "fellatio." We employed precise phrases to describe each behavior, e.g., "female oral contact with male genitals." While these phrases sound awkward and formalistic, we can be quite certain that the respondent understands the behavior of interest and that his or her responses will be more valid. We hoped that any cost to rapport would be minimized by placing the assessment of sexual behavior late in the questioning. Thus, we believe strongly that both vernacular and highly scientific terminology should be avoided. The behaviors included and the phrases used to describe them are indicated in table 4.1.

Lifetime Behavior

There is widespread agreement among researchers that lifetime behavior refers to those activities in which the person has ever participated. Generally, the actual questions have assumed that the person has engaged in the behavior. Thus, Schofield (1965) used the form, "When did you first . . . ?" Simon and Gagnon (1968) apparently asked "How often have you . . . ?" Schofield stated the rationale as follows:

> This placed the onus of denial on the interviewee. It also helped to assure the young person that the interviewer would not be surprised or shocked if he had had such an experience. Many boys and girls said this approach helped them considerably because this assumption about their experience made them feel less embarrassed. . . . (p. 267)

We found the rationale convincing. Because of our interest in measuring the development of sexual behavior, we wanted to know the age of first experience with each of the behaviors; therefore, we asked "How old were you when you first engaged in . . . ?"

We noted in Chapter 2 that Schofield did not ask about more intimate behaviors after the respondent indicated that he or she had not participated in a given behavior. This results in a potentially incomplete set of data and may produce a false appearance of sequential ordering in sexual activity. Accordingly, we asked each person about all nine of the behaviors in our measure.

Current Behavior

Ehrmann (1959), who introduced the concept of current behavior, employed two different definitions in the course of his research. The questionnaire completed by the first 200 students surveyed asked them "to report their behavior for a typical or representative month during the preceding year" (p. 15). He discovered that this was not satisfactory if the person had had an irregular or unstable behavior pattern. Accordingly, the instructions were changed, and subsequent respondents were asked to report their behavior "on a monthly basis" with the maximum period covered being the preceding year. Alternatively, "subjects with very low frequencies were asked to include a monthly average covering a period of one year" (p. 15). As he indicated, the time period specified is important. If questioning is limited to the preceding month (as in Sorensen's study), some respondents will have experienced atypically high or low frequencies. Use of "a typical month" avoids this problem but creates difficulties in answering accurately for those whose patterns of behavior have been fluctuating from month to month. Limiting reported behavior to the past year is desirable to minimize the impact of memory errors on the data.

Considering these problems, we chose the following approach, partly on the basis of our interest in the couple and their relationship. The first question regarding current activity was whether the person had "gone out with a male/female within the past year." If the respondent had not, the remaining questions about current behavior were skipped. If the respondent had, he or she was then asked about "the person you have most recently dated or are currently dating." If the respondent was currently seeing more than one person, he or she was asked to answer in terms of the one he or she had *most recently* been out with; a later series of questions asked about behavior with other current partners. Each person was next asked how many times they had ever been together. "Current behavior" was then assessed by asking whether "you and your partner [have] ever engaged in . . ." each of the behaviors; for each behavior reported, the respondent was asked the percentage of the times they had been together in which they had engaged in that activity. Thus, we measured current behavior in terms of relationships, rather than in terms of dates as used by Ehrmann; we also included all behavior with the partner(s) the person had been out with within the past year. Some of these relationships extended over a longer period; some had terminated prior to the interview. We can control for such temporal variations, since we asked about the total length of the relationship and whether it was continuing or when it had been terminated.

SOCIOPSYCHOLOGICAL CHARACTERISTICS

Self-Image and Self-Esteem

We were particularly interested in finding appropriate measures of self from among the large number already in existence. Based upon the information given by Robinson and Shaver (1969), we selected Sherwood's (1962) measure as a starting point. It was particularly appropriate because of its semantic differential format, with pairs of bipolar adjectives separated by seven spaces. By selecting one space, the respondent indicated the degree to which one or the other of the adjectives more accurately described him or her. The social or interactional nature of the adjectives employed, relative to other measures, also made this potentially more valid for our purposes. Finally, Sherwood's scale asks the respondent to characterize himself or herself as he or she is at present ("real self") and as he or she aspires to be ("ideal self"). We had planned to use real-ideal discrepancy as a measure of self-esteem following Sherwood, but as the following results indicate, an alternative approach is more straightforward. We did *not* include the second part of Sherwood's measure, which asks for a ranking of the relative importance of each dimension to one's total self evaluation.

We included this modified version of Sherwood's scale in our pre-test (see DeLamater, 1974a); it contained 25 bipolar scales. Separate correlational and factor analyses were performed on the responses of men and women to these items. These analyses indicated that 10 of the dimensions were not related to the remaining 15 scales, or to other variables in which we were interested. These dimensions were dropped from the final version. The instructions and the measure itself are reproduced in figure I.1.

We originally planned to develop measures of both ideal and real self. However, the results showed little variation in ratings of ideal self; a large majority of our respondents wanted to be extremely moral, honest, intelligent, etc. It seems that people responded in terms of a social stereotype, and thus their answers did not provide information about themselves as individuals. There was much greater variation in ratings of self at present, and these, therefore, could be more meaningfully related to other variables.

Answers to the individual items were coded so that the most socially desirable responses received the highest scores. The results of factor analyses of these self ratings indicated a single, large, unrotated factor. All 15 items had high loadings on this factor with positive relationships between more socially desirable responses on each bipolar dimension. Inspection of this factor suggested that it essentially represents self-esteem, the extent to which the person perceives himself or herself

FIGURE I.1. Self-Description Measure

Instructions

The following characteristics have been found to be used by many persons in describing themselves.

Each characteristic is represented graphically by a scale.

1. Please indicate the location on the scale where you *presently* picture yourself by an: X Please do *not* be concerned if you see yourself as being different in different *situations* (e.g., cooperative-competitive). You are to indicate how you picture yourself in general or most usually.

In addition to your present picture of yourself, we are also interested in the aspirations which people have for themselves. All persons have a desired picture of themselves toward which they see themselves to be *realistically* striving. This is *not* meant to be the person's ideal—rather, that picture of yourself which you actually aspire to attain in the future.

2. Please indicate the location on the scale where you aspire to picture yourself by an: 0

Do not restrict yourself to a particular range on the scale, feel free to place your responses anywhere on the scale. The only requirement is that you be honest with yourself. Please do not be concerned with the way your answers would be judged by others, this is completely irrelevant here. Remember, you are describing yourself to yourself—not to other people.

The scale runs continuously from one labeled extreme to the other with the varying degrees being indicated by spaces (—).

Please mark both an X indicating your present picture of yourself and an 0 for your aspired picture of yourself. Place your marks in the middle of the (—) not on the boundaries.

SELF-DESCRIPTION

Value myself low	— — — — — —	Value myself high
Comfortable with others	— — — — — —	Awkward with others
Moral	— — — — — —	Immoral
Insightful about self	— — — — — —	Lack insight about self
Honest	— — — — — —	Dishonest
Fair	— — — — — —	Unfair
Not likable	— — — — — —	Likable
Lack self-confidence	— — — — — —	Self-confident
Unintelligent	— — — — — —	Intelligent
Dependent	— — — — — —	Independent
Personally undesirable	— — — — — —	Personally desirable
Physically attractive	— — — — — —	Physically unattractive
Weak	— — — — — —	Strong
Bad	— — — — — —	Good
Sensitive to others	— — — — — —	Insensitive to others

positively. Accordingly, we obtained a measure of self-esteem by simply adding the numerical codes for each of the 15 items, weighting each item equally.

We then performed varimax roations of the real self ratings. Varimax procedures are designed to maximize the independence of the factors, to produce dimensions with minimal intercorrelations. The best solution, in terms of independence and the amount of variance explained, identified two dimensions. This solution is presented in table I.1, which indicates the loading of each item on each of the two factors. In general, the items which are most highly related to Factor I (identified by asterisks in the table) are: value myself, comfortable with others, likable, self-confident, desirable, and strong. These qualities all involve interpersonal skills or relative evaluations of one's ability to relate to others; accordingly this factor seems to represent what we will call perceived social desirability. As the percentages at the bottom of the table indicate, this factor was quite strong, accounting for 14 to 18 percent of the total variation in the items, and more than 50 percent of the variance explainable by the factors identified in the analysis. Note that the items included on this factor varied somewhat in the nonstudent female subsample; in addition to the items noted above, the intelligence, insight, and physical attractiveness items also loaded on Factor I. For nonstudent males, the comfortable-with-others item did not load highly enough to justify its inclusion.

Factor II is comprised generally of the bipolar scales whose positive ends are moral, insightful, honest, and fair. In addition, self rating of sensitivity loaded on Factor II in all but the student male subsample. The underlying dimension here seems to be a moral one, the extent to which the person perceives himself or herself

TABLE I.1. Self-concept–real self: factor loadings
Principal factor procedure—2 rotations

	SM		NM		SF		NF	
	I	II	I	II	I	II	I	II
Value myself	.670*	.115	.647*	.159	.606*	.199	.676*	.114
Comfortable with others	.498*	.121	.268	.287	.405*	.209	.436*	.088
Moral	.096	.434*	.043	.425*	.122	.541*	.154	.438*
Insightful	.221	.439*	.200	.423*	.246	.436*	.405*	.124
Honest	.009	.671*	.069	.649*	.072	.690*	.068	.722*
Fair	.170	.599*	.129	.702*	.169	.684*	.166	.695*
Likable	.533*	.180	.501*	.202	.397*	.235	.528*	.253
Self-confident	.676*	−.003	.557*	.089	.614*	.054	.667*	.023
Intelligent	.368	.235	.399	.307	.477	.186	.473*	.284
Independent	.301	.108	.279	−.021	.463	−.043	.204	.076
Desirable	.593*	.271	.671*	.187	.641*	.222	.670*	.355
Physically attractive	.274	.248	.344	.231	.323	.175	.439*	.161
Strong	.476*	.242	.441*	.155	.539*	.122	.420*	.242
Good	.394	.468	.276	.422*	.365	.278	.290	.467*
Sensitive	.140	.355	.121	.492*	.133	.536*	.164	.479*
% factor variance	58.1	41.9	51.7	48.3	55.5	44.5	57.7	42.3
% total variance	17.2	12.4	14.7	13.7	17.2	13.8	18.6	13.6

*Items chosen for factor.

as a moral individual. Among students, the loadings of the good/bad item tended to be similar on both Factors I and II; among nonstudents, this item loaded more strongly on Factor II. This was also a relatively strong factor, as evidenced by percent of both total and factor variance for which it accounted.

Factor scores for perceived desirability and morality were constructed for each respondent by simply summing the numerical codes associated with his or her answers to the appropriate items (that is, by assigning unit weights).

Body Image

The body-image measure was adapted from the Body-Cathexis Scale introduced by Secord and Jourard (1953). We initially selected 25 of the 46 characteristics which they used. We generally eliminated highly specific traits, e.g., ankles, wrists, and fingers, and items which referred to bodily functioning, e.g., appetite, elimination, and energy level. Again, the initial version, employing the five response categories which they used, was included in the pre-test, and the responses obtained were analyzed. The analysis indicated that 16 of the characteristics were interrelated and/or correlated with other measures of interest to us. The scale employed and the instructions for its completion are reproduced in figure I.2.

We also factor analyzed responses to these items. Again, principal factor procedures with varimax rotations were employed in an attempt to identify independent or uncorrelated factors. The analyses identified two underlying factors or dimensions. Table I.2 presents the loadings of each of the items on these.

FIGURE I.2

Physical Evaluation (Body Image) **Measure**

Consider each item listed below and circle the number which best represents your feelings according to the following scale:
1. have strong feelings and wish change could somehow be made
2. don't like, but can put up with
3. have no particular feelings one way or the other
4. am satisfied
5. consider myself fortunate

hair	1	2	3	4	5
facial complexion	1	2	3	4	5
distribution of hair over body	1	2	3	4	5
waist	1	2	3	4	5
body build	1	2	3	4	5
width of shoulders	1	2	3	4	5
chest/breasts	1	2	3	4	5
eyes	1	2	3	4	5
hips	1	2	3	4	5
legs	1	2	3	4	5
teeth	1	2	3	4	5
face	1	2	3	4	5
weight	1	2	3	4	5
genitals	1	2	3	4	5
stomach	1	2	3	4	5
birthmarks/scars	1	2	3	4	5

TABLE I.2. Body image: factor loadings
Principal factor procedure—2 rotations

	SM I	SM II	NM I	NM II	SF I	SF II	NF I	NF II
Hair	.051	.398	.307	.260	.089	.312	.080	.330
Complexion	.106	.454*	.123	.458*	.057	.418	−.045	.439*
Distribution of hair	.151	.337	.214	.325	.173	.377	.065	.414*
Waist	.560*	.308	.743*	−.034	.637*	.188	.728*	.134
Body build	.685*	.162	.497	.453	.717*	.191	.722*	.108
Width of shoulders	.689*	−.023	.111	.632*	.421	.386	.300	.434
Chest/breasts	.722*	.010	.198	.656*	.154	.370	.154	.330
Eyes	.045	.340	−.061	.303	−.030	.456*	.013	.185
Hips	.511*	.228	.457	.412	.724*	.006	.614*	.030
Legs	.479*	.240	.441	.415	.611*	.048	.552*	.064
Teeth	.044	.336	.106	.263	−.022	.371	.022	.251
Face	.218	.629*	.220	.500*	.149	.653*	.069	.573*
Weight	.527*	.223	.609*	.176	.768*	.006	.739*	.062
Genitals	.280	.405*	.390	.395	.194	.460*	.169	.473*
Stomach	.464	.364	.710*	.052	.555*	.229	.616*	.228
Birthmarks/scars	.113	.336	.069	.244	.029	.286	.045	.368
% factor variance	62.1	37.9	50.8	49.2	61.5	38.5	63.2	36.8
% total variance	18.4	11.2	15.7	15.1	18.9	11.8	17.6	10.3

*Items chosen for factor.

Factor I is generally comprised of the following items: waist, body build, hips, legs, weight, and stomach. Note that only waist and weight are included on Factor I in all four subsamples; the other items are included for three of the four. The build, hips, and legs items were not included on this factor for nonstudent males because they also loaded highly on Factor II. For the same reason, the item concerning evaluation of stomach was not included on Factor I for student males. In general, all of these items deal with bodily build, in contrast to characteristics such as complexion, eyes, and teeth. Thus, the underlying dimension seems to be satisfaction with overall build and the body's relative proportions. Factor I was relatively strong; it accounted for 6 to 19 percent of the variation in responses to all the items and half or more of the factor variance.

Only three items had consistently high loadings on Factor II: complexion and face in all four subsamples and genitals in three of them. In the student female group, eyes was also highly loaded on this factor. Additional anomalous results are the high loadings on this factor of shoulders and chest in the nonstudent male subsample and the hair item in the nonstudent female subsample. To some extent, this factor involves evaluation of one's face and the related aspects of complexion and eyes. This would be understandable, since facial features are among the first characteristics people notice and are important aspects of handsomeness and beauty. But this pattern is confounded by the fact that genitals also are consistently associated with this factor. Among nonstudent males, this factor seems to be comprised of bodily characteristics above the waist, i.e., face, complexion, shoulders, and chest. This factor was generally weaker than the first, in the percentage of both factor and total variance for which it accounts.

Again scores were constructed by summing the individual's responses to the relevant items, employing unit weighting.

Internal-External Control

The concept and original measure of internal-external control were developed by Rotter (1966). He reported several factor analyses which supported his position that the measure he employed is unidimensional. However, Gurin et al. (1969) have introduced some important distinctions and presented empirical evidence suggesting that it is in fact multidimensional. Using the Rotter items and a variety of additional ones in the same format, they found four factors: control ideology (beliefs about the determinants of outcomes generally in the culture), personal control (beliefs about the extent to which one controls his or her own life), system modificability (beliefs about the extent to which various social phenomena can be controlled by man), and race ideology. The analysis and data of Gurin et al. convinced us to begin with their measure. Since the race ideology factor was not relevant for our purposes, we omitted the items which loaded on it. Thus, the pre-test included a 22-item measure, comprised of the items which loaded on their first three factors. An "item" in both the Rotter and Gurin et al. measures actually includes two statements; in each case the respondent is asked to choose the one of the pair which is most accurate. In our pre-test, we found that many respondents objected to this absolute, forced-choice format. While they often found that one was more true, or true more of the time, they felt that selecting that one in the context of the measure misrepresented their beliefs. As a result, there were considerable missing data and many comments written on the questionnaires. Accordingly, we revised the format to provide for degrees of agreement with one or the other.

To the extent that we could, we analyzed the pre-test results, and found evidence of the three factors. However, there was also some evidence of a fourth factor in the responses of women to the scale; items which involved the importance of being liked by and pleasing others seemed to constitute a somewhat independent set. This was suggestive of an "interpersonal control" factor, beliefs about the extent to which friends and acquaintances control what happens to the individual. We wrote several additional items of this nature. Having both revised the response format and added items, we decided to obtain additional pre-test data; we were able to obtain access to several university classes, which yielded about 180 completed scales. Again, we factor analyzed the responses, both for all respondents and separately for males and females. These results did not yield clear-cut factors. A substantial number of the items loaded on more than one factor; in most of these cases, it appeared that the two statements introduced more than one of the four factors or concepts, and these were revised to limit their content. We were forced by pressures of time to produce the final scale, and so, with these revisions and the inclusion of new items to provide nine items whose content might relate to each factor, a 36-item scale resulted. This final scale is reproduced in figure I.3; in order to conserve space, the repetition of the response categories, which appeared in the original on the right half of the page, has been omitted.

As noted, this scale was initially taken from Gurin et al. (1969). We had hoped to measure three of the factors which they found (control ideology, personal

Figure I.3. Internal-External Control Measure

On the following pages are some pairs of statements. Read each statement, and decide which item in the pair you agree with more. Then select the response which most closely represents your opinion. For example, consider these two statements:

    a. Ice cream is good for the soul
    b. Ice cream is bad for the soul

Agree much more with *a*	Agree somewhat more with *a*	Agree slightly more with *a*	Agree slightly more with *b*	Agree somewhat more with *b*	Agree much more with *b*
___	___	___	___	___	___

You do not have to make an absolute choice between these two. Suppose you agree with *a* a little more than with *b*; then you would check "agree slightly more with *a*." If you agree with *b* much more than *a*, you would check "agree much more with *b*."
Be sure you select only one response for each pair of items.

1.   a. Most people's lives are controlled to a large extent by accidental happenings.
     b. Accidental happenings play a relatively small part in people's lives.
2.   a. It is always wise to plan ahead.
     b. It is not always wise to plan too far ahead because many things turn out to be a matter of good or bad fortune anyhow.
3.   a. People can have almost no control over the things politicians do in office.
     b. People can control the things politicians do in office.
4.   a. Who gets to be boss depends on who has the skill and ability; luck has little or nothing to do with it.
     b. Who gets to be boss is determined primarily by luck; skill and ability have little or nothing to do with it.
5.   a. I have very little control over what happens to me.
     b. What happens to me is my own doing.
6.   a. I consider my life to be like a piece of artist's clay; I can shape it into anything I wish.
     b. I have little control over the shape my life will take.
7.   a. When I am in an unfamiliar setting, I carefully watch people around me so that I will know how to behave.
     b. I rely on myself to know how to behave; that is far more important than what other people are doing.
8.   a. I am a person who does not change greatly in different kinds of situations.
     b. Since I am many different kinds of people, the situation at the moment determines who or what I am.
9.   a. Racial discrimination can be eliminated.
     b. Racial discrimination cannot be eliminated.
10.   a. The people cannot control world events.
     b. By taking an active part in political and social affairs, the people can control world events.
11.   a. It is usually more important to please yourself than to please other people.
     b. It is usually more important to please other people than to please yourself.
12.   a. Rational thinking will result in decisions which will, in the long run, prove to be wise.
     b. Only time and later developments can determine whether a decision was a wise one; therefore, it is useless to spend much time trying to be rational.
13.   a. The average citizen can have an influence in government decisions.
     b. The average citizen can have no influence in government decisions.
14.   a. We are capable of bringing about a permanent world peace.
     b. There is very little we can do to bring about a permanent world peace.
15.   a. Things often work out much differently than you expect they will, so I consider it a waste of time to make careful plans.
     b. I consider it very important to make careful plans for the future.
16.   a. I feel helpless in the face of what's happening in the world today.
     b. I feel that I can do something about what's happening in the world today.

Figure 1.3—*Continued*

17. a. Many times we might just as well decide what to do by flipping a coin.
    b. Flipping a coin is an unreasonable way to make a decision.
18. a. Governments are the result of the ideas and personalities of people and can be shaped by deliberate design.
    b. Governments are the result of historical and accidental events and cannot be shaped by deliberate design.
19. a. When I make plans, I am almost certain that I can make them work.
    b. Even when I make plans, I usually cannot make them work.
20. a. Trusting to fate has never turned out as well for me as making a decision to take a definite course of action.
    b. Trusting to fate has always worked better for me than deciding to take a definite course of action.
21. a. People can control the bureaucracies which are supposed to serve them.
    b. It is impossible for people to control the bureaucracies which are supposed to serve them.
22. a. Becoming a success is a matter of hard work; luck has little or nothing to do with it.
    b. Becoming a success is basically a matter of luck.
23. a. When making a decision about my life, I attempt to weigh very carefully the wishes and interests of the people around me.
    b. I attempt to make decisions about my life independent of the wishes and interests of the people around me.
24. a. People like me have very little chance of changing society.
    b. People like me can change society.
25. a. Since there is little I can do to control my future, I believe in being the type of person who can adjust to whatever happens.
    b. I am more likely to control events to suit myself than to shape myself to fit events.
26. a. Careful plans for the future will probably be changed greatly by fate or luck.
    b. If one makes careful plans for the future, fate or luck will probably not change them much.
27. a. The decisions I make for myself depend heavily on what other people are doing or saying.
    b. I tend to make decisions for myself that depend very little on what other people are doing or saying.
28. a. When I am trying to make up my mind about something, I pay little attention to the opinions of other people.
    b. When I am trying to make up my mind about something, the opinions of people I like are very important.
29. a. There is nothing I can do about the things happening in the world today.
    b. I can do something about the things happening in the world today.
30. a. I know whether I am right, regardless of whether other people agree with me.
    b. If a lot of people disagree with my decision I know that I am probably wrong.
31. a. I cannot determine the pattern of my life.
    b. I can determine the pattern of my life.
32. a. Unpredictable events usually make it impossible for me to carry out the plans I make for my future.
    b. While unpredictable events do make a difference, I can manage to carry out whatever plans I make for my future.
33. a. In my case, getting what I want has little or nothing to do with luck.
    b. Getting what I want depends largely on luck.
34. a. Many people never get the respect they deserve in this world.
    b. In the long run people get the respect they deserve in this world.
35. a. Chance determines almost everything; making decisions is therefore a waste of time.
    b. Decisions will determine the future; chance plays a very small part.
36. a. It is not important to me to have other people respect and approve the important decisions I make.
    b. I think it is very important to have other people respect and approve of important decisions I make.

control, and system modificability) and the interpersonal control dimension which was suggested by some of our pre-test results. However, factor analyses of the 36 items consistently identified only three dimensions. The results of the final analysis are presented in table I.3. The composition of Factor I is almost identical in all four subsamples. It is comprised of items which concern the importance of planning for the future (15, 26), deciding on a course of action (20, 35), hard work in determining success (22), and luck (33) and an item dealing with whether the individual can carry out his or her plans (32). In addition, items 6 (control over one's life) and 17 (decision making) each load in one subsample. This is fairly clearly a personal control dimension. In three of the subsamples, this is the strongest factor, accounting for proportionately more of the factor variance (40 to 47 percent) as well as total variance. In the NF subsample, this factor is slightly weaker than Factor II.

The second dimension is quite different in content. Its composition also varies more across the four subsamples. Questions with large loadings in three or four of the groups concern people's control over politicians' actions (3), citizen influence on government (13), and whether the individual can affect world events (10, 29). In the student subsamples, item 21, concerning people's ability to control bureaucracies, also has a high loading. Among nonstudent females, items 14 (whether people can bring about peace) and 24 (the ability of people to control society), and among nonstudent males, item 16 (helplessness in the face of world events), load on this factor. These items all relate to the system control/control ideology aspects of internal-external control. Factor II was almost as strong as Factor I in variance accounted for.

Factor III was consistently the weakest, accounting for 17 to 22 percent of the factor variance and only 4 to 5 percent of the total variance in the items. Four items had high loadings in at least three of the four groups: the extent to which others influence personal decisions (23, 27), the importance of others' opinions (28), and the importance of their approval of one's decision (36). Other items had high loadings in one or more of the subsamples: the extent to which one watches others for behavioral cues (7), the importance of pleasing others (11), whether others influence one's feeling of being right (30), and the extent to which one can control events (25). In general, the underlying dimension deals with interpersonal control, the extent to which the individual is sensitive to and influenced by others. To our knowledge, such a factor has not been identified in previous research.

Thus, we have three scores for each of our respondents: personal control, the extent to which they feel in control of what happens to them; system control, the extent to which they feel people in general can influence society and large-scale events; and interpersonal control, or the extent to which others control their behavior. Again, the numerical codes for each person's answers on the relevant items were summed to arrive at his or her scores.

Role Definitions

A large number of measures have been used to assess the individual's orientations toward male and female roles. Most of these have been used in only one or two

TABLE I.3. Internal-external control: factor loadings
Principal factor procedure—3 rotations

Item number	SM I	SM II	SM III	NM I	NM II	NM III	SF I	SF II	SF III	NF I	NF II	NF III
1	.261	-.070	.019	.381	.130	.061	.307	.075	.115	.285	.041	.029
2	.411	-.124	-.059	.213	-.185	.321	.413	-.020	-.021	.336	.093	.115
3	.057	.599*	-.237	.050	.569*	.006	.126	.591*	-.054	.080	.595*	-.010
4	.446	.084	-.095	.378	.067	-.227	.363	.123	.192	.159	.172	.343
5	.295	.187	.055	.399	.076	.178	.302	.236	.006	.207	.169	.042
6	.293	.132	.017	.444*	-.109	.005	.250	.148	.115	.113	.279	.044
7	.117	.201	.400*	.251	.072	.244	.033	.126	.431*	.216	.104	.189
8	.253	.022	.011	.086	-.087	-.151	.018	.187	.139	.236	-.031	.073
9	-.010	.308	.168	.049	.325	-.059	.105	.376	.102	.038	.274	-.115
10	.050	.529*	.031	.111	.572*	.070	.042	-.093	.049	.125	.445	.105
11	-.076	-.111	.237	-.114	.161	.120	.389	.098	.444*	-.127	.044	.373*
12	.474	-.015	-.091	.312	.168	-.089	.135	.638*	-.019	.280	.178	.086
13	.167	.485*	-.300	.130	.519*	-.223	.092	.564	-.086	.045	.584*	-.035
14	.084	.425	.006	.083	.564	-.170	.535*	.040	.037	.135	.548*	.107
15	.555*	.016	-.083	.445*	.119	-.059	.186	.543	.099	.433*	.208	-.118
16	.178	.533	.050	.226	.622*	.166	.368	.072	.008	.175	.531	.169
17	.287	.158	.077	.239	.100	.209	.308	.375	-.053	.450*	.094	-.051
18	.319	.256	-.015	.174	.167	-.271	.463*	.134	.109	.208	.393	-.088
19	.445	.203	.045	.391	.053	-.001	.532*	-.022	.066	.314	.219	.062
20	.536*	.055	-.042	.346*	.100	-.156	.138	.680*	-.039	.583*	-.011	.132
21	.178	.559*	-.179	.192	.470	-.250	.527*	.175	-.140	.337	.420	-.185
22	.633*	.031	-.056	.530*	.098	.335*	-.083	-.040	-.140	.418*	.178	-.317
23	.028	-.041	.475*	-.025	.076	.235	.062	.565	.408	.129	-.027	.420*
24	.090	.541	.106	.103	.491	.305*	.226	.170	.260	.028	.542*	.255
25	.381	.152	.277	.408	.031	-.008	.571*	.083	.313	.146	.238	.314
26	.536*	.120	.047	.529*	-.106	.367*	.147	.142	.095	.517*	.097	.012
27	.261	-.110	.480*	.320	-.062	.223	.030	.008	.514*	.231	.055	.345*
28	-.069	-.062	.376*	-.050	.001	.057	.201	.640*	.456*	.103	-.044	.459*
29	.130	.740*	-.074	.159	.645*	.306*	.181	-.010	.116	.032	.610*	.091
30	.026	.037	.326	.040	-.176	.078	.435	.233	.393	.001	.083	.325
31	.445*	.242	.165	.376	.185	-.001	.492*	.151	.151	.238	.423	.210
32	.519*	.268	.047	.499*	.240	-.163	.508*	.149	.173	.519*	.202	.019
33	.549*	.114	.163	.603*	.102	.214		.093	.126	.547*	.095	-.173
34	.180	-.002	.011	.064	-.061	-.116	.211	.144	-.016	.069	.199	-.126
35	.551*	-.137	-.003	.510*	.119		.649*	.079	.040	.508*	.235	-.115
36	-.072	-.073	.406*	-.103	-.161	.411*	-.076	.042	.564*	-.035	-.010	.520*
% factor variance	46.9	35.8	17.3	43.6	38.1	18.2	40.5	38.7	20.7	37.2	41.1	21.7
% total variance	11.2	8.6	4.1	9.6	8.4	4.0	10.4	10.0	5.3	8.2	9.1	4.8

*Items chosen for factor. I = personal control and efficacy of planning   II = system control   III = interpersonal control

251

studies, and there is no measure which is generally considered better than any others. In developing our measure, we selected the best items, either in terms of their reported statistical characteristics or their content, from a variety of scales. This pool was included in our pre-test, and on the basis of correlational and factor analyses, 12 items seemed to be worth retaining. The 12 items are reproduced in figure I.4.

Factor analyses of responses to these items consistently identified one large factor; other factors which were found consisted of only one or two items and generally accounted for very little variance. Item three, concerning responsibility for discipline of children, did not correlate highly with the remaining items nor did it load systematically on the factor. Accordingly, it was dropped from the scale. The role definition scale thus consists of the remaining 11 items with codes summed to arrive at an individual's score. Low scores reflect agreement with "traditional" role definitions, such as fewer grounds of divorce should be permitted wives, obedience is a wifely virtue, and women should be guided by men's views of decency in dress. High scores reflect more egalitarian views, such as women can decide proper dress for themselves, there should be no legal restrictions on night work by women, and women are as capable as men of contributing to economic production.

SEXUAL IDEOLOGY

We discussed at length both Ehrmann's (1959) and Reiss's (1967) measures of individual standards. Reiss inquired about the acceptability of three behaviors within each of four types of relationships. He employed 12 items, each pairing one behavior with one relationship, to measure standards for males and repeated the items for females. In general, Reiss (1967) found that respondents were highly consistent in their answers. For example, if an individual accepted intercourse when two people were in love, he or she accepted it when they were married; however, he or she might not if they were single and felt only strong affection or felt no affection. We believed that a more efficient question format could be designed. We listed categories representing relationships, ordered in terms of emotional intimacy, on a card which was handed to the respondent and simply asked at what point in the development of the relationship each of three behaviors was acceptable. We assessed ideology for males and females separately; thus, our measure consists of 6 items instead of 24, although it yields essentially the same information and can be scored to produce a permissiveness scale which is similar to Reiss's.

We then needed to select (1) the specific behaviors and (2) the categories of relationships to be included. The behaviors employed by Reiss were kissing, petting, and intercourse. We felt that for college-age young people in 1972–73, kissing was not a particularly meaningful behavior. Instead, we used breast fondling, genital fondling, and intercourse.

Simon and Gagnon (1968) employed five categories in measures characterizing the quality of relationships: not before marriage, if engaged, if in love, if feel

FIGURE 1.4. Role Behavior Scale

Instructions

On the following pages is a list of statements with which you are asked to express either agreement or disagreement. After the statement, circle the response category which most closely corresponds to your attitude.

For example, if you were to strongly agree with the following statement, you would mark the category in this way:

Ice cream is good for the soul.   1   2   3   4   5   6

When you have completed the twelve items, please return the questionnaire to the interviewer.

ROLE BEHAVIOR SCALE

	Strongly Agree	Moderately Agree	Slightly Agree	Slightly Disagree	Moderately Disagree	Strongly Disagree
A. Women who insist upon removing the word "obey" from the marriage service make themselves appear foolish.	1	2	3	4	5	6
B. A husband has the right to expect that his wife should always be faithful and dutiful.	1	2	3	4	5	6
C. Parental authority and responsibility for discipline of the children should be equally divided between husband and wife.	1	2	3	4	5	6
D. Women have the right to decide for themselves what is appropriate dress for females.	1	2	3	4	5	6
E. It is senseless to regard scrubbing floors as more proper for women than mowing the lawn.	1	2	3	4	5	6
F. Fewer grounds for divorce should be permitted the wife as compared with the husband.	1	2	3	4	5	6
G. It is absurd to regard obedience as a wifely virtue.	1	2	3	4	5	6
H. There should be no legal restrictions upon night work by women.	1	2	3	4	5	6
I. A woman who continues to work outside the home after marriage is shirking her fundamental duty to home and children.	1	2	3	4	5	6
J. On the average women should be regarded as less capable of contributing to economic production than are men.						
K. Women should not be permitted to hold political offices that involve great responsibility.	1	2	3	4	5	6
L. Women should be guided by men's view of decency in dress.	1	2	3	4	5	6

affection, and if both want it. Three of these are equivalent to those used by Reiss, and the addition of "not before marriage" seemed appropriate, so these were the types of relationships we included. When we discussed this measure with colleagues, they frequently argued that "times have changed," that young people no longer think of relationships in such "narrow, tradition-bound" terms. Since prior research has shown that standards depend on the type of relationship, it was very important to have categories which were meaningful to our respondents. We decided to determine empirically whether the categories used made a difference. We developed a set of categories which employed "feel a long-term commitment" instead of engaged. In our pre-test, half of the respondents were interviewed using the former and half using the latter in all questions dealing with intimacy of relationships. The procedures used and the results are described in greater detail by DeLamater (1974a); generally, we found no difference in responses or results, and so in the final interview schedule we used the more "traditional" terms.

The same measure was employed to assess the ideology of the respondent's current partner, with the referent changed from how "you personally feel" to how "your partner feels."

MEASURES OF GROUP INFLUENCE

There has been considerable variation in measures used to assess the influence of peers on the individual's premarital sexuality. Reiss (1967) argued that the individual derives his or her standards from peers. This implies that it is important to measure friends' standards. From a symbolic interactionist point of view, we would expect that it is the individual's *perception* of his or her peers' standards that influences him or her, that is, what the person knows about their beliefs, which may or may not correspond with the beliefs themselves. Therefore, we wanted to assess perception of peers' ideology. We employed the same format used to measure the person's own attitudes. There has also been variation in the definition of "peers." Mirande (1968) asked about the individual's two closest friends. Others (Walsh, 1970; Vandiver, 1972; Walsh, Ferrell, and Tolone, 1976) have asked about his or her close friends. In both cases, gender is apparently not specified. Borgatta and Bohrnstedt (1970) used "your five best friends of the same sex" as an operational definition of peers, and this seemed the best of those which have been used. This measure of peer influence is termed *friends' ideology* and refers to questions concerning the acceptability of the three behaviors to the respondent's "five close friends." "Friends" was defined as "people who you know best, whom you confide in on occasion, and who confide in you."

The individual probably has some information about his or her friends' sexual standards. It occurred to us that he or she might believe, realistically or not, that these friends had different standards for him or her. We do make exceptions for our friends and may rationalize their behavior to the extent that it departs from the norms we hold. When the individual's behavior is different from peers' standards and they do not attempt to influence him or her to change, he or she may conclude that they accept the difference, that is, that they have different expectations for him or her compared to others. We therefore also asked the ideology questions in terms of when in his or her relationship, your "five close friends" believe a given behavior "is acceptable for you." This measure will be referred to as *friends' expectations*. To our knowledge, this is the first time such a measure has been employed.

Thus far we have considered perception of peers' attitudes. Some social psychologists have argued that equally or more important is the person's beliefs about friends' behavior. We may recognize that others do not always adhere to their beliefs, and we may be influenced more by what they do than what they say. Borgatta and Bohrnstedt (1970) employed perception of one's five best friends' behavior in a variety of areas (alcohol consumption, drug use, as well as sexuality) as their primary measure of peer influence. We followed their lead and asked how many of one's five close friends engaged in each of the nine heterosexual activities included in our behavioral scale. This is referred to as *friends' behavior*.

Simon and Gagnon (1968) used different measures in an apparent attempt to assess peer influence. Their questions concerning peer standards asked "When do you think girls/boys at this college" or "most boys/most girls feel ——— is acceptable?" Similarly, they inquired about peer behavior by asking "How many boys/girls at your college ———?" Their respondents were selected from 12 colleges and universities, ranging from quite small (a few hundred students) to a university with more than 30,000 students. Their questions may be quite valid in a very small college, where intensive interaction conceivably produces a great deal of homogeneity of attitude. We felt that students in a large university or community would find it difficult if not impossible to assign a single standard to boys and to girls. We were intrigued by their questions concerning behavior; this is one way to assess the respondent's perception of the larger community of young people, and it may tap a more general aspect of social influence. We thus included questions which asked "what percentage of males/females engage in" each of four behaviors: breast fondling, genital fondling, oral-genital contact, and intercourse. We call this a measure of *context* and do not consider it a measure of peer influence in the strict sense of that term.

Thus, we measured a variety of aspects of peer influence. In our analyses we were particularly interested in assessing their relative explanatory significance. If we find substantial differences between them, such that we can conclude that some are more useful than others, this will be a contribution to the literature on peer or group influence.

These measures of peer influence as well as the measures of ideology discussed earlier involve references to members of the two sexes. We were struck by the fact that different researchers have employed different terms; Reiss (1967) used male/female in his scales, Simon and Gagnon (1968) used boy/girl. We became concerned that such variation might be important; the connotation of youth, and possibly immaturity, associated with boy and girl may produce differences in responses compared to male and female. Accordingly, we systematically varied the gender terms in our pre-test, always using boy/girl in half of the interviews, and male/female in the other half. The results, discussed by DeLamater (1974a), indicated that this variation made no difference. Since our sample would consist of people 18 and older, we felt that male/female was more appropriate and used these terms in our final interview schedule.

CHARACTERISTICS OF RELATIONSHIPS

The development of a valid measure of the quality of specific heterosexual relationships was of particular concern. As discussed in Chapter 2, we believe that the specific sexual behavior which occurs is influenced by the quality of the relationship, that is, by whether or not the relation has the intimacy required by the person's ideology. It was obviously desirable to use the same categories as those included in the ideology measure: engaged, in love, and feel affection ("married" was omitted since all respondents would be single). Simon and Gagnon's (1968) measure included three additional categories: someone the person dated casually, "pick-up," and prostitute. These seemed relevant, though we did not like the connotations of the last two; we used the phrase "someone you dated only once or twice" and "paid sexual partner" instead.

Again the issue arose over whether traditional categories such as dating and engaged were meaningful to young people. As with the ideology measure, we developed an alternate set of categories, which employed "seeing" instead of "dating" and "expected to marry" instead of "engaged." In our pre-test, those for whom the ideology measure used traditional terms were given such categories in the measure of quality of relationships; for the other half, both measures employed the alternate terms. Again, as reported by DeLamater (1974a), there was no evidence that these differences in wording affected the results.

The relationship measure was used to assess quality of the relationship with the person's partner in their first intercourse experience and with all the persons they were currently dating.

FAMILIAL CHARACTERISTICS

We believe that parents are the original source of the individual's sexual standards. Thus, we wanted to measure at least the person's perception of his or her parents' standards and attitudes regarding his or her sexual behavior. In the pre-test research, we included a large number of questions concerning how a parent would respond to a particular situation involving the child, for example, to knowledge that the person was having sexual intercourse with someone he or she loved. Questions were asked separately about mothers' and fathers' reactions. In general, we found that responses to these did not relate significantly to either the standards or behavior of the person. It occurred to us that such items perhaps included two elements, both the parents' standards and their response to a particular situation. Accordingly, in the final schedule we used the basic ideology measure presented earlier and asked the respondent when in a relationship his or her mother and father felt each of the behaviors was acceptable for the person. We did retain separate questions about how each parent would respond to the individual living with a member of the opposite sex, being pregnant (asked of women) or getting a girl pregnant (for men), and what each parent would expect the person to do if a pregnancy occurred.

Appendix II

Quality Of The Data

The purpose of including the methodological variations discussed in Chapter 3 was twofold: we could determine whether there were differences in response associated with these differences in technique, and checks could be made on the quality of the data. Insofar as these variations do not affect the responses obtained, we can have additional confidence in the quality of the data. We analyzed the effects of the methodological variations before performing any of the substantive analyses because if a variation had significantly affected the responses, we would have had to control for it in subsequent analyses.

There are two types of factors that could affect the responses and the quality of the data. First, there are respondent characteristics, including willingness to answer, truthfulness, and response error. The interviewer's characteristics, attitudes, and skills are the second potential source of variation. Each of these is examined in turn.

RESPONDENT ASPECTS

Uncontrolled Respondent Variation

Various characteristics of the respondent could affect the quality of the data. He or she could react to the interview in ways that would affect his or her response. If the respondent was unwilling to answer some questions and either refused to answer or said "don't know" where it was an inappropriate response, the response rate on those questions would be low. Overall, the response rate within the schedule was extremely high; there were few missing data. The vast majority of the items have responses for every respondent who was asked the question. The items with the most missing data lack only 14, 15, 18, and 20 responses out of 432 (SM), 220 (NM), 431 (SF), and 293 (NF) interviewees, respectively. The questions on sexual behavior should be particularly sensitive to respondent unwillingness to answer. However, even these questions have high response rates. In the series of questions assessing lifetime sexual behavior, one female student did not answer the last six questions; among the nonstudents, two males have missing data on one and four items and two females on two and five questions. For student males, the answers are complete to all the questions. The resulting response rate for the lifetime behavior measure is 99.2 percent. All respondents answered each of the current sexual behavior items. In general, a complete set of answers was obtained for nearly every question in the interview schedule.

Given this high response rate, the next problematic aspect would be whether the respondents were answering truthfully. In order to assess the respondent's reactions to the interview, after the interview had been completed he or she filled out a questionnaire that described his or her feelings during the interview. The written and oral instructions told the respondent that the interviewer would not see the questionnaire, which was to be placed in an envelope and sealed by the respondent. In addition, the written instructions said that the information gathered would not be used to evaluate the interviewer, although comments about the interviewer could be made in a space provided at the bottom of the post-interview reaction sheet. The interviewer explained that the purpose of the questionnaire was to help the researchers learn how best to conduct this type of study. The first set of questions involved semantic differential scales in which the interview was to be characterized as boring/interesting, innocuous/offensive, trivial/relevant, comfortable/uncomfortable, pleasant/unpleasant, and unimportant/important. The second part asked how much of the time the respondent had felt embarrassed, that his or her privacy had been invaded, that he or she didn't want to answer, had been worried about confidentiality, and how much of the time it was easy to be frank. Two final questions asked "How much of the time did you answer truthfully?" and if the respondent had not answered the questions about sexual behavior truthfully, whether sexual behavior had been overreported or underreported.

Answers to these questions provide evidence that the quality of the data was not affected to any great extent by variation in the truthfulness of the respondents. About a third of the respondents answered that it was easy to be frank all the time, with an additional 40 percent indicating that it was easy most of the time. Even though some respondents may not have found it easy to be frank, they apparently were honest. Three-quarters of the respondents reported answering truthfully all the time [75 (SM), 77 (NM), 78 (SF), and 75 (NF) percent]. An additional 19 to 23 percent reported answering truthfully most of the time. Some respondents commented verbally or in writing that they had reported less than total honesty because they had had trouble remembering some of the information requested or had been just estimating. These comments suggest that some of the variance in honesty was due to the accessibility of the answer to the respondent rather than a desire not to answer or report accurately due to the interview situation or topic. Of those who did not answer truthfully all the time, 7.9, 10.4, 5.6, and 4.8 percent had reported too much sexual behavior, and 7.9, 5.4, 7.0, and 10.2 percent had reported too little sexual behavior among student males, nonstudent males, student females, and nonstudent females respectively. Thus, while the over-reporting and underreporting is more balanced among the students, in general non-student females tended to underreport and nonstudent males to overreport. In regard to the questions on sexual behavior, 84 to 87 percent reported complete candor. As pointed out by Johnson and DeLamater (1976), with the assumption that the post-interview reactions were valid, it does not appear that the sexual topic of some questions was the only source of the repondents' lack of truthfulness.

In order to see if the answers of those who were less than totally truthful affected the obtained rates of sexual behavior, the percentage of persons engaging in each behavior was computed for those who reported telling the truth about their sexual behavior. The resulting percentages are not significantly different from those obtained for the total sample. Of the 36 comparisons of lifetime sexual activity (nine behaviors in each of the four subsamples), only five are 2 percent or larger; none are larger than 5 percent. Comparisons of current sexual behavior show 14 differences greater than 2 percent, 8 of those more than 3; none are larger than 5 percent. If the candid percentages are assumed to be more valid, the differences in lifetime behavior represent underreporting by the total sample while 21 of the 24 differences in current behavior show overreporting by the total. Because the largest difference in the smallest sample (NM) falls well within the 98-percent confidence interval, these differences are not significant and did not warrant further analysis.

In summary, if one assumes that the post-interview reactions were answered truthfully, it seems that nearly three-quarters of the respondents answered truthfully most of the time. A larger percentage told the truth about their sexual behavior. The frequency of sexual behavior reported by candid respondents does not seem to be significantly different from the total sample. The data do not appear to have been affected by unwillingness to answer or lack of truthfulness on the respondent's part.

A third way of measuring the respondent's reaction to the interview was by having the interviewer rate the degree of tension or discomfort the respondent evidenced. The interviewer checked a position on a seven-point scale unobtrusively at four times during the interview. The first rating followed the demographic, political, and religious questions; the second followed the section on contraceptives; the third occurred after the demographic questions on the family; and the last one was after completing the questions on sexual attitudes and behaviors. The mean for each interviewer was computed and compared to the grand mean. This comparison proved to be uninterpretable, since each interviewer happens to have had a different perception of what a given value on the scale corresponded to in terms of the respondent's tension. There were, therefore, great differences in the base rate. Instead, an overall mean was computed for each interviewer and the first and last tension ratings he or she gave his or her respondents was compared to this grand mean. Overall, there is an increase in tension throughout the interview which would be expected, since the questions dealing with sexual behavior are placed at the end. The largest increase for students was 3.38 points on the seven-point scale; it was 2.28 for the nonstudents. It should be noted, however, that even with the increase in tension ratings, the grand means fall on the relaxed side of the scale.

In an examination of each interviewer's mean first and last tension rating, a difference-between-means test was calculated to see if the increase in tension was statistically significant. For the nonstudent respondents, the difference was not significant; for students, the increase was significant ($p < 0.05$). There are several possible explanations for this difference between students and nonstudents. Several interviewers left the project after the students were interviewed; several of these interviewers had large difference scores, indicating increasing tension. The non-students were, therefore, interviewed by a smaller number of interviewers who were also better on our measures of technical competence and rapport. Thus, these interviewers may have been more comfortable with the interviewing and rated tension as lower, or they may actually have put more of the respondents at ease. Finally, since the nonstudents were interviewed after the students, the inter-viewers who remained had had considerable experience, making them better inter-viewers or changing their perceptions of the respondents over time.

Since the tension rating is dependent upon the interviewer's perceptions of the respondents, which varied between interviewers and perhaps also over time, the conclusions to be drawn are limited. Overall, the tension rating tended toward the relaxed side of the scale throughout the interview. In addition, there was a small increase in tension from the first to last tension rating. Because of the various interpretations of the difference between students and nonstudents, no conclusion as to the cause or meaning of the increase can be drawn. The tension-rating technique of measuring the respondent's reaction to the interview, is, therefore, of limited usefulness.

Planned Interview Variations

The variations in techniques described in Chapter 3 were included to test their effect on respondents. The results of these variations are discussed briefly here and have been examined in greater detail elsewhere (DeLamater and MacCor-quodale, 1975). First, the order or sequence of the questions on current sexual behavior, partner's sexual ideology, and attributes of the relationship were varied. Six forms of the schedule were prepared representing the six possible orders for these three sets of questions. The form which the respondent received was deter-mined by the order of scheduling within each educational status–gender category. Since the number of respondents was large, the assignment to form of the interview constituted essentially random assignment. Because of the noncontinuous nature of this variation, analysis of variance by form was used to look for differences in each of the component variables. These analyses were run separately for each educational status–gender subsample. Age was entered as the other factor.

Analysis of variance is a technique for assessing the statistical significance of differences between groups. The groups can be determined by variations in a numerical amount of some characteristic or treatment, in the experimental case, or by qualitative differences. A statistically significant difference is one that is unlikely to occur because of chance alone: if the same variables were measured on a different sample drawn from the sample population, one would expect the results to be the same. Because it is easier to obtain statistical significance with large samples, attention must be paid to the pattern of statistically significant results and to the meaningfulness of relationships.

There were 28 items involved in the three sets of questions. As previously reported (DeLamater and MacCorquodale, 1975), the Fs obtained for form were almost all nonsignificant, indicating that varying the sequence of questions did not affect the responses obtained. The variation in question ordering had been included because it seemed that respondent's beliefs about how physical intimacy, quality of relationship, and partner's sexual ideology should be related might lead them to misrepresent one of these aspects toward consistency with earlier responses. We found, however, no effect of sequence on responses to these questions. In the absence of any order effect, it seems that the interview simply elicits the respondent's preexisting characterization of the relationship. In this context, asking about sexual behavior first, for example, does not substantially affect the later reports of emotional intimacy, or vice versa.

The second variation involved interviewer versus self-assessment of lifetime sexual behavior. Half the respondents received a questionnaire with the same questions and ordering that had been used by the interviewers for assessing lifetime sexual behavior for the other half. The assignment to type of assessment depended on the identification number. Over the large samples involved, the assignment to type of assessment was random. The independent variable was dichotomous, so analyses of variance were used to examine the effect of type of assessment on reported lifetime sexual behavior and age at first experience. The analyses were performed within each educational status–gender group; for example, student females who were questioned by the interviewer were compared to the student females who filled out the questionnaire. Age was entered as the other factor, in order to control for its strong, positive association with sexual behavior.

The results (DeLamater and MacCorquodale, 1975) indicate that there was no substantial or systematic effect by type of assessment. Nineteen variables in each of the four samples were analyzed; of the resulting 76 F values, only seven are statistically significant. Six of the seven occur in the reports of the more physically intimate behaviors. The direction of the difference is the same in all six cases; respondents who were asked the question were more likely to report having engaged in the behavior. Since it seems unlikely that these people would falsely report having engaged in intimate sexual behaviors, it follows that the questionnaire resulted in some underreporting of behavior. Besides the questions asking whether the person had ever engaged in each behavior, and age at first experience, a summary measure of lifetime behavior was constructed. This is discussed in detail in Chapter 4. At this point, it is sufficient to note that there are no significant differences in this lifetime score as a function of type of assessment. Therefore, there were few statistically significant effects of this variation, and the overall conclusion is that type of assessment did not substantially affect reported sexual behavior.

The comparison of the first and second assessments of lifetime and current sexual behavior provides information on the effect of the placement of these questions within the interview as well as on the reliability of the responses. The lifetime behavior of half the respondents, and the current behavior of the other half, was reassessed at the end of the interview. The identification numbers were used to determine which behavior was assessed twice: if the respondent's number ended in an even digit, lifetime was assessed again, and if it ended in an odd digit, there was a second assessment of current behavior. Again, this assignment is essentially random with the large Ns involved. If the respondent's answers differed the second time, the interviewer politely indicated that there was a discrepancy and asked which of the two responses was more correct.

The yes or no responses given to both assessments of lifetime and current sexual behavior can be compared to see if they were identical or different. Since there were only a very small number of changed responses, only the sums across the nine behaviors were considered. Nine answers for each respondent are, thus, included in the "lifetime totals" and in "current totals." As the results discussed elsewhere (DeLamater and MacCorquodale, 1975) indicate, virtually all the responses were identical; only 68 out of 11,910 sets of paired responses were different (0.0057 %). The changes usually involved the more physically intimate behaviors, and the second assessment was reportedly more valid in 53 of these cases. Thus, there was slightly greater honesty associated with behavior reported at the end than with the assessment in the middle of the interview. In terms of the direction of the 68 changes, when the first assessment was more correct, 12 of the 15 changes were to "No" on second assessment, i.e., in the direction of less reported behavior. The changes were almost equally divided between reporting less (24) and more (29) behavior when the second assessment was correct.

The ages at first experience for lifetime behavior were compared by examining the product-moment correlations between the two responses. The correlation coefficient is an estimate of the (linear) relationship between two variables. A correlation coefficient of zero means that the variables are completely unrelated; as the magnitude of the coefficient approaches one, there is a stronger relationship between the variables. If the coefficient is positive, high scores on one variable are associated with high scores on the other. A negative coefficient indicates that high scores on one are associated with low scores on the other.

Generally, there was close to perfect agreement between the ages reported on the first and second lifetime assessments (see DeLamater and MacCorquodale, 1975). Thirty of the 36 correlations were greater than 0.95. We also computed the product-moment correlations between the two assessments of the percentages of the time the respondent reported engaging in the behavior with the current partner. While only seven of these correlations are greater than 0.95, 29 are above 0.90. The somewhat greater differences between the responses reflected by these correlations undoubtedly reflect the more judgmental nature of the percentage reports. By contrast, the age at which one first experiences a given behavior is more concrete and may be easier to remember as it is more salient.

The conclusion drawn from the two assessments of lifetime and current behavior is that the reports of sexual behavior were highly reliable within the interview; there were very few changes. This reliability seems to reflect the nature of the questions which asked whether the respondent had ever engaged in precisely defined, salient behaviors, age of first experience, and whether and how often these same behaviors had been engaged in with one's current partner. The small differences between reports at the middle and end of the interview indicate that the placement of questions did not produce large enough differences to substantially change the findings. There were no differences in extent of agreement by gender or educational status.

INTERVIEWER ASPECTS

The interviewer can also be a potential source of variation in responses. Through the interaction between the respondent and the interviewer, the interviewer may create a certain atmosphere that elicits certain responses. The respondent may infer from personal characteristics or behavior of the interviewer that the interviewer holds certain attitudes and may change his or her answers accordingly. Second, interviewers vary in the quality of their interviewing, both in the extent to which they encourage a businesslike, friendly interaction and in the asking, recording, and explaining of the questions themselves. These variations in interviewer aspects could affect the obtained responses and thus, the quality of the data. Accordingly, the data were analyzed for evidence of such effects. A more detailed discussion of interviewer effects is presented by Johnson and DeLamater (1976).

As discussed in Chapter 3, interviewer gender was varied in each status-gender subsample. One-quarter of the interviews were randomly selected among the female samples for cross-sex interviews and among the male sample for same-sex interviews. This variation was included because, while earlier research had suggested that same-gender interviews were more accurate (Benney, Reisman, and Star, 1956; Schofield, 1965), it was unclear from the pre-test data (DeLamater, 1974a) that interviewer gender significantly affected responses obtained, especially those relating to sexual attitudes and behavior.

The majority of the respondents were interviewed by females. In the student sample, 23 percent of the females (99 of 431) and 21 percent of the males (92 of 432) and among the nonstudents, 15 percent of the men (34 of 220) and 19 percent of the females (55 of 293) had male interviewers. Since approximately the same proportion of males were interviewed same-gender as females cross-gender, and since the gender variation is a qualitative one, analyses of variance were used. The dependent variables that were tested for interviewer-gender effects included both lifetime and current sexual behaviors, sexual attitudes, and responses to the post-interview reactions.

As indicated in table II.1, only six of the 72 separate comparisons of sexual behavior yielded significant F values: three in lifetime behavior and three in current behavior. Nonstudent females reported younger ages of heterosexual breast fondling and genital fondling, and fewer current experiences of necking and french kissing, when interviewed by males. On the sexual attitude questions, only one significant difference was found; male students expressed more permissive attitudes about genital fondling to same-gender interviewers. In general, interviewer gender had little effect on reported sexual behavior or attitudes.

The respondents did have different reactions to the interview depending on the gender of the interviewer. As shown in table II.1, there were only two differences among the males; male students rated the interview significantly more interesting when interviewed by a female, and male nonstudents reported telling the truth more to female interviewers. Among the female respondents, gender of interviewer had a more systematic effect. Student females rated the interview significantly more interesting and important, less offensive and embarrassing, and reported greater willingness to answer and more truthfulness when the interviewer was

Table II.1. Effects of variations in four interviewer variables on reported sexual behavior, attitudes, and reactions to the interview: F values

INTERVIEWER VARIABLE

Dependent variables	Gender				Sexual experience				"Rapport"				Technical competence			
	SM	NM	SF	NF	SM	NM	SF	NF	SM	NM	SF	NF	SM	NM	SF	NF
Lifetime sexual behavior																
Necking	3.48	0.17	0.32	0.14	0.87	1.21	0.74	3.64[a]	0.21	1.11	0.45	0.49	0.04	1.19	1.00	0.63
Age at first experience	0.64	0.03	0.01	0.01	3.36[b]	0.60	0.21	0.62[b]	1.59	0.89	0.01	0.75	4.48[b]	2.12	2.10	0.15
French kissing	1.49	0.06	0.04	1.14	1.06	0.59	1.38	2.91[b]	0.33	0.20	1.29	0.60	0.03	0.40	3.24[c]	1.23
Age at first experience	0.00	1.02	1.31	2.49	2.01	0.29	0.14	1.49	2.18	1.97	0.46	2.00	1.30	0.77	0.96	1.16
Breast fondling	1.40	0.05	0.02	2.31	0.16	1.60	1.89	2.81[c]	0.54	0.75	0.46	1.38	0.61	1.76	2.66	2.15
Age at first experience	0.16	0.90	0.01	3.92[c]	2.05	1.89	0.18	1.41	3.69[c]	0.65	2.07	2.41	2.29	0.74	0.78	1.55
Male fondling of female genitals	5.17[b]	0.00	0.16	0.15	0.63	0.40	1.03	2.17	0.51	0.35	0.26	0.27	0.43	0.66	1.00	2.80
Age at first experience	0.15	1.47	0.74	5.35[b]	1.24	0.78	0.43	1.18	2.10	1.76	0.59	0.89	1.55	0.62	1.31	0.45
Female fondling of male genitals	3.16	0.00	0.17	0.01	1.07	0.27	1.03	1.63	0.90	0.37	0.07	0.08	1.00	0.18	1.71	2.24
Age at first experience	0.41	1.72	0.07	1.28	0.73	1.18	0.56	1.16	0.84	1.89	0.36	1.35	1.01	0.48	1.16	0.17
Genital apposition	2.40	0.00	0.32	0.04	1.03	0.23[c]	0.80	2.09	0.65[b]	0.18	0.25	0.60	3.45[c]	0.46	5.29[a]	1.73
Age at first experience	1.40	1.63	0.06	1.16	2.13	2.70[c]	0.42	0.83	4.05[b]	1.77	0.77	0.51	0.30	1.15	0.38	0.29
Intercourse	0.79	0.65	1.05	0.04	1.79	0.81	0.74	0.39	2.06	1.60	1.03	0.65	2.18	0.47	0.44	0.05
Age at first experience	0.49	1.29	0.24	0.07	0.47	0.96	0.21	1.05	0.14	0.61	1.56	1.21	0.05	0.49	0.28	0.07
Male oral contact with female genitals	0.07	0.45	2.16	0.01	0.63	2.43	0.80	0.51	1.26	1.11	0.22	0.43	4.26[b]	0.24	2.06	0.41
Age at first experience	0.42	3.67	2.30	3.00	1.89	0.24	1.10	0.67	0.74	0.09	1.03	0.99	1.22	1.11	1.29	0.28
Female oral contact with male genitals	1.37	0.14	0.45	0.24	0.41	3.16[b]	0.93	0.40	0.30	1.30	1.73	0.47	0.99	0.17	2.87	0.17
Age at first experience	0.31	1.66	3.04	2.43	1.62	0.30	0.13	0.50	0.18		0.78	0.37	0.07	0.96	0.16	0.10
Sexual behavior with current partner																
Necking	0.07	1.27	1.32	0.95	0.60	0.19	1.81	1.12	1.11	0.17	1.68	0.72	0.37	2.18[b]	0.14	0.57
Percent of times together	0.08	0.39	0.95	4.27[c]	1.48	0.60	2.24	1.41	8.18[a]	2.14	0.05	2.12	4.76[b]	4.68[b]	1.05	1.28
French kissing	0.53	1.22	0.69	0.00	0.71	0.61[b]	3.22[b]	0.54	0.47	0.49	0.39	0.16	1.08	1.39	0.44	0.29
Percent of times together	0.01	0.55	2.39	4.53[c]	2.29	3.02[b]	2.37	1.47	3.32[c]	2.10	0.13	1.50	4.15[b]	2.98	1.23	1.69
Breast fondling	1.04	1.05	1.30	0.00	1.39	0.22	0.83	2.05	0.95	0.76	0.96	0.51	0.90	1.36	0.40	1.21
Percent of times together	0.42	0.46	0.52	1.61	2.84[c]	1.89	2.34	0.32	1.91	1.57	0.88	2.17	1.05	2.25	1.19	1.33
Male fondling of female genitals	1.01	1.82	2.80	0.08	0.99	0.56	0.76	1.18	1.85	0.73	0.06	0.38	2.74	0.26	2.47	1.29
Percent of times together	0.00	0.00	1.18	1.03	0.83	0.72	0.73	0.99	3.67[c]	0.59	0.03	1.39	0.36	1.78	0.23	1.94
Female fondling of male genitals	0.72	2.73	1.43	0.11	0.98	0.80	0.78	1.36	1.02	0.47	0.82	0.34	1.72	0.48	1.27	1.75
Percent of times together	0.13	0.43	1.52	2.75	1.50	1.41	0.79	1.14	3.42[c]	0.26	0.02	2.38	0.25	2.44	0.09	2.14
Genital apposition	0.37	0.64	3.54	0.16	0.70	0.43	0.66	1.63	0.88	0.44	1.33	4.35[b]	0.84	0.45	2.24	1.29[c]
Percent of times together	0.23	1.52	0.06	2.13	1.36	1.41	0.23	1.08	4.88[a]	0.18	0.59	7.93[c]	2.31	0.14	1.17	3.55[c]
Intercourse	0.64	0.85	2.82	0.26	1.25	2.29	0.98	0.71	0.57	0.65	1.19	2.56	1.00	0.03	0.63	0.19
Percent of times together	0.16	0.04	0.58	3.14	1.32	1.37	0.98	0.76	1.60		0.37		0.01	2.84	0.58	1.55

Table II.1—*Continued*

	df 1,120				df 4,120				df 2,120				df 2,120			
Male oral contact with female genitals	0.01	0.00	5.77[b]	0.20	0.86	2.17	1.59	0.77	0.25	1.15	2.70	0.83	0.49	0.05	0.86	0.46
Percent of times together	0.80	1.46	1.82	0.00	1.24	0.38	0.44	0.37	2.10	0.20	0.48	0.52	0.14	1.33	0.39	1.18
Female oral contact with male genitals	0.54	1.52	2.94	0.48	0.99	2.35	0.73	0.91	0.66	0.75	2.31	0.62	0.09	0.53	1.45	0.51
Percent of times together	2.21	0.94	2.57	0.00	1.40	0.69	0.56	0.78	1.11	0.18	0.17	0.43	0.47	1.52	2.31	0.94
Number of times respondent had intercourse	0.47	0.00	0.24	1.90												
Number of partners respondent had intercourse with	0.15	0.24	2.15	1.43												
Sexual attitudes or ideology																
Acceptability of breast fondling for males	3.56	1.23	0.81	2.21	0.97	2.25	1.15	0.73	1.53	0.02	2.82	2.16	0.64	0.33	2.03	1.14
Acceptability of breast fondling for females	3.19	1.17	0.10	2.17	1.02	2.17	1.05	0.57	1.93	0.23	1.50	1.76	1.18	0.94	1.32	1.68
Acceptability of genital fondling for males	4.41[c]	3.74	0.05	1.18	0.78	2.54[c]	0.90	1.24	1.11	0.61	1.61	1.49	1.73	0.91	0.27	2.45
Acceptability of genital fondling for females	3.89	2.38	0.11	0.79	0.64	1.85	0.94	1.18	1.54	0.19	1.68	1.79	2.20	1.07	0.29	3.07[c]
Acceptability of intercourse for males	1.97	2.30	0.23	0.30	0.55	1.97	1.69	0.98	0.94	0.07	2.10	1.83	1.21	1.20	0.28	0.85
Acceptability of intercourse for females	2.28	1.26	0.52	0.28	0.47	1.92	1.06	1.02	1.10	0.03	1.46	1.72	1.75	0.80	0.56	1.33
Reactions to interview																
Interesting	15.55[a]	2.28	5.58[b]	0.85									2.68	1.44	1.82	0.40
Offensive	1.12	0.85	4.92[a]	2.63									0.13	0.36	0.13	0.10
Uncomfortable	0.31	0.45	8.31[a]	7.98[a]									4.59[b]	0.63	1.31	0.58
Important	2.98	1.04	9.37[a]	7.55[a]									0.03	0.17	2.39	0.68
Embarrassing	0.56	2.09	0.00	1.56									4.94[a]	1.72	0.61	0.15
Made you concerned about privacy	1.57	0.16	9.03[a]	1.93									0.67	0.39	0.17	0.18
You didn't want to answer	1.62	0.19	0.05	1.22									2.05	0.49	1.10	0.05
You worried about confidentiality	0.25	2.63	1.18	0.04									0.72	6.28[a]	0.18	0.53
It was easy to be frank	1.71	0.00	0.00	0.01									0.04	0.58	0.65	0.55
You told the truth	1.50	5.13[c]	5.62[b]	0.09									1.02	0.30	0.30	0.54

df 1,120 — 3.92 / 5.15 / 6.85
df 4,120 — 2.45 / 2.89 / 3.48
df 2,120 — 3.07 / 3.80 / 4.79
df 2,120 — 3.07 / 3.80 / 4.79

[a] p ≤ .01
[b] p ≤ .025
[c] p ≤ .05

265

a female. Nonstudent females felt that the interview was more comfortable but less important when the interviewer was of the same gender. Thus while gender of interviewer had little effect on reported sexual behavior or attitudes, it did seem to have an effect on the reactions of female respondents to the interview. This effect was particularly consistent for student females who rated same-gender interviews more positively.

A second effect of the interviewer could originate in the interviewer's own sexual experience. Gender, for example, theoretically affects responses because the respondent may infer the interviewer's sexual ideology from this characteristic. The interviewer, however, could communicate his or her own ideology through subtle verbal and nonverbal cues that would convey disapproval or approval of various behaviors. In order to check for the effect of the interviewer's own sexual experience, each interviewer completed the entire schedule, including the sexual behavior measures, before the actual training started. It served the joint purpose of familiarizing the interviewer with the questions and providing information on each interviewer's own experiences. For the analyses, each female interviewer was coded into one of five categories: married, living with someone of the opposite sex, experienced (more than two lifetime coital partners), inexperienced, and virgin. The male interviewers were so few in number that similar analyses were not possible.

There are few significant differences in reported sexual behavior or attitudes as shown in table II.1. While ten of the F values are statistically significant, a pattern of differences was found only for female nonstudents. In these cases, respondents were more likely to report that they had not experienced the first three lifetime behaviors to interviewers with the least sexual experience. Since the F values decrease in both size and significance, and since there are no other systematic differences, the interviewer's sexual experience seems to have had very little effect on the data obtained. It should be noted that efforts were made during the training to minimize the possibility of the interviewer's conveying personal opinions to the respondents; interviewers were carefully instructed about the use of probes and routine ways of delaying or avoiding personal questions addressed to them. They were also told not to wear jewelry or buttons which might convey particular political or social beliefs. These efforts plus the wide range of responses to which each interviewer was exposed could have reduced the likelihood of the interviewer's communicating personal viewpoints.

Throughout the training sessions, it was stressed that the interviewer maintain a friendly yet businesslike atmosphere. The relationship between the interviewer and the respondent has conventionally been thought to influence the quality of the data. This interaction between respondents and interviewers is best described by the term "rapport," although the choice of this word should not be confused with its application in peer groups designating informal rapping.

The post-interview reactions were used to determine the interviewer's ability to develop rapport. Over the large number of respondents being asked essentially the same questions, differences in the post-interview reactions should be at least partially attributed to differences in the interviewer's interpersonal skills. A "rapport" score for each interviewer was constructed by comparing the average rating of each interviewer's respondents on a particular question to the overall average. For example, it could be determined if a particular interviewer's respondents were above or below average on feeling comfortable. The ratings for each interviewer were summed across the 12 post-interview reaction items resulting in possible scores from $-$ 12 (below average on each item) to $+$ 12. The actual range, from $-$ 12 to $+$ 10, was divided into three categories: below average, average, and above average.

These categories were used in an analysis of respondents' answers to questions on sexual attitudes and behavior. From an analysis of variance, only nine of the resulting comparisons were significant. Of these significant F values, seven were found among male students. Five of these suggest a pattern; in reports of current behavior, with increasing interviewer rapport, there were greater percentages reported for engaging in necking, french kissing, genital fondling, and genital apposition. The same differences were not found among male nonstudents. It should be remembered that most of the males were interviewed by females; thus student males may have underreported to female interviewers where there was low rapport. Overall, rapport did not systematically affect the data obtained in the various subsamples.

The interviewer's competence is composed of technical as well as interpersonal skills. The completeness and accuracy with which he or she records responses are important to the quality of the data. The pauses between questions as well as the time taken and difficulty evidenced by the interviewer in recording the responses may convey important cues to the respondent. As a check on technical proficiency, the same respondent was interviewed by 22 of the 24 interviewers. This female respondent gave identical answers to each interviewer to the best of her ability. These interviews were checked for completeness; an error was recorded for each instance of inappropriately skipping or asking a question or incorrectly coding or recording a response. The scores of total errors ranged from 1 to 24, and were divided into three categories: below average, average, and above average. These categories were also used in analyses of variance to look for differences in reported sexual behavior, sexual ideology, and post-interview reactions; this analysis included data for 21 interviewers.

As shown in table II.1, 13 significant differences were found. Two of these significant F values were found in each of three subsamples, nonstudent males and both female groups. The pattern of these results, however, was not consistent. The remaining seven significant differences were in the student male subsample. They reported earlier average age of necking, more genital apposition, and more male oral contact with females' genitals, as well as more current necking and french kissing to above-average interviewers as compared to average or below-average groups. In the post-interview reactions, however, male students interviewed by interviewers with average technical competence scores rated the interview more comfortable and less embarrassing than those interviewed by the other interviewers. Thus, the above-average interviewers received more reporting of sexual behavior from male students, while average interviewers got high post-interview reactions from this same group. Since this pattern was not consistent and was not repeated in the other subsamples, technical competence did not seem to influence the data in any systematic manner.

The interviewer characteristics of gender, sexual experience, rapport, and technical competence have, at best, modest effects on the data. To the extent that patterns emerge from the scattered findings, the significant differences seem to reflect ordering of questions, with earlier items affected more than later items. As pointed out by Johnson and DeLamater (1976), 9.5 significant differences would be expected by chance (where $p = 0.05$) out of the 190 comparisons we made for the four interviewer variables; in fact, 14 of the resulting Fs are significant. The data, therefore, did not seem to be affected by interviewer aspects, thus providing additional evidence of its quality.

The "paid respondent" also provided a check on the reliability of the questions. The responses recorded by each of the interviewers could be compared for errors in recording, skipped questions, inappropriate questions, or varying interpretation of questions that can affect the response. Using the 352 questions that were coded and appropriate to ask, the error rate was 0.0329. This error rate is very low. If the total number of questions in the schedule were used, the error rate would be lower, as the interviewers would get credit for correctly skipping questions that were inappropriate to ask. There was 100 percent agreement on 253 questions. Of the remaining 99 where there were differences, there were 70 questions on which agreement was 85 percent or more and 51 of those questions had a rate of over 90 percent.

These control interviews were conducted in the middle of the student interviewing. Meetings with all the interviewers were held to clear up the common misconceptions and conferences were held with each of the 22 interviewers to discuss individual problems. Therefore, many of the variations in interpretation and erroneous skipping of questions were corrected before the rest of the interviewing was done. Since the overall error rate was low, there is every reason to believe that the quality of the interviewing improved even above this level. The high reliability of the questions indicated by these comparisons adds more evidence of the high quality of the data.

References

Adams, Bert. *The Family: A Sociological Interpretation.* 2nd ed. Chicago: Rand McNally, 1975.

Bell, R., and J. Chaskes. "Premarital Sexual Experience Among Coeds, 1958 and 1968." *Journal of Marriage and the Family* 32 (1970): 81–84.

Benney, M., D. Reisman, and S. A. Star. "Age and Sex in the Interview." *American Journal of Sociology* 62 (1956): 143–152.

Berscheid, Ellen, and Elaine Walster. *Interpersonal Attraction.* 2nd ed. Reading, Mass.: Addison-Wesley, 1978.

Borgatta, Edgar, and George Bohrnstedt. Personal communication, 1970.

Burgess, Jane. *Influence of Family Relationships on the Sexual Behavior of College Students in Norway and the United States.* Doctoral dissertation, University of Illinois-Champaign, 1973.

Carns, Donald. "Talking About Sex: Notes on First Coitus and the Double Standard." *Journal of Marriage and the Family* 35 (1973): 677–687.

Christensen, Harold T., and Christina Gregg. "Changing Sex Norms in America and Scandanavia," *Journal of Marriage and the Family* 32 (1970): 616–627.

Clayton, Richard. "Premarital Sexual Intercourse: A Substantive Test of the Contingent Consistency Model." *Journal of Marriage and the Family* 34 (1972): 273–281.

DeLamater, John. "Methodological Issues in the Study of Premarital Sexuality." *Sociological Methods and Research* 3 (1974a): 30–61.

DeLamater, John. "Review of Sorensen: Adolescent Sexuality in Contemporary America." *Contemporary Sociology* 3 (1974b): 157–158.

DeLamater, John, and Patricia MacCorquodale. "The Effects of Interview Schedule Variations on Reported Sexual Behavior." *Sociological Methods and Research* 4 (1975): 215–236.

Edwards, A. L. "Scalogram Analysis." In *Techniques of Attitude Scale Construction.* New York: Appleton-Century-Crofts, 1957. Pp. 172–199.

Ehrmann, Winston. *Premarital Dating Behavior.* New York: Henry Holt, 1959.

Elder, Glenn, Jr. *Adolescent Socialization and Personality Development.* Chicago: Rand McNally, 1968.

Ferrell, Mary Z., William Tolone, and Robert Walsh. "Maturational and Societal Changes in the Sexual Double Standard: A Panel Analysis (1967–1971); 1970–1974). *Journal of Marriage and the Family* 39 (1977): 255–271.

Gagnon, John, and William Simon. *Sexual Conduct: The Social Sources of Human Sexuality.* Chicago: Aldine, 1973.

Gorden, Raymond. *Interviewing: Strategy, Techniques and Tactics.* Homewood, Ill.: Dorsey Press, 1969.

Grinder, Robert, and Sue Schmitt. "Coeds and Contraceptive Information." *Journal of Marriage and the Family* 28 (1966): 471–479.

Gurin, P., G. Gurin, R. Lao, and M. Beattie. "Internal-External Control in the Motivational Dynamics of Negro Youth." *Journal of Social Issues* 25 (1969): 29–53.

Hampe, Gary, and Howard Ruppell. "The Measurement of Premarital Sexual Permissiveness: A Comparison of Two Guttman Scales." *Journal of Marriage and the Family* 36 (1974): 451–464.

Hardy, Kenneth. "An Appetitional Theory of Sexual Motivation." *Psychological Review* 71 (1964): 1–18.

Heise, David, and George Bohrnstedt. "Validity, Invalidity and Reliability." In *Sociological Methodology 1970.* Edited by Edgar Borgatta and George Bohrnstedt. San Francisco: Jossey-Bass, 1970. Pp. 104–129.

Hunt, Morton. *Sexual Behavior in the 1970's.* Chicago: Playboy Press, 1974.

Johnson, Weldon, and John DeLamater. "Response Effects in Sex Surveys." *Public Opinion Quarterly* 40 (1976): 165–181.

Kaats, Gilbert R., and Keith E. Davis. "The Dynamics of Sexual Behavior of College Students." *Journal of Marriage and the Family* 32 (1970): 390–399.

Kaats, Gilbert, and Keith Davis. "The Social Psychology of Sexual Behavior." In *Social Psychology in the Seventies.* By Lawrence Wrightsman et al. Monterey, Calif.: Brooks/Cole, 1972. Pp. 549–580.

Kantner, John and Melvin Zelnik. "Sexual Experience of Young Unmarried Women in the United States." *Family Planning Perspectives* 4 (1972): 9–18.

Kantner, John, and Melvin Zelnik. "Contraception and Pregnancy Experience of Young Unmarried Women in the United States." *Family Planning Perspectives* 5 (1973): 21–35.

Kinsey, A. C., W. B. Pomeroy, and C. E. Martin. *Sexual Behavior in the Human Male,* Philadelphia: W. B. Saunders Co., 1948.

Kinsey, A. C., W. B. Pomeroy, C. E. Martin, and P. H. Gebhard. *Sexual Behavior in the Human Female.* Philadelphia: W. B. Saunders Co., 1953.

Libby, Roger. *A Multivariate Test of Reference Group and Role Correlates of Reiss' Premarital Permissiveness Theory.* Doctoral dissertation, Washington State University, 1974.

LoSciuto, L., A. Spector, E. Michels, and C. Jenne. "Methodological Report on a Study of Public Attitudes toward and Experience with Erotic Materials." In *Technical Report of the Commission on Obscenity and Pornography.* Vol. VI. Washington, D.C.: U.S. Government Printing Office, 1971. Pp. 139–256.

Lundy, James. "Some Personality Correlates of Contraceptive Use Among Unmarried Female College Students." *Journal of Psychology* 80 (1972): 9–14.

MacCorquodale, Patricia. *Premarital Contraception and Conception.* Master's thesis, University of Wisconsin–Madison, 1974.

Mirande, A. M. "Reference Group Theory and Adolescent Sexual Behavior." *Journal of Marriage and the Family* 30 (1968): 572–577.

Newcomb, Theodore. *The Acquaintance Process.* New York: Holt, Rinehart and Winston, 1961.

Perlman, Daniel. "Self-Esteem and Sexual Permissiveness." *Journal of Marriage and the Family* 36 (1974): 470–474.

Podell, L., and J. C. Perkins. "A Guttman Scale for Sexual Experiences: A Methodological Note." *Journal of Abnormal and Social Psychology* 34 (1957): 420–422.

Rains, Prudence. *Becoming an Unwed Mother.* Chicago: Aldine, 1971.

Reiss, Ira. *Premarital Sexual Standards in America.* New York: Free Press, 1960.

Reiss, Ira. *The Social Context of Premarital Sexual Permissiveness.* New York: Holt, Rinehart and Winston, 1967.

Reiss, Ira, Albert Banewart, and Harry Foreman. "Premarital Contraceptive Usage: A Study and Some Theoretical Explorations." *Journal of Marriage and the Family* 37 (1975): 619–633.

Richardson, Stephen, Barbara Dohrenwend, and David Klein. *Interviewing: Its Form and Functions.* New York: Basic Books, 1965.

Robinson, John, and Phillip Shaver. *Measures of Social Psychological Attitudes.* Ann Arbor, Mich.: Institute for Social Research, 1969.

Rotter, J. B. "Generalized Expectancies for Internal vs External Control of Reinforcement." *Psychological Monographs* 80 (1966): Whole Number 609.

Schofield, Michael. *The Sexual Behaviour of Young People.* London: Longmans, Green, 1965.

Schwartz, Michael, and Sheldon Stryker. *Deviance, Selves and Others.* Washington, D.C.: American Sociological Association Rose Monograph Series, 1970.

Secord, P. F., and S. M. Jourard. "The Appraisal of Body-Cathexis: Body Cathexis and the Self." *Journal of Consulting Psychology* 17 (1953): 343–347.

Sherwood, J. J. *Self-identity and Self-actualization: A Theory and Research.* Doctoral dissertation, University of Michigan, 1962.

Shibutani, Tamotsu. *Society and Personality.* Englewood Cliffs, N.J.: Prentice-Hall, 1961.

Simon, J. H., and W. Gagnon. *Youth Cultures and Aspects of the Socialization Process:* College Study Marginal Book. Bloomington, Ind.: Institute for Sex Research, 1968.

Simon, J. H., A. Berger, and W. Gagnon. "Beyond Anxiety and Fantasy: the Coital Experience of College Youth." *Journal of Youth and Adolescence* 3 (1972): 203–222.

Sorensen, Robert. *Adolescent Sexuality in Contemporary America.* New York: World Publishing Company, 1972.

Stratton, J. R., and S. P. Spitzer. "Sexual Permissiveness and Self-evaluation: A Question of Substance and a Question of Method." *Journal of Marriage and the Family* 29 (1967): 434–441.

Sudman, Seymour, and Norman Bradburn. *Response Effects in Surveys.* Chicago: Aldine, 1974.

Thomas, William (with Dorothy Swaine Thomas). *The Child in America.* New York: Alfred Knopf, 1928.

Udry, J. Richard, Karl Bauman, and Naomi Morris. "Changes in Premarital Coital Experience of Recent Decade-of-Birth Cohorts of Urban American Women." *Journal of Marriage and the Family* 37 (1975): 783–789.

U.S. Bureau of the Census. *Census of Population: 1970. General Social and Economic Characteristics.* Final Report PC(1)–C51. Wisconsin. Washington, D.C.: U.S. Government Printing Office, 1972.

Vandiver, R. *Sources and Interrelation of Premarital Sexual Standards and General Liberality-Conservatism.* Doctoral dissertation, Southern Illinois University, 1972.

Vener, A. M., and C. J. Stewart. "Adolescent Sexual Behavior in Middle America Revisited." *Journal of Marriage and the Family* 36 (1974): 728–735.

Vincent, Clark. *Unmarried Mothers.* New York: Free Press, 1961.

Walsh, Robert. *A Survey of Parents and Their Own Children's Sexual Attitudes.* Doctoral dissertation, University of Iowa, 1970.

Walsh, Robert, Mary Z. Ferrell, and William Tolone. "Selection of Reference Group, Perceived Permissiveness, Personal Permissiveness, Attitudes and Behavior: A Study of Two Consecutive Panels (1967–1971; 1970–1974)." *Journal of Marriage and the Family* 38 (1976): 495–507.

Ward, Russell. *Growing Old: Stigma, Identity and Subculture.* Doctoral dissertation, University of Wisconsin–Madison, 1974.

Wells, L. Edward, and Gerald Marwell. *Self-Esteem: Its Conceptualization and Measurement.* Beverly Hills, Calif.: Sage Publications, 1976 (Sage Library of Social Research; Vol. 20).

Zelnik, Melvin, and John Kantner. "Sexuality, Contraception and Pregnancy Among Young Unwed Females in the United States." In *Demographic and Social Aspects of Population Growth,* Vol. 1. Edited by C. Westoff and R. Parke, Jr. Washington, D.C.: U.S. Government Printing Office, 1973.

INDEX

DESIGNED BY GARY GORE
COMPOSED BY FOCUS/TYPOGRAPHERS, ST. LOUIS, MISSOURI
MANUFACTURED BY THOMSON-SHORE, INC., DEXTER, MICHIGAN
TEXT IS SET IN PALATINO, DISPLAY LINES IN HELIOS AND OPTIMA

Library of Congress Cataloging in Publication Data
DeLamater, John.
    Premarital sexuality.
    Bibliography: p.
    Includes index.
    1. Young adults—Sexual behavior.   2. Socialization.
      3. Sexual ethics.   4. Sex role.
    I. MacCorquodale, Patricia, joint author.   II. Title.
    HQ27.D39   301.41'75   78–65019
              ISBN 0-299-07840-X